George Gissing
Essays & Fiction

Also by Pierre Coustillas

Les Carnets d'Henry Ryecroft (bilingual edition with introduction and notes)
Collected Articles on George Gissing
George Gissing at Alderley Edge
Gissing's Writings on Dickens: A Bio-Bibliographical Survey
Isabel Clarendon (critical edition)
The Letters of George Gissing to Gabrielle Fleury

George Gissing

This photograph, by Russell, appeared in *The Album* for February 25, 1895.

George Gissing
Essays & Fiction

Edited with an Introduction by
Pierre Coustillas

The Johns Hopkins Press
Baltimore and London

Copyright © 1970 by The Carl and Lily Pforzheimer Foundation, Inc.
"Cain and Abel" copyright © 1970 by Alfred C. Gissing.

Manufactured in the United States of America

The Johns Hopkins Press, Baltimore, Maryland 21218
The Johns Hopkins Press Ltd., London

Library of Congress Catalog Card Number 78-100702

International Standard Book Number 0-8018-1115-5

This book has been brought to publication with the generous assistance of a
grant from The Carl and Lily Pforzheimer Foundation, Inc.

The engraving reproduced on the endpapers is from Punch *for December 3, 1887.*

To Professor Shigeru Koike
of the Metropolitan University of Tokyo

Contents

Acknowledgments

MY MAJOR DEBT is to Carl H. Pforzheimer, Jr., President of The Carl and Lily Pforzheimer Foundation, through whose kindness and confidence I was permitted the agreeable and absorbing task of editing this collection. The first stages of my work in New York were greatly facilitated by the staff of the Carl H. Pforzheimer Library, whom I also wish to thank for answering my queries from Paris with promptness and accuracy. I am indebted to the late John D. Gordan, Curator of the Henry W. and Albert A. Berg Collection of the New York Public Library, Astor, Lenox, and Tilden Foundations, for making available the manuscript of "Cain and Abel." Herman W. Liebert of the Yale University Library gave permission to quote from various unpublished documents. To Louis Bonnerot, of the Sorbonne, I am grateful for constant encouragement and very useful advice. I also wish to thank my friends John Fletcher and C. S. Collinson for reading the typescript. The texts are printed by permission of Alfred C. Gissing.

George Gissing
Essays & Fiction

Introduction

THOUGH HE HAD barely reached middle age when he died in 1903, George Gissing left behind him twenty novels and five other volumes of prose, among which were *The Private Papers of Henry Ryecroft*, his best-known though by some standards not his best work. Posthumous publication substantially increased those figures: forgotten short stories were unearthed from the files of English and American journals, two more novels were brought out, and his introductions to the Rochester edition of Dickens' works were gathered in one volume.[1] Yet, when all this pious work was done—mainly by his family—there remained some Gissing scholars who demanded more, and their demand is neither surprising nor unreasonable. Once a man has read a book by the apostle of pessimism (unless he be a Douglas Goldring or a Frank Swinnerton), contagion often seizes upon him, and he falls to reading any other Gissing volume he can lay hands on. Then too, there are gaps of varying degrees of importance in the published works. Whole novels have disappeared which, whatever opinion their author may have held of them, might shed some light on his personality as well as provide a link between the published stories. Who, for instance, would not like to discover the manuscript or the galley proofs of *Mrs. Grundy's Enemies,* which Bentley finally refused to issue for fear that the readers of Mr. Mudie's Select Library would be repelled by its bitterness?[2] Similarly, one longs to

[1] Most of the early short stories written in America in 1877 were collected in *The Sins of the Fathers and Other Tales* and in *Brownie*. The short stories of the mature years were gathered in *The House of Cobwebs, A Victim of Circumstances*, and *Stories and Sketches*, whereas a selection from *Human Odds and Ends* and the 1906 and 1927 volumes was published by Harrap in 1929 in the series *Short Stories of To-day and Yesterday*. The novels were the unfinished romance of Roman and Goth, *Veranilda*, and *Will Warburton*. The Dickens pieces appeared first in *Critical Studies of the Works of Charles Dickens* and in *The Immortal Dickens*. Footnote references are to the editions of the novels cited in the Bibliography unless otherwise indicated.

[2] For a detailed account of the history of the book, see Royal A. Gettmann, *A Victorian Publisher* (Cambridge: Cambridge University Press, 1960), pp. 196-97 and 215–22, and "Bentley and Gissing," *Nineteenth Century Fiction*, March, 1957, pp. 306–14. Richard Bentley the younger retired from business in 1898,

recover a three-decker about the theatrical world, *Clement Dorricott*, written with a view to serialization in *Temple Bar* and relegated to some drawer by Gissing, who turned down an offer of publication in book form because, in his estimation, it was unworthy of succeeding *Thyrza*. It would be of great interest to compare its outlook and treatment with other novels of the period which describe the same milieu—Zola's *Nana* (1879) and Moore's *Mummer's Wife* (1884). One's curiosity is further aroused by a satire of the spiritualist movements which flourished in England at the turn of the century, a novel with which he eventually grew dissatisfied and which he ordered his agent to burn. One laments over the loss of this new attack on sham and intellectual vacuity, the main object of which must have been Mrs. Annie Besant and her followers.

Yet the disappearance of *Among the Prophets*, first called *Oracles*, or of *Clement Dorricott* create no alarming lacuna. Gissing's works of the late eighties and nineties were written and published in such close succession that we are left in no great doubt as to the evolution of his technique and political and social ideas. Quite a different situation exists, however, concerning the years to which *Mrs. Grundy's Enemies* belongs—the four years between the publication of *Workers in the Dawn* in 1880 and *The Unclassed* in 1884. While there is no hope of recovering the manuscript of "Will-o'-the-Wisps," which must have been longer than the average three-decker volume when it was discarded, and very little expectation of unearthing the proofs of *Mrs. Grundy's Enemies,* which may have been destroyed when the business of Richard Bentley passed into the hands of Macmillan and Company, some consolation for these losses is provided by the group of manuscripts published in the present volume. With one exception—"Their Pretty Way," not written until 1894— they belong to the years between Gissing's first and second published

---

and the books distributed by his firm passed into the hands of Macmillan. Up to that date the manuscript and proofs of *Mrs. Grundy's Enemies* doubtless survived, as it cannot be imagined that the publisher would destroy a novel he had bought, even though he had decided not to publish it. Besides, it seems that when the firm closed down Gissing's manuscript was never returned to him: neither his correspondence nor his diary for the late nineties alludes to it, and his Account of Books for the years 1880–1892 merely reads: "MS still in Bentley's hands."

novels. Eight of these manuscripts are held by the Carl H. Pforzheimer Library in New York City; the manuscript of "Cain and Abel" is in the possession of the Berg Collection of the New York Public Library. Apart from "The Hope of Pessimism," which Jacob Korg has summarized and briefly commented upon in his biography of Gissing, they have never been mentioned by the critics. They consist of two essays, one on pessimism and a description of the banks of the Thames entitled "Along Shore"; a novella, "All for Love," which will probably surprise many admirers of Gissing; and six short stories, ranging in tone from boyish optimism to gruesome despair: "The Last Half-Crown," "Cain and Abel," "The Quarry on the Heath," "The Lady of the Dedication," "Mutimer's Choice," and "Their Pretty Way."

I: The Young Gissing

In order to see the texts in a proper light, we should recall briefly the salient facts of Gissing's life and the main steps in his literary career prior to the composition of the first piece in this volume. He began life with fairly hopeful prospects. Born in Wakefield, Yorkshire, on November 22, 1857, he was the eldest son of a pharmaceutical chemist of some local note, Thomas Waller Gissing, and of Margaret Bedford, the daughter of a Droitwich solicitor. George spent his infancy and childhood in his native town, and, much to his father's satisfaction, distinguished himself early at school. His passion for learning was so strong that he once ran off to school with a herring bone in his throat rather than miss a lesson. At an age when most boys still prefer the playground to the study, he devoured the volumes in his father's modest library and wrote poems, plays, and accounts of his activities.

Even as a child he seems to have been haunted by a sense of the brevity of life and the necessity of turning his time to the best possible account. He satirized his younger brothers, William and Algernon, because they preferred shallow books like Ballantyne's *Martin Rattler* to more serious literature and the corrosive irony of Hogarth's pictures. Even before his father's death in 1870, Gissing had an almost abnormal awareness of his duty to his brothers and sisters as well as to himself. The loss of his father convinced him more

3

than ever that if he was to make his way in life and gain an honorable position, it would be through the power of a trained intellect and hard work alone.

Early in 1871, with the help of a few friends, his mother was able to send her three sons to Lindow Grove School, Alderley Edge, Cheshire, a Quaker boarding establishment. There George continued to draw the attention of pupils and masters alike. More than thirty years later, one of his school-fellows recorded his impressions of the youthful Gissing: "Energy of character, self-reliance, and an exorbitant passion for study were his chief characteristics at this time. Into whatever task he entered he threw his whole soul. On the great 'speech nights' it was Gissing who mouthed the most brilliant Greek and Latin orations, and who filled the most important parts in the French plays."[3] At Lindow Grove he had few rivals in the humanities—the only branch of study he cared for—and, in 1872, he accomplished his greatest academic feat. He sat for the Oxford Local Examination and came out first in the whole of England. In those days the Senate of Owens College, Manchester, offered free tuition for three sessions to the best candidate in this examination, and thus Gissing entered the College under circumstances which must have greatly alleviated his mother's financial worries.

His years at Owens College were brilliant. He continued to win prizes and exhibitions, and his precocity is indicated by his poem "Ravenna,"[4] a poetic evocation of the history of the Italian town in twenty-one Spenserian stanzas, written when he was a little over fifteen. In June, 1874, he matriculated with high honors in the University of London and in 1875 won the top place in the first class with the University Exhibition in Latin and English in the examination for honors following the Intermediate B.A. One of his last successes was the Shakespeare scholarship of forty pounds per annum, tenable for two years, the award of which to Gissing is recorded in the Minute Book of Proceedings of the Council for November 5, 1875.

[3] Arthur Bowes, "George Gissing's School Days," *TP's Weekly*, January 22, 1904, p. 100.
[4] See *Manchester University Verses, 1868–1912*, published in Manchester in 1913, pp. 22–28; also reprinted in *Selections Autobiographical and Imaginative from the Works of George Gissing*, pp. 176–84.

Though at first he continued to live with his brothers at Alderley Edge and came to Owens College only to attend lectures, he now took lodgings near the college and, at the age of eighteen, enjoyed a degree of personal freedom which proved disastrous. Probably early in 1876 he met Marianne Helen Harrison ("Nell"), who, though she was a year younger than Gissing, made her living by prostitution. Love and pity soon got the better of common sense and prudence, and Gissing tried to save her. He began by giving her whatever money he could spare from his scholarships, and even bought her a sewing machine so that she might earn her living honestly. However, Nell had also begun to drink heavily, and Gissing's donations were not sufficient to meet her demands. In his eyes she was a victim of society, and society was to pay for its cruel indifference toward her. Accordingly, when he could no longer supply her with money of his own, he began to rifle the locker room of the college. To the puzzlement of both students and staff, the thefts went on through the winter and spring of 1876 until, on May 31, a private detective hired by the college authorities caught Gissing in the act of stealing marked money from an overcoat.[5] He was taken into custody and, on June 6, was convicted and sentenced to one month's imprisonment at hard labor. Thus ended in disgrace his remarkable academic career, and it is no exaggeration to say that he never recovered totally from that blow.

Because they thought that employers' doors would be closed to him, some of his and his mother's friends gathered together some money and, a couple of months after his release from prison, sent him to America, where they hoped that he could make a new start. Letters of recommendation made his first steps easier. By October 5 he was in Boston, and spoke enthusiastically of his new country. There he made a friend of William Lloyd Garrison, the poet, who occasionally read poetry to him until the small hours of the morning.

---

[5] On the Manchester episode, the main authority remains Morley Roberts in *The Private Life of Henry Maitland* (1912; new editions in 1923 and 1958), but new light has been shed on this affair by Arthur C. Young in *The Letters of George Gissing to Eduard Bertz, 1887–1903,* and by the author in "George Gissing à Manchester," *Etudes Anglaises,* July–September 1963, pp. 254–61. The latter article reproduces four vital letters from John George Black to Gissing prior to the outbreak of the scandal, as well as quotations from the official records of Owens College, now Manchester University.

Garrison knew the editor of the *Atlantic Monthly* and did his best to help Gissing place articles in American journals. The first of these appeared on October 28 in the Boston *Commonwealth*;[6] its author proudly sent it to his mother, doubtless to prove that he was getting a foothold in America. But the little writing he did for newspapers and periodicals was insufficient to support him, and, when the new year came, his financial worries had become so serious that he could no longer continue free-lance journalism. He took a post at Waltham High School, some ten miles outside Boston, and there taught English, Latin, French, and German for two months, to everyone's satisfaction. The reason for his sudden departure, on March 9, 1877,[7] remains obscure. From then until his return to England in the autumn his movements were irregular. It was in Chicago, where he had gone with an immigrant's ticket, that he started his literary career proper. Goaded by starvation, he turned to the writing of short stories and succeeded in placing a number of them with the editors of local papers like the *Tribune*, the *Evening Journal*, and the *Post*; even a New York monthly, *Appleton's Journal*, accepted one of his manuscripts.[8] Whatever comfort, intellectual and financial, these modest successes may have brought him, he had to acknowledge his defeat when the summer drew to a close. He borrowed money and on October 3 was again in Liverpool.

Gissing then began a life reminiscent of that led by Grub Street hacks in the age of Pope and Johnson. The London sections of *The Private Papers of Henry Ryecroft* give a faithful image of this existence, though he was not quite the lay anchorite of that book.[9] Nell, with whom he had kept in touch during his stay in America, now joined him in London. His resolve to reclaim her had not altered, though he soon had to acknowledge his failure. He scraped

[6] "Art Notes. 'Elaine'—Rosenthal and Tojetti." It is unsigned, but there are proofs at Yale that bear Gissing's initials, "GRG."

[7] See the *Waltham Sentinel* and *Waltham Free Press* for that date.

[8] For Gissing's short stories from his stay in America to his death, see my bibliography in *English Literature in Transition*, 7, no. 2 (1964): 59–72.

[9] I have discussed and analysed at some length the autobiographical aspects of *Henry Ryecroft* in the introduction and notes of my bilingual edition of the book (Paris: Aubier, 1966).

a living from private tutoring and from clerical work for a metropolitan hospital, while boldly launching himself into the writing of fiction, which he considered his only legitimate work. A first novel, which must have been very immature, was rejected in July, 1878, but, while he could be depressed for hours by a passing remark, Gissing could also be dauntless. With characteristic brevity he wrote to his brother Algernon: "Just what I anticipated. The next must be better."[10] In spite of Nell's constant ill health and irresponsibility, life in lodging houses on the fringes of the slums, and grinding poverty, he managed to complete a second novel known to us as *Workers in the Dawn*. Were it not for the help of a new friend, Eduard Bertz, a socialist whose ideas had led to his exile from Bismarck's Germany, it might well never have been completed. Not only did Bertz encourage him to finish it, but he contributed the material for an additional chapter consisting of excerpts from the heroine's diary during her student years in Germany. After many delays—some of them caused by insufficient planning in the development of his plot— Gissing succeeded in finishing his huge manuscript toward the end of October, 1879. He had been working on it for about fifteen months. On November 3 he summed up his effort to Algernon: "It consists of 46 chapters, of some 450 MS.pp., and will, I fear, make three good volumes."[11] About mid-November, after some corrections and the insertion of the chapter sketched by Bertz, the manuscript was sent to Chatto and Windus.

On November 26 Gissing and Nell, now newly married,[12] moved to Islington.[13] There Gissing, whose imagination had been sorely tried by *Workers in the Dawn*, attempted some shorter fiction, three specimens of which are presented in the pages that follow. When he wrote

[10] July 24, 1878, *Letters of George Gissing to Members of His Family*, p. 32 (hereafter referred to as *LMF*).

[11] *LMF*, p. 49.

[12] The marriage was celebrated on October 27, 1879, in St. James's Parish Church, Hampstead Road. The reason for this belated ceremony remains unknown.

[13] 5 Hanover Street, now 60 Noel Road. The two-story house turns its back on the Regent's Canal—*"maladetta e sventurata fossa,"* as Gissing called it in *Demos* (chap. 3).

"The Last Half-Crown," "Cain and Abel," and "All for Love," it was with little experience. The American tales, whatever biographical and psychological interest they may have, were scarcely more than a gifted youth's exercises, and the value of the two full-length novels had not yet been recognized. On February 7, 1880, by which time these three stories were completed, his situation was taking a tragic turn: "I write hard at some tales, of which I have several in the hands of Magazine editors. If none of these are taken, I shall be *au désespoir*."[14] Some other stories which bear the Islington address of 5 Hanover Street have been preserved: "An Heiress on Condition," which did not come to light until 1923, when a Gissing collector, George J. C. Graberger, had it published by the Pennell Club of Philadelphia in an edition limited to forty-eight numbered copies (the manuscript is now in the Berg Collection of the New York Public Library), "My First Rehearsal," which I edited for *English Literature in Transition* in 1966 (vol. 9, no. 1; the manuscript is at the Yale University Library); and "My Clerical Rival" (the manuscript is also in the Berg Collection), soon to be published in London by the Enitharmon Press along with "My First Rehearsal" as a monograph in the Enitharmon Gissing Series. These three stories show Gissing in a gay, youthful mood. None of them, although they were apparently sent to the popular reviews early in 1880, were accepted.

With the exception of "Their Pretty Way," the stories collected in the present volume add much to our knowledge of a period in which Gissing's surviving production consists mainly of non-fiction. In chronological order, the list of these writings runs as follows: three essays in the *Pall Mall Gazette* for September 9, 11, and 14, 1880, entitled "Notes on Social Democracy";[15] eight quarterly articles in *Vyestnik Evropy* (*Le Messager de l'Europe*), Turgenev's review, from February, 1881, to November, 1882, dealing with English political, social, and literary affairs; a letter to the editor of *The Daily News* for February 5, 1883, on theatrical questions; "Song," a fifteen-line poem in *Temple Bar* for November, 1883; a descriptive essay entitled "On Battersea Bridge" in the *Pall Mall Gazette* for November

---

[14] *LMF*, p. 57.
[15] Reprinted in the *Pall Mall Budget* on September 11 and 17, 1880.

30, 1883; and, finally, two short stories, "Phoebe" and "Letty Coe," in *Temple Bar* for March, 1884, and August, 1891.[16]

It will be noted that of the writings presented here only two out of the eight early pieces, "Cain and Abel" and "The Hope of Pessimism," are mentioned in the author's correspondence and other papers. It seems that Gissing, chastened by the rejection of his contributions by reviews and magazines, maintained a discreet silence about his less ambitious literary efforts, at least until their merit had been recognized. It is characteristic, for instance, that references to "On Battersea Bridge" abound, whereas there is no mention of its twin essay, "Along Shore." There remains, however, the possibility that allusions to these stories were made in letters which have disappeared or have not found their way into public collections. Because of Gissing's secretiveness regarding these modest manuscripts, as well as his tendency to pass severe judgment on his early work, one is grateful that they did not perish together with his many abortive attempts at novels. I do not claim that they are works of the first order or that they upset our notions about the novelist's art in his early career, but, as will be seen, their interest for the Gissing scholar is considerable, and the essay on pessimism has relevance far beyond the question of its writer's own intellectual and philosophical development.

II: The Manuscripts

The contents of this volume have escaped the notice of scholars for over sixty years, and it may be appropriate to inquire into the history of these manuscripts, though not so fascinating as that of the novelist's letters to Bertz.[17] In his will Gissing named his brother Algernon and his friend Clara Collet as his executors. Their task, when he died in the remote village of Ispoure, near Saint-Jean-Pied-de-Port, Basses-Pyrénées, was a difficult one. All his papers should have been gathered together and put in order, but because he had been neither willing nor able to look on France, and in particular

---

[16] "Letty Coe" was written in June, 1884, paid for by Bentley in December (£6.6.0), and finally kept by him for publication until the success of *New Grub Street*.

[17] See Arthur C. Young's Introduction to that volume, pp. xii–xv.

Ispoure, as his permanent home, many of his belongings were in Madame Fleury's Paris flat and at Wakefield, his mother's and sisters' home, as well as at the Maison Elgue, his last abode. Gradually, however, most of his personal papers reached Algernon.[18] Out of vanity and a misconception of his own capacities, his brother had taken up the career of a novelist in the eighteen-eighties and, with a wife and five children to maintain, was constantly in a state of financial embarrassment. It must be added that, although George's two sons, Walter and Alfred, had obtained a yearly pension of seventy-four pounds on the Civil List, largely through the good offices of H. G. Wells, they inevitably increased the financial strain on the family. Thus Algernon soon felt obliged to make whatever money he could out of his brother's most valuable papers.

The piecemeal sale began in 1912, the year in which Walter came of age. Algernon may have thought that the moment had come for higher prices. For one thing, the publication, almost simultaneously of Swinnerton's *Critical Study* and Morley Roberts' fictionalized biography, *The Private Life of Henry Maitland,* because of the violent controversy they aroused, had drawn considerable attention to Gissing's name. Moreover, a series of important reprints of his novels and other works by such firms as Sidgwick and Jackson, Smith, Elder and Company, John Murray, Constable and the Gresham Publishing Company made almost all his books available; the interest of the public in them had not been so high since 1904. With apparent reluctance, Algernon began to part with the manuscripts of the published works, which he sold to Frank Redway of Wimbledon, a bookseller and dealer in literary relics who succeeded Walter E. Peck in 1908. In the two years before the war nine manuscripts of the novels passed into Redway's hands at the remarkably low price of eleven guineas each.[19]

[18] But by no means all. Among other examples, the corrected proofs of *Our Friend the Charlatan*, a letter from the Spanish and Oriental scholar Butler Clarke, and many books in his library as well as his own works remained in Gabrielle's hands until her death in 1954.

[19] Here is the list in the order of sale, with the present-day location: *Denzil Quarrier, The Whirlpool, The Crown of Life, Thyrza, The Nether World, In the Year of Jubilee* (all in the Huntington Library); *Demos* and *The Emancipated* (both in the Berg Collection of the New York Public Library); and *Our Friend*

As the war increased his difficulties, Algernon was compelled to dispose of the unpublished works. In August, 1915, he probably sold "The Last Half-Crown" to an unknown dealer for twelve guineas, after Redway had rejected his conditions.[20] On September 16 he made a new offer of two other manuscript short stories, "My Clerical Rival" and "The Lady of the Dedication," on the same terms. This time, though he complained loudly, Redway bought both stories for twenty-one pounds. The latter tale was purchased from him by the Carl H. Pforzheimer Library in January, 1925. Five other pieces in the present volume, "All for Love," "Mutimer's Choice," "The Hope of Pessimism," "Along Shore," and "The Quarry on the Heath," entered the Pforzheimer collection via Walter T. Spencer, the well-known bookseller, in September, 1922. They are listed and briefly described in his *Forty Years in My Bookshop* (1923).[21] Two more stories, "The Last Half-Crown" and "Their Pretty Way," were purchased by the Pforzheimer Library from Charles Boesen of Detroit in November, 1954. They had previously belonged to the Bandler Library. "Cain and Abel" was in the possession of Arthur Pforzheimer before it passed into the Berg Collection.

III: *"The Hope of Pessimism"*

"The Hope of Pessimism" is an unparalleled achievement in Gissing's career. Of the few essays he wrote—some critical, like "The

---

the Charlatan (in the Alexander Turnbull Library, Wellington, New Zealand). That the sums obtained by Algernon were abnormally low is shown clearly by a footnote on p. 187 in Edward Clodd's *Memories* (1916). While correcting the proofs of his book, Clodd received a bookseller's catalogue offering the manuscript of *The Emancipated* as a bargain at £120.

[20] On the 25th, Algernon offered him two manuscripts of short stories of twenty and thirteen pages, respectively, both signed with the middle R and bearing the Islington address. "The Last Half-Crown" was doubtless the second one, since its description corresponds exactly with that given by Algernon. Redway would only give twelve pounds for the two, though he was asked twelve guineas each or twenty-five pounds for both. On September 2, 1915, Algernon informed his correspondent that he had obtained the price he asked from another dealer.

[21] P. 219. Algernon sold "All for Love" in March, 1916. The letters in which he negotiated the sale of the story with Spencer, dated March 7 and March 11, are in the Carl H. Pforzheimer Library. "The Quarry on the Heath" probably passed into Spencer's hands in the following September.

Place of Realism in Fiction," some descriptive and reminiscent, like "At the Grave of Alaric"[22]—none shows him so deeply involved in abstract issues. One may recall Morley Roberts' statement that his life-long friend hated speculative thought and that "the one philosopher he sometimes read" was Schopenhauer,[23] but, as almost always, one feels compelled to qualify such statements. Although it is true that at the end of his life Gissing found the discussion of metaphysical problems unrewarding and, in fact, disturbing, this attitude did not develop until about 1885, when he became a professional novelist for good. He was always interested in the history of religions (his voluminous notes for *Veranilda* bear eloquent testimony to this), and his letters of the late seventies and early eighties contain occasional remarks which clearly indicate an interest in philosophy.[24]

In "The Hope of Pessimism" Gissing ceases to cloak his thoughts in the garb of fiction and adopts the language of the philosopher. This passionate essay presents two opposing views of existence, two doctrines he had himself espoused. The optimism of Auguste Comte is contrasted with the pessimism of Arthur Schopenhauer, and this bitter attack on Positivism, the idol he had once revered, and its dethronement in favor of a creed of hopelessness is the climax of a spiritual crisis which had been latent for several years. It is wrong to assert, as Morley Roberts did,[25] that Gissing took up the Positivist cause out of gratitude to Frederic Harrison, the leader of Comte's English disciples. His interest in the movement grew naturally and was quite free from external pressures and solicitations. As early as

---

[22] Published in *The Humanitarian* for July 1895, pp. 14–16, and *The Daily Chronicle* for May 31, 1898, p. 6, and reprinted in *Selections Autobiographical and Imaginative from the Works of George Gissing*, pp. 217–21 and 238–44.

[23]*The Private Life of Henry Maitland*, p. 131.

[24] Thus he wrote to his brother Algernon on May 2, 1880, that he "must get some excellent history of Philosophy, and master the current of thought from the beginning of Indian wisdom—in its large phases" (*LMF*, p. 69). About a month before, he had asked William: "Did it ever occur to you to study Philosophy of any kind? I wish you could get a peep into that world. I suppose you know the names of Spinoza, Kant, Schopenhauer, etc? I hardly know whether such studies would be in your line, but I wish they were" (March 27, 1880, *LMF*, p. 67).

[25] *The Private Life of Henry Maitland*, p. 115: "His temporary Positivist pose . . . was entirely due to his gratitude to Harold Edgeworth [i.e., Frederic Harrison] for helping him."

October, 1878, he recommended that his younger brother Algernon read the current number of the *Fortnightly Review* because it contained an article by Harrison, and a month later, on November 9, he wrote him enthusiastically about Comte's fundamental work, which he had just read in the translation of Harriet Martineau: "His 'Philosophie Positive' consists of a most wonderful *résumé* of all human knowledge, classed thus: Mathematics, Astronomy, Physics, Chemistry, Physiology and Social Physics. His idea is to deduce from all our positive knowledge a theory of social life, which shall in time be developed into an exact science and free us, by direct attention to its laws, from the state of social anarchy into which we are at present plunged. By all means read his book if you ever get a chance."[26] He persisted in the attempt to impress Algernon with Comte's ideas, but his brother, down in Yorkshire, whose intellectual curiosity was at a fairly low level, was only mildly intrigued by motions of progress and evolution. Gissing's growing admiration for Comte led him to pass from reflection to action. Like his partially autobiographical character Arthur Golding in *Workers in the Dawn*, he sought out workingmen's clubs and addressed their audiences on themes like "Faith and Reason" and "The State Church from a Rationalist Point of View." He read voraciously in history, religion, and philosophy with a view to aiding the intellectual emancipation of the masses. Though he admitted that Comte had doubtless been too sanguine, he was quite prepared to excuse him: "When one has pierced so deeply into the secret of history and gained so clear an insight into the future of the human race as Comte had, it is hardly possible to help believing that others will at once, and for ever, be convinced by our clear proofs and statements."[27] He went on to deplore the fact that the average man was incapable of reflection and reasoning; however, that seemed to him no reason why one should renounce the attempt to win the people away from their apathy and traditional religious beliefs.

The year 1879 was mainly occupied by the writing of *Workers in the Dawn*, a fact which partly explains Gissing's gradual desertion of radical clubs and lecture rooms, but his faith in Positivism did not

[26] To Algernon, November 9, 1878, Berg Collection.
[27] To Algernon, January 26, 1879, *LMF*, p. 42.

abate. He resumed his discussion of it in letters to Algernon in the spring of 1880, and one such, which has escaped the notice of his biographers and critics, is worth quoting at length for the contrast it provides with "The Hope of Pessimism":

Though metaphysics interest me much, I shall never make a metaphysical system the *guide of my life*. That is the whole question, what is to be the guide of our lives? And in this sense I am sure you have the *desire* to be a philosopher, though I grant you, you have not yet time and opportunity to give grave thought to the matter. I myself can only call myself a *philosopher* in the literal meaning of the word,—a *lover* of wisdom, not necessarily its possessor. And so far from seeking the guide of my life in metaphysical speculations, I have adopted the Positive Philosophy of Auguste Comte, which expressly throws away all metaphysics and speaks thus: "All thinking men are tortured perpetually by the involuntary questions—What am I? Whence come I? Where do I go? How shall I conduct my life? Now the experience of the world has shown us that an *absolute* answer to the first three questions is impossible for human intelligence; life, as such, is what we call an ultimate fact; we must accept it, and not endeavour to seek *what* it is. But upon life in the more every-day sense, science is ever throwing greater light, ever giving us more power to answer the last question—How shall I live?" So the Positive Philosophy bids us keep our eyes on science, to do our best to collect all the results of human knowledge, and to deduce therefrom a scheme of *the history of the world,* and from an intimate knowledge of the past to discover a number of general rules which shall enable us in a certain sense to predict the future, and so to lead our political, social and individual lives more in consonance with reason. Just as there is a science of astronomy, and men can predict eclipses etc., just so we believe that there is a science of human life, that the total of the world's history is already fully planned out, and that we are able to learn sufficient of the rules of this new science to see for some distance into the mists of the future.

Now with all this I feel you must sympathize, for I know you *must* sometimes (inasmuch as you are an educated man,) ask yourself the above questions, and it is your human nature that you should be restless till you get some definite answer. The Christian religion is one of the thousand answers that men have made for themselves, and for a long time it sufficed; but *only* till science had grown sufficiently to dispense with the aid of a blind faith and to find natural laws for itself. The dogmas of religion the world has outgrown, at all events the thinking portion of it; they were good in their time, but that time has gone by. And mark,—men become more modest as they get wiser. The Christian religion was not content with asking—How shall I live? but persisted in putting impossible questions as to the *origin* of the world and life, of which man *can know nothing.* Now-a-days, as I have said, we only ask for a history of the *growth and progress of life,* and are content to smile at those who come to us with their cut-and-dried theories of the origin of all things.[28]

[28] To Algernon, May 9, 1880, Yale University Library.

Workers in the Dawn appeared in early June, and it soon became obvious to its author that it would be an outright failure if he did not take steps to promote it. The publishers, who had consented to bring it out only at Gissing's expense, spent as little as possible on advertisements, and it was clear that the novel would not receive public attention. Naturally enough, Gissing turned to the man whose writings had led him to Comte. On July 9, 1880, he sent Harrison a copy with a letter in which he confessed that it was mainly to Comte that he owed the ideas set forth in the book. Harrison's reply is well known:[29] he praised the novel highly even before he had finished reading it and promised help of various kinds. In his second letter to Harrison, Gissing freely vented his opinion of the traditional forms of Christianity:

> The satire upon churchly institutions which some of course find so offensive, I could not help; I have been at times driven to frenzy by what one reads and sees of clerical audacity and impotence. And, whether it be, in my case, youthful presumption, or, as is very probable, inherited temperament, I have never, since I reasoned on such things, known one moment of enthusiasm for, one instant of belief in, the dogmas of religion. For me they are something apart, something of historical interest. Thus, I may not say that I have ever undergone that struggle out of the bondage of creeds of which so many speak. I have strayed about in thick gloom, and all the more glorious does the light of Positivism shine before me, inasmuch as my memory holds no gleam of revelation with which to contrast it.[30]

Impressed by Gissing's scathing observations on Christianity, Harrison wrote to many of his friends recommending *Workers in the Dawn*. Although his efforts failed to win the book even a semblance of recognition by the public at large, they drew Gissing out of his social and intellectual isolation. He was introduced to John Morley (afterwards Lord Morley), who was then editor of the *Pall Mall Gazette* and the *Fortnightly Review,* and was invited to contribute articles to both journals. A few months later, when Turgenev was looking for a British correspondent to review the political, social, and literary news of England every quarter for his *Vyestnik Evropy,* it was Gissing who was offered the assignment by Professor Beesly, acting for the Russian editor, because Harrison had mentioned his

[29] It is printed in full in *LMF*, pp. 77–79.
[30] July 23, 1880, Carl H. Pforzheimer Library.

name. By early November, 1880, Gissing had become a member of the Positivist Society and attended its meetings regularly. During the first six months of 1881 he dated his letters by the Positivist calendar. At the end of January he wrote to Algernon, "To Positivism is the future, I am convinced. It gives one an entirely new spirit in all human matters, makes you understand *why* you follow such and such a course, indeed points your course to you at every juncture. It is the science of social life,—which has hitherto been the most miserable empiricism."[31] He was attracted by the idea of devoting oneself to the advancement of the human species through the study of history and the consequent planning of the development to come. Although he felt no interest in the practical aspects of the religion of humanity, he admitted the appeal of the cult of the race underlying it.

His attendance at Positivist meetings, which he had always found time-consuming, ceased in the early summer of 1881 after one meeting with Laffitte, the leader of the French Positivists, and another at which Gissing acted as interpreter in the course of a debate on the prosecution of the *Freiheit*, a German socialist journal. His domestic difficulties had by then put a serious strain on the optimism engendered by Comte's doctrine. Nell's behavior, which was extremely disorderly, had had a serious effect on his health. By his own admission, he had become so nervous that "the doorbell ringing . . . or the postman's sudden knock" put him into "palpitation and head-swimming."[32] At the same time, he was gradually discovering his dislike for the masses, and his reluctant contacts with them had made him doubt their ability to improve themselves. He had ceased contributing to the *Pall Mall Gazette* after his articles on social democracy were published, and now he deserted workingmen's gatherings and lecture halls. His original enthusiasm had spent itself. With increasing boredom he continued to compile his quarterly reports for the Russian review until the end of 1882, but the only personal contact he retained with the Positivists was with Harrison (he had become the tutor of two of Harrison's sons in December, 1880, and derived a sizeable portion of his income from this benefactor). In the early autumn of 1882 Gissing's state of mind was very similar

[31] January 30, 1881, Yale University Library.
[32] To Algernon, May 4, 1881, *LMF*, p. 97.

16

to that of Osmond Waymark, quoted on p. 43 below. His adherence
to Positivism was nothing more than a stage on the way to the rejection
of all creeds, whether religious or politico-social.[33]

If the rise and fall of his interest in Comte's philosophy can be
traced with reasonable accuracy, his exposure to Schopenhauer's
doctrine is somewhat less well documented. One thing at least appears
to be certain: it is to his friend Eduard Bertz that Gissing owed his
discovery of the German philosopher. In this regard it is significant
that the passage on Schopenhauer in *Workers in the Dawn* occurs
in the chapter known to have been sketched by Bertz (vol. 1, chap. 14,
"Mind-Growth"). Helen Norman, the heroine, becomes acquainted
with Schopenhauer through the two volumes of *Parerga und Paral-
ipomena* and, quaintly enough, finds that "his pessimism is the least
valuable part of Schopenhauer's teaching." It would be bold to assert
that by the time the novel was completed Gissing had read more
than these two volumes, which do present Schopenhauer's views in
their most attractive and least somber garb. Helen Norman could do
what her creator would have deemed a sheer impossibility or a sign
of mental vacuity, namely, discard Schopenhauer in favour of Comte.
Whatever knowledge he had gained of the former in 1882 was derived from the original works, probably from the *Sämmtliche Werke*
published in six volumes at Leipzig in 1873 and 1874, which he could
consult at the British Museum. The first English translation of *Die
Welt als Wille und Vorstellung* by Haldane and Kemp did not begin
to appear until 1883. Gissing knew German well and could go
through Schopenhauer's fat volumes without undue difficulty. As he
was an attentive reader of periodicals, it is also very likely that his
curiosity about the works of the German philosopher was fostered
by a number of magazine articles on the value and hopelessness of
life which appeared in England in 1879, while he was completing

---

[33] Later allusions to Comte and Positivism in the correspondence and the
works are extremely scarce. Let us note the short dialogue between Robert
Asquith and Ada Warren in *Isabel Clarendon* (1:61):

"What are you reading?" Asquith inquired.
It was a volume of Comte. She showed the title without speaking.
"You are a Positivist?"
"No, merely an atheist."

Workers in the Dawn.[34] At any rate, when Gissing wrote his essay Schopenhauer's name was little known in England, and it would be a deplorable mistake to dismiss "The Hope of Pessimism" on the grounds that it is largely based on Schopenhauer's ideas, since these were not common knowledge at the time.

The stimulus to write the essay came from Sir John Robert Seeley's *Natural Religion*, which appeared in the early summer of 1882. In a letter of July 30 to Algernon,[35] Gissing remarked that Seeley's book was well reviewed everywhere and expressed his desire to obtain a copy through a library. He could have indulged his wish after he moved to Chelsea that summer, where he was nearer to the free library in Westminster, all the more so as he had just completed *Mrs. Grundy's Enemies* and was free to pursue this new interest. Speculation had taken such a hold upon his mind that, as in his socialist days, he tried to convert his brother: "I cannot give up the hope that you will—in settled days—apply your mind to the wider sense of things and have a struggle with the problems of life. Of course it is to me amazing that any man *can* refrain from such lines of thought. But I suppose I under-rate the importance of that second birth into philosophical consciousness which can only come with much reading of a special kind."[36]

"The Hope of Pessimism" opens with a passionate and sarcastic attack upon optimism. The average man's thinking, says Gissing, displays a combination of short-sightedness, naiveté, forgetfulness, selfishness, and contradiction. Man will more naturally obey his instinct of self-preservation and cling to earthly life than adhere to a belief in another life, though on reflection he will admit the misery of human fate on this side of the grave. Gissing then darts a special shaft at the advanced Christian who is prepared to find on earth signs of the blessed state to be enjoyed in the existence to come. Not only does this new type of Christian indicate his abysmal incapacity for observation but he violates his creed, the pessimism of which Gissing implicitly accepts as an asset. The religion of humanity "improves"

[34] See Ralph Goodale, "Schopenhauer and Pessimism in Nineteenth Century English Literature."

[35] Yale University Library.

[36] October 6, 1882, Yale University Library.

upon rationalistic Christianity in that it becomes a lay religion and discards all reference to a life beyond the grave. In it, man becomes the source and the end of all things. The agnostic optimism of Comte, whose spiritual and moral sides Gissing summarizes, rests on the assumption that human thought and knowledge passes through three main stages: the theological, the metaphysical, and the scientific. It is the aim of the French philosopher's program to bring mankind to the third and last stage, whatever vestiges of the earlier ones may linger on in the age of science. But it is significant that he retained the word "religion," which he took pains to redefine in his *Positivist Catechism* as the source of harmony within and between individuals. Gissing refrains from attacking that word; he is content to show the weaknesses resulting from the rejection of the supernatural element in religion. For the promise of a reward in a future life has been substituted the satisfaction of doing good to one's fellow beings. The religion of humanity, Gissing satirically remarks, makes a virtue of necessity, but it underestimates a well-nigh ineradicable urge in man, the religious instinct, which cannot be satisfied by the prospect of "subjective immortality" guaranteed by our generous behavior to our fellow creatures. Here Gissing calls Schopenhauer to his aid. The religious instinct is a manifestation of what the German thinker called the metaphysical urge, which originates in the realization by man of the irrevocability of death, for "if our life were endless and painless, it would perhaps occur to no one to ask why the world exists and is just the kind of world it is."[37] The doctrine of agnostic optimism hopes to triumph over other creeds, on the assumption that it is possible to eliminate the metaphysical urge and that its absence is compatible with the altruism which, on account of the "subjective immortality" it gives man, will replace and satisfy the desire for reward in another world.

At this stage of his essay Gissing declares his goals: to show that the metaphysical instinct's yielding to a realistic philosophy is not inevitable and that hope lies in the hopelessness of human fate. Far from discouraging metaphysical speculation, science, because of its very progress, will stimulate it, and agnosticism will not be trans-

[37] *The World as Will and Idea*, 2:360.

mitted automatically from one generation to the next. To the average man agnosticism remains a superficial creed which suffering and the approach of death are likely to reduce to nothing; moreover, death makes all men equal. As man distinguishes himself more clearly from the animal or the savage, he becomes more and more self-conscious, and the problem of his destiny is not likely to lose its importance in his mind. If anything, knowledge and education can but increase the intensity of this awareness.

Gissing then demonstrates that "universal realism," that is, the general recognition that this life is an end in itself, can lead to nothing. Can man reasonably admire himself as he admired a deity? The world, says Gissing after Schopenhauer, is nothing but evil, and evil will become rampant if the fear of some superior justice no longer somehow checks the flood of human vices and if the religion of humanity is the sole agency "to counteract threatening ill." Self-seeking will become the general law. Gissing, who no longer believed in a Positivist utopia, which, he felt, could but multiply the iniquities of the present world, lavishes his irony on the latter, where commercialism and competition reign supreme. Comte said: "Le service collectif de l'Humanité repose continuellement sur deux dispositions connexes: le dévouement des forts aux faibles; la vénération des faibles pour les forts."[38] The incentive for such an ideal state of things offered by the religion of humanity will be ludicrously inadequate.

After devoting two-thirds of his essay to undermining the foundations of Positivism, Gissing passes on to an exposition of his solution to the world's woes; from then on he more openly relies on Schopenhauer. Egoism, being a manifestation of the will to live and the cause of war between individuals and nations as well as of the greater part of the misery in the world, can only be combated successfully by refusing life. Since man is the incarnation of evil, he can only move toward good by denying his very nature. On all sides he is confronted with problems which overwhelm his poor intellect, and the sole consolation he can hope to find is in self-pity and pity for others. There lies the source of future good. Man will reach that stage through asceticism, by which is meant not self-mortification, but

[38] Quoted by André Cresson in his *Auguste Comte. Sa vie, son oeuvre, sa philosophie*, p. 152.

celibacy (the sexual instinct is a form of the will to live), self-imposed poverty, avoidance of all pleasure-seeking and humility.

In our world of woe, says Gissing after Schopenhauer, there is but one kind of optimism which is not a delusion—that which stems from artistic creation. This was an idea particularly appealing to a man who, at all times, placed the artist's work high on the scale of human activities. The artist at work frees himself from the influence of the will; his enthusiasm deadens the pain of life in him—thus compensating for his lowly position in society—but it does so only temporarily, during the act of creation. Hence Gissing's benevolent gaze upon the optimistic religion of ancient Greece, the religion of a race of artists.

Now that the myth of Christianity is no longer acceptable to man's reason, now that Christianity has equated itself with egotism and the will to live, Schopenhauer's doctrine contains the only possible salvation for mankind. By refusing to perpetuate itself and by developing mutual compassion, mankind will move toward extinction and will regard death as the ultimate happiness. The essay might have fittingly concluded with this description of the man who has succeeded in stilling his passions and looks upon the grave placidly:

> Nothing can alarm or harass him any more, nothing can move him; for he has cut all the thousand filaments of willing which hold us bound to the world and which, as appetite, fear, envy, and rage, drag us hither and thither in constant pain. He now looks back, calm and smiling, upon the illusions of this world, which were once able to move and agonize even his mind, but which now stand before him as indifferently as chessmen when the game is ended, or as fancy-dress cast off the morning after, whose forms teased and disquieted us on the carnival night. Life and its forms now merely hang before him as a fleeting appearance, like a morning dream to one who is half awake, through which reality already shines and which can no longer deceive; and like such a morning dream they too, without any violent transition, finally vanish.[39]

On the personal plane, "The Hope of Pessimism" stands as an important landmark. Though he did not try to publish it, Gissing drew a certain solace from the writing of it. It acted as a safety valve all the more effective because the intransigence of his views did not have to be softened in the process of their embodiment in a novel. The

[39] *The World as Will and Idea*, 1:504–5.

bitter satire on the nineteenth-century exponents of optimism has the ring of intense disillusionment, which derives its vigor in part from the self-mortification attendant upon the denunciation of a state of mind common enough among advanced thinkers. Like a jilted lover, the author takes refuge in cynical statements. The image of man finding salvation in self-condemnation gives him an unavowed yet keen pleasure, and, as sometimes happens when he voices his despair, his manner verges on lyricism; the conclusion of the essay, with its well-balanced sentences demanding to be read aloud, has an eloquence which anticipates the description of Emily Hood's ordeal in *A Life's Morning* or the last paragraph of *The Nether World*. Schopenhauer's comments on the privileged situation of the artist helped Gissing to clarify his own position regarding his art. It is largely through this influence that he turned from socialist lecturer to a novelist who kept his distance from all political and philosophical movements, endeavoring to record without passion the life around him. Half a year after writing this essay he remarked to his sister Margaret that "the only thing known to us of absolute value is artistic perfection. The ravings of fanaticism—justifiable or not—pass away; but the works of the artist, work in what material he will, remain, sources of health to the world."[40] And on July 18, 1883, he was even more explicit to his brother:

I am by degrees getting my right place in the world. Philosophy has done all it can for me, and now scarcely interests me any more. My attitude henceforth is that of the artist pure and simple. The world is for me a collection of phenomena, which are to be studied and reproduced artistically. In the midst of the most serious complications of life, I find myself suddenly possessed with a great calm, withdrawn as it were from the immediate interests of the moment, and able to regard everything as a picture. I watch and observe myself just as much as others. The impulse to regard every juncture as a "situation" becomes stronger and stronger. In the midst of desperate misfortune I can pause to make a note for future use, and the afflictions of others are to me materials for observation.[41]

Both passages read like a personal expression of Schopenhauer's development of the notion of art as the flowering of life in *The World as Will and Idea*. Together with the essay itself they confirm to the point of being embarrassingly obvious, the views expressed by C. J.

[40] Letter of May 12, 1883, *LMF*, p. 126.
[41] *LMF*, pp. 128–29.

Francis,[42] who was more happy in his research than Ralph Goodale some thirty years before,[43] though he did not benefit by any single material discovery made in the interim. In Goodale's opinion, Gissing's highly subjective experience offered sufficient explanation of his pessimism, and Schopenhauer need not be called to the rescue. Yet, though Schopenhauer's name occurs only rarely in Gissing's fiction, his philosophy is frequently reflected in the demeanor of leading characters. In *The Unclassed* Waymark compares Maud Enderby's distrust of the urge to live, which in her is solely the result of the influence of Christianity, with the teachings of Schopenhauer. He remarks that Maud expresses herself as though she had read the German philosopher[44] and mentions the resemblance of his ideas to those of Buddhism.

From here on, there is an undercurrent of Schopenhauerian thoughts and attitudes in Gissing's most characteristic works. Bernard Kingcote, the hero of *Isabel Clarendon*, who has too often been dismissed by unperceptive reviewers and critics as a morbidly depressed and depressing character, assumes a new dimension seen in this particular light. All passion spent, crushed in spirit, he renounces his former ambitions, literary and emotional, and, not unlike Will Warburton in the novel of that name, makes his peace with the world: "He began with thoughts of glory; he would finish his career as a shop-keeper."[45] Kingcote is convinced that we were born for suffering[46] and derives his only mental pleasure from renunciation. In him,

---

[42] "Gissing and Schopenhauer." Francis, who did not know of the existence of "The Hope of Pessimism," based his demonstration on Gissing's published letters to his family and the novels.

[43] "Schopenhauer and Pessimism in Nineteenth-Century English Literature."

[44] Vol. 3, chap. 3, in the original version (London: Chapman and Hall, 1884) and chap. 27 in subsequent editions. The chapter is entitled "The Will to Live." When he revised his novel in 1895 Gissing canceled such over-explicit references. Thus this comment, made by Maud Enderby before Waymark has pronounced the name of Schopenhauer, only occurs in the first edition: "To feel and enjoy the fulness of life, to assert your existence, to hope and fear for the future,—these things were forbidden to whosoever sought the higher ends of being. Abnegation, mortification of the desires, this alone could save. We were sent into the world only that we might renounce it, and our renunciation must extend even to the instinct which bids us cling to life" (p. 50).

[45] Vol. 2, p. 279.

[46] *Ibid.*, p. 275.

as in other characters downtrodden in the battle of life, passivity is associated with goodness, pity, and a craving for justice. Gilbert Grail in *Thyrza* and Sidney Kirkwood in *The Nether World* submit to their fate with the same resignation, but the two most convincing instances are Edwin Reardon and Harold Biffen, the penniless novelists of *New Grub Street*. In Reardon we witness the ultimate battle between self-denial and the will to live. "The man Edwin Reardon," he says of himself, "whose name was sometimes spoken in a tone of interest, is really and actually dead. And what remains of me is resigned to that. I have an odd fancy that it will make death itself easier; it is as if only half of me had now to die."[47] Yet, though he wishes nothing as much as to finish his life in peaceful retirement, he obeys his wife's appeal when their son's life is in danger. The sexual urge has not been annihilated in him, and a reconciliation is at hand. Again he hopes for happiness, but he dies quoting *The Tempest*: "We are such stuff as dreams are made on," which, as C. J. Francis remarks, fittingly illustrates Schopenhauer's opinion of human existence. Similarly, Biffen yields to the will to live when he falls in love with Reardon's widow, but when he realizes the vanity of his desire, the thought of death takes hold of him. The prospect soothes him, and his mood becomes "one of ineffable peace."[48] He dies remembering Reardon's last words.

Like Schopenhauer, Gissing occasionally stresses the fact that man's fate is ruled by capricious powers. (Alfred Yule, in *New Grub Street,* is such a victim. This middle-aged hack becomes blind and dies a miserable death far from the literary world.) He shows, however indirectly, that man cannot escape himself. Heredity and circumstances mould his character and, strive as he will, he cannot alter it. Between Bernard Kingcote and Reardon, Gissing offers a number of variants on this theme, a pathetic intermediate case being James Mutimer, whose acquaintance we shall make in "Mutimer's Choice." The resignation with which Gissing endows him, his calm acceptance of his destiny, will recur in the character of Henry Ryecroft. That Grub Street veteran writes in a strain which the German philosopher would not have disapproved:

47 Vol. 3, p. 189.
48 *Ibid.*, p. 294.

24

It may well be that what we call the unknowable will be for ever the unknown. In that thought is there not a pathos beyond words? It may be that the human race will live and pass away; all mankind, from him who in the world's dawn first shaped to his fearful mind an image of the Lord of Life, to him who, in the dusking twilight of the last age, shall crouch before a deity of stone or wood; and never one of that long lineage have learnt the wherefore of his being. The prophets, the martyrs, their noble anguish vain and meaningless; the wise whose thought strove to eternity, and was but an idle dream; the pure in heart whose life was a vision of the living God, the suffering and the mourners whose solace was in a world to come, the victims of injustice who cried to the Judge Supreme—all gone down into silence, and the globe that bare them circling dead and cold through soundless space.[49]

Thus "The Hope of Pessimism" confirms Gissing's participation in a wide-ranging movement—the revival of pessimism stimulated by the progress of scientific and critical thought and by the disappointment of the hope for a better society which science had for a time aroused. The foundations of religious belief had been undermined and man's solitude in the universe reinforced. Gissing's despair did not stem from the realization of this solitude but from his dread that science might, in a supreme irony, mean the reverse of progress. At this very early stage of his career, therefore, he is expressing what remained one of his most deeply felt beliefs: "I hate and fear 'science' because of my conviction that, for long to come if not for ever, it will be the remorseless enemy of mankind. I see it destroying all simplicity and gentleness of life, all the beauty of the world; I see it restoring barbarism under a mask of civilization; I see it darkening men's minds and hardening their hearts; I see it bringing a time of vast conflicts, which will pale into insignificance 'the thousand wars of old,' and, as likely as not, will whelm all the laborious advances of mankind in blood-drenched chaos."[50]

IV: "Along Shore"

After *The Unclassed* Gissing devoted himself exclusively to fiction for nearly a decade, and his literary activities up to 1884 were varied. This diversity did not indicate that he was still feeling his way, however: as early as January, 1880, when *Workers in the Dawn* was seeking a publisher, he confidently asserted to Algernon,

[49] *Henry Ryecroft* (Autumn X).
[50] *Ibid.* (Winter XVIII).

"You will see that I shall force my way into the army of novelists, be my position there that of a private or of a general."[51] It was rather that he believed all types of creative writing to be his province. If philosophical essays ran the risk of wounding his patron's sensibilities, he could safely compose descriptive pieces, fairly innocuous in tone, and try to place them with newspapers whose coverage was not strictly limited to political, social, and general events.

"Along Shore" is one such attempt, and the fact that the manuscript was found in Gissing's papers at his death makes it almost certain that it never achieved publication, for a newspaper editor would not normally have troubled to return to its author the manuscript of an article that had been printed, and Gissing's handwritten versions of his printed essays and articles have not survived. Like "On Battersea Bridge," it was inspired by the Thames and its embankment, a region which Gissing haunted when he lived, as he did then, at 17 Oakley·Crescent. Wapping, the setting of the essay, he knew from the long walks he took along the river, perhaps coming back by steamer, as his letters suggest. Chelsea was too decent a district to supply him with "copy" for his proletarian novels. A letter to his sister Ellen tells of such an outing:

> I spent an evening in the east end on Saturday. It is a strange neighbourhood, totally different from the parts of London in which my walks generally lie. The faces of the people are of an altogether different type, and even their accent is not quite the same as that of the poor in the west end. I rambled till midnight about filthy little courts and backyards and alleys, and stumbled over strange specimens of humanity. I had a long conversation with a curious Welshman. He informed me that he was "something of a scholar," for he constantly read the newspapers. He was rambling about the crowded streets in his slippers, looking for his wife, who was shopping.[52]

After the manner of Zola and Charles Reade he hunted for "documents" and was not satisfied until he was surrounded by notebooks full of observations of the kind of life he wished to describe. His picture of the waterside docks and yards and the jumble of mean, lower-class habitations nearby shows him as close as he ever came to the naturalist school. He dwells on sensory images, transcribing not only what he sees and hears but also the peculiar smells of the stored goods, of "rope and tar, canvas and cargo." In the same way, when

[51] Letter of January 25, 1880, *LMF*, p. 57.
[52] February 27, 1883, *LMF*, p. 124.

writing *Thyrza*, he found it necessary to go round a hat factory and repeatedly visited Lambeth, which he was using as the background of his story, "doing my best to get at the meaning of that strange world, so remote from our civilization." On bank holidays he rarely missed going out, as "there is always much matter to be picked up on such days."[53] For instance, while he was working on chapter 12 of *The Nether World* he spent the Easter Monday of 1888 at the Crystal Palace, of all places one of the best in which to observe the holiday-making populace. Artistically, "Along Shore" resembles that novel: both texts bear witness to the same care for concrete details, usually of a low order. But in this vignette of waterfront life on a winter night, he manages to keep in check pity, indignation, and contempt. The human element is more implicit than truly present. No pathetic heroine like Emma Vine in *Demos* or Jane Snowdon in *The Nether World* intervenes, and the description does not convey the impression of personal involvement created by his often-quoted page on Manor Park Cemetery in the earlier novel.

Man does appear in the second part, in the guise of a working man, as at the end of "On Battersea Bridge," but whereas there the passerby notices nothing of the fine sunset[54] and is only capable of

[53] Letter to Margaret, July 31, 1886, *LMF*, p. 182.

[54] It may be relevant here to publish for the first time a sonnet inspired by a sunset Gissing had watched a few months before (the manuscript is in the Rare Book Room at Yale University Library):

To AFG

One evening of a summer that is dead
  From a hill-top we watched the sun fall low,
  And marked, in clouds with green and gold aglow,
The track of waves about a bold sea-head,
So clear that, each by the other's fancy led,
  We heard the very billows' magic flow;
  Then o'er the vision saw the darkness grow,
Till all the glory of the sky was shed.

The memory dwells with me. So far apart
  We wander in the cheerless world;—though nought
  Of sunder'd circumstance or varying thought
Disturbs the kindness of the kindred heart;—
  I gladden when we see and think as one,
  As in that vision o'er the sunken sun.

GG
5.5.83

making a symbolic remark about the muddy waters of the Thames, the old waterman is not altogether without the author's approval. He is the symbol of a passing age, and Gissing, whose radical period was over, deplores with him the death knell of the picturesque and the natural. The passionate conservatism of *Isabel Clarendon* and *Demos* is heralded in the waterman's nostalgic look at "his idle boat below." As for the rhythmic, occasionally stilted prose born of the study of common things, it is again conspicuous in *Henry Ryecroft*.

V: "All for Love"

The idea of writing "All for Love" seems to have originated in a letter Gissing wrote to Algernon on November 21, 1879. After some satirical comments on the attack published by a man named Stewart (Algernon's employer in Wakefield) on Charles Bradlaugh, the notorious atheist who refused to take the oath before taking his seat in the House of Commons, Gissing begged his brother to shake off the atmosphere of a country town, adding that he contemplated writing a novel of provincial life.

The contrast in tone and aim between this story and the recently completed *Workers in the Dawn* is so great that, if the chronology was not firmly established, one would be tempted to reverse the order. In none of his American short stories did Gissing appear committed to a social mission, nor does he in "All for Love," whereas from *Workers in the Dawn* down to his last novel of contemporary life the depiction and denunciation of social evils and injustices is never absent. Obviously, the two works are aimed at different publics: after a desperately earnest book from which he had endeavored to exclude sensational elements and in which he had tried, however unsuccessfully, to vie with the greatest names in fiction, he bowed to the tastes of the common run of readers of novels and with the popular magazines in mind, resolutely set aside for a while his ambition to carve out for himself an honorable place in English literature.

Yet, when it has been conceded that "All for Love"—a title used by Dryden for a play in 1678—is an immature production with a fairly low artistic standard, the many points of similarity with Gissing's mature works must be stressed. Of all resemblances, those with *Denzil Quarrier* (1892) are the most striking. Both novels tell stories of polyandry. In each, the protagonist marries another man's wife, the legitimate husband comes back to haunt and torture the illicit couple, and the tension is relieved dramatically by one or several violent deaths. Whereas almost all of Gissing's stories are set in London, here we are in unattractive provincial towns where local affairs have pride of place. The resemblances are not limited to the general outline of the narrative and the location of the action; they cover a number of details. Apart from the similarity of their positions, both heroines are frail, sweet, sad, quiet, and fundamentally innocent creatures who have been lured into marriage by older men who turn out to be rascals. While Bertha is compared with a lily, Quarrier's "wife" symbolically bears the Christian name of Lilian. Before their second marriages, they have identical occupations, that of governess in a middle-class family. Lilian later becomes a schoolmistress in Bristol, and we read of Bertha that "upon her mother's death, she obtained a situation as governess in a family residing in the south of England" and after that "earned a scanty living by keeping an infants' school" (chap. 2).[55] When their former husbands disturb their new lives, they show similar agitation and fright at the prospect of scandal. Finally, death is the price of their error.

Their husbands, who in each case have been in prison—Vanstone for robbery, Northway for forgery—both took advantage of the girls' inexperience and romanticism to achieve their ends. The mechanism for their reappearance on the stage is comparable, involving secret appointments, and their ultimate aim is to wring money from their rivals. Their dishonorable lives make it necessary for them to be known by several names: Northway shortens his surname to North, and Vanstone has a good many aliases. In *Denzil Quarrier*, Glazzard also enters into relations with Northway under an assumed name. The sum paid to buy silence is five hundred pounds in each case.

If we turn from the main characters to secondary figures, other

[55] One might be tempted to accuse Gissing of poverty of invention, but it must be remarked that, as he had not published "All for Love" and had no intention of doing so, he was entitled to borrow from it whatever parts he thought useful for another story; further, there were very few occupations that young ladies of moderate education with no personal fortune could contemplate. Gissing was simply trying to make his heroines' activities plausible.

parallels suggest themselves. Miss Chad and Mrs. Wade are witnesses to meetings between the deserted wives and their worthless husbands and play a determining, though indirect, role in the denouements. Miss Chad's indiscretions tempt Harriet Golland to write a second anonymous letter which brings about Laurence Bloomfield's suicide; in like manner, Mrs. Wade, by not coming to the help of Lilian, whom she hears throw herself into Bale Water, has a passive role in the final tragedy. In the background, Serena Mowbray and Harriet Golland indulge in similar bickerings with their respective mothers, even though the cause in each case is different. Eventually they both marry in haste and find a new bondage away from parental surliness. Harriet's jealousy is echoed by the Reverend Scatchard Vialls' envy and pettishness.

The background consists of two imaginary provincial towns characterized by a slow-going existence, animated gossip, and female inquisitiveness; the arrivals of Bertha and Lilian are watched and commented upon by the virtuous ladies of Market Leyton and Polterham in a suspicious and self-righteous manner which seems only mildly amusing to the present-day reader. It is understandable that Dr. Bloomfield and Denzil Quarrier at one time contemplate settling abroad to escape such an atmosphere.

The eleven years which separate "All for Love" from *Denzil Quarrier* probably account for the discrepancy in technical ability between the two works, but some major alterations result not so much from a change in artistic taste as from a different conception of the story. The novel is, of course, much more than the typical Victorian fictional predicament: an "irregular union" imperiled by the return of the lady's legal husband. It is also a political satire, which the original title, "The Radical Candidate," clearly indicated, as well as a plea for women's education.[56] Mrs. Wade bears the standard of female emancipation as Rhoda Nunn and Mary Barfoot later do in *The Odd Women*. Moreover, Denzil's amateur writing on the Vikings sounds like a faint reflection of *New Grub Street*. Of these ele-

---

[56] The subject of his next novel is announced with great accuracy on p. 85 of the first edition: "There was still twenty minutes, and he decided to use the time in offering solace to the army of women who, by force of mere statistics, are fated to the frustration of their *raison d'être*."

ments which fill the canvas of *Denzil Quarrier,* only the preoccupation with woman's place in society and her victimization by· man-made laws are foreshadowed in "All for Love" (unless this impression merely reflects the temptation to see in the early work the promise which was fulfilled in Gissing's mature years).

Because the satire of provincial life is, so to speak, the only flesh on this skeleton of a story, the plot plays a more important part in "All for Love" than in *Denzil Quarrier*. Whereas Northway's arrest for forgery as he comes out of church on his wedding day and Glazzard's recourse to private inquiry agents are the only details in the novel which might fit into a detective story, in 1880 Gissing relied on such elements to a considerable degree. In terms of plot, "All for Love" is closer to *The Town Traveller* (1898) than to Denzil's adventures. A note of mystery is struck in the very first chapter—a burglary with an uncommon motive has been committed—and not until the last page do we learn the full consequences of the marriage that took place before the narrative opens. Throughout, Gissing resorts to devices familiar to the sensational tale rather than those of the realistic social novels on which his fame rests. Burglary with the connivance of a servant in the house and a neighboring innkeeper, robbery, anonymous letters, murder, and suicide give "All for Love" a melodramatic atmosphere.

These elements are considerably toned down in *Denzil Quarrier*. Gissing no longer thought it necessary to kill off his three leading characters; he grounded his catastrophe on the treachery of the hero's friend, a device which had the advantage of replacing a series of plot incidents with one psychological element—Glazzard's secret determination to cause Quarrier's downfall.[57] A psychological study,

---

[57] Some critics have complained that Glazzard's behavior is not justified in the eyes of the reader. Thus, George Cotterell wrote in *The Academy,* "The perfidy of Denzil's friend . . . is somewhat unaccountable" (April 9, 1892, p. 347), and the anonymous reviewer in the *New York Daily Tribune* commented on Glazzard's betrayal, "It is so objectless, so purely malicious and spiteful, as to be scarcely human" (March 27, 1892, p. 18). Both critics must have read the book very casually. As early as chap. 3, they could have found many details showing the great pains Gissing took to justify Glazzard's conduct. In Lilian's presence Denzil's tone when addressing his friend is extremely provoking, and Lilian is quite aware of it. Many a person, in the place of Glazzard, would at least wish to give Quarrier a rap on the knuckles for his rather insolent remarks.

perhaps somewhat thankless in Glazzard's case, was better suited to Gissing's imagination than a sequence of spectacular episodes. Another change in the same direction was to make Denzil aware of Lilian's past, indicating a preference for credibility over suspense. During the first half of "All for Love" the reader shares Laurence Bloomfield's ignorance of his wife's past, to the detriment of the psychological interest which his knowledge would have created. The reticences of his bride are far less readily acceptable in the novella than in *Denzil Quarrier*. By 1891 Gissing had learned to make motivation more plausible. His desire to avoid being psychologically arbitrary led him to more commonplace, and consequently more realistic, situations.

To the Gissing reader "All for Love" will suggest a few other parallels. For instance, Bertha's former occupation and all the miseries attendant upon it were to develop into a full-length analysis in *A Life's Morning*, written in the autumn of 1885 and published in 1888. In his protestations of love, Laurence recalls Wilfrid Athel's passionate impulse towards Emily Hood in the same novel. As with Arthur Golding, the hero of *Workers in the Dawn* (1880)—indeed, as with Gissing himself—love seems to have sprung from pity. But it is perhaps with some episodes of *Demos* (1886) that the resemblance is most compelling. Mrs. Mewling, like Miss Chad (their names are self-explanatory), plays the part of gossiper-in-chief; the amiable doleful relations between Laurence and Mrs. Bloomfield have something in common with the uneasy filial and parental love between Hubert Eldon and his ageing mother. As Mrs. Bloomfield is assailed by housebreakers, so the home of the Eldons is attacked by the riotous workingmen of New Wanley, though the consequences are different. Finally, Bertha's maiden name recurs in the anti-socialist novel, where it is one of the aliases of Alice Mutimer's scoundrel of a husband. This intricate network of associations with the rest of Gissing's works would probably convince us, if we needed further proof, that he soon gave up the idea of publishing "All for Love"; after it was discarded he freely used this or that element of it in a new story. No such close parallels can be found among the works he published in his lifetime.

However uncharacteristic it may appear at the first casual reading, some highly significant Gissing touches can be discerned in this brief story, in which one vainly seeks for traces of social or philosophical commitment. When he describes Laurence's face as "handsome, intellectual," he reveals a notion which was close to his heart. His diary and correspondence show how sensitive he was to people's physiques and to their facial features in particular. His dislike for Walter Besant, for instance, can be partly accounted for by the latter's nondescript personal appearance; to Gissing, he was nothing more than a plain-faced, dull-witted tradesman. On another occasion he noted how unlike his idea of a poet's Verlaine's face was. After first meeting A. H. Bullen, the publisher and Elizabethan scholar, he recorded his disenchantment: "A much younger man than I expected, and rather less intellectual. How consistently I am disappointed when I meet men of whom I have heard!"[58] The juxtaposition of the two adjectives "handsome" and "intellectual" was for Gissing a natural one; his ideal lay in the conjunction of the two qualities.

When Gissing has Laurence get rid of Philip Vanstone, he manifests a temperamental tendency to violence coexisting in him with a reluctance to resort to physical strength, a trait which such friends of his as Morley Roberts, H. G. Wells, and Henry Hick stigmatized as muscular cowardliness. Like many shy individuals whose patience is tried to the breaking point, he would dream of removing the obstacles in his way by violent means (which, incidentally, prompts me to believe that he made a wise decision when he left his second wife in the autumn of 1897, for the only alternative to flight would certainly have been an irreparable outburst of fury). Gissing is not known to have been a wife-beater or a thrasher of blackguards. His urge to strike out at insolent or idiotic people when he was exasperated found its outlet in writing. He relished Laurence's murder of Vanstone, just as he may be said to have acted out his impulse to deal a deadly blow to his wife's head vicariously, in his critical study of Charles Dickens.[59] A few traces of this feeling have survived in

[58] Diary, November 6, 1891.

[59] See, for instance, his violence in the following passage: "Mrs. Gargery shall be brought to quietness; but how? By a half-murderous blow on the back of her head, from which she will never recover. Dickens understood by this time

Denzil Quarrier, in which this piece of dialogue occurs (chap. 3):

"Every now and then I feel I should like to thrash some one. I read in the paper this morning, of some son of a ——" (Denzil's language occasionally reminded one that he had been a sailor) "who had cheated a lot of poor servant-girls out of their savings. My fists itched to be at that lubber! There's a good deal to be said for the fighting instinct in man, you know."

"So thinks 'Arry of the music-halls."

Glazzard's reply reflects the other, dominant side of Gissing's personality. This self is to be found in the pacifist chapters of *The Whirlpool* (1897) and *The Crown of Life* (1899) and in an essay entitled "Tyrtaeus,"[60] written just before the outbreak of the Boer War, strongly condemning the warlike spirit in the poetry of Swinburne and Kipling.

From the artistic point of view, "All for Love" indicates that Gissing was still seeking his own way. It is easier to determine the influences under which he was laboring than to trace in the book the development of themes which go to form the warp and woof of his great social novels. The recourse to the horrible, which is conspicuous in most of the American short stories reprinted in *Brownie* (1931), can still be noticed in the last chapters. He had recently read Poe's tales with great admiration[61] and tried to emulate them in "Cain and Abel,"[62] and the death of Philip Vanstone seems to proceed from the same fountainhead. But Gissing also looked toward Dickens, whose *Oliver Twist* offered him the combined themes of fear and violence. He used melodramatic devices to facilitate the creation of appropriate feelings in his characters. Threat causes fright, which in turn provokes brute force.

Yet, like Dickens and in conformity with the tendencies present in the bulk of his works, he chose to base his story on everyday life. Such fantastic devices as an infernal machine or a woman charmed

---

that there is no other efficacious way with these ornaments of their sex. A felling and stunning and all but killing blow, followed by paralysis and slow death. A sharp remedy, but no whit sharper than the evil it cures" (*Charles Dickens: A Critical Study*, p. 143).

[60] *The Review of the Week*, November 4, 1899, pp. 6–7.
[61] See his letter to Algernon dated August 20, 1879, in the Berg Collection.
[62] See Section VII below.

by a rattlesnake, which occur in the tales written in Chicago, were now dismissed in favor of more realistic agencies. He may have been following the example of Wilkie Collins, who combined terror with very careful plot construction;[63] at any rate, he was aiming at a plausible rendering of life and removed from his story all supernatural elements. As he later suggested to his brother during Algernon's apprenticeship in the art of fiction, each chapter contains some incident or revelation which keeps the reader's interest alive; hence one has the impression of staginess and mechanical unfolding of the narrative, which, one feels, is almost too cleverly constructed. But it is just possible that Gissing intended to submit his story for serialization, in which case his method would appear more justified. At all events, the search for literary effects in the most unusual aspects of everyday existence soon ceased to interest him. With the exception of *The Town Traveller*, inspired by a contemporary scandal,[64] he increasingly avoided presenting events out of the ordinary, a forbearance which reaches its height in his short stories of the middle nineties, with their total rejection of romanticism and sensationalism.

In this short novel Gissing was too much concerned with the

---

[63] There are good reasons to assume that Gissing was thinking of Wilkie Collins. If the presence of Collins' favorite themes or devices or situations (mysterious identity, anonymous letters, blackmail, family secrets, attack by thieves, enticement of the heroine into matrimony) fails to convince, one may quote Collins who said that in the character of Sarah Leeson, the heroine of *The Dead Secret* (1857), he attempted to trace "the influence of a heavy responsibility on a naturally timid woman, whose mind was neither strong enough to bear it, nor bold enough to drop it altogether," a description which might well apply to Bertha. The titles of Collins' novels—*Man and Wife, Miss or Mrs?, Hide and Seek*—at least suggest the type of situation on which Gissing's imagination was then working. It is also curious to note that *The Frozen Deep* might have served for the title of any of the last three chapters of "All for Love," in which the villain's name, Vanstone, happens to be that of the heroine of Collins' *No Name* (1862), Magdalen Vanstone. The resemblance, however, remains superficial, and if, with Collins, villains are generally likable, in Gissing's works they never are, nor does the protest against the injustice of English marriage laws uttered by Collins find much of an echo in "All for Love." Thus, the influence of Collins' mystery stories appears to be diffuse but none the less certain.

[64] The Druce-Portland affair, on which two books can be consulted: *The Druce-Portland Case* by Theodore Besterman (London: Duckworth, 1935), and *Painful Details* by Michael Harrison (London: Max Parrish and Co., 1962), chap. 12.

concatenation of events to pay great attention to psychology. Not only can a minor character like Harriet Golland be reduced to spitefulness and jealousy and a universal newsmonger like Miss Chad be censured for her lack of originality, but the trio round whom the plot revolves are observed rather perfunctorily. Vanstone is a villain who could not be left unpunished in a moral tale dealing with lapses from virtue; his intelligence should not have empowered him to escape from the hands of the police unless Gissing meant them to be his inferiors in that respect. Her sentimentality and helplessness give Bertha the appearance of a complete victim, when she should have been less innocent; compared with Carrie Mitchell, her immediate predecessor, she is no more than a child-wife, the model for whom Gissing found in Dora Copperfield. In Laurence's love for her, which is bloodless and idealized, we sense Gissing the undergraduate, trying to rescue Nell from her life of shame. His final burst of energetic action is compatible with great moral weakness, as was also the case with his creator.

Doubtless Gissing could—and would—have selected a bolder subject had not the repressive moralism of Mrs. Grundy forbidden him to show adultery in its natural colors. Roberts has described his friend's complaints about the intolerable restrictions that were imposed on the novelist as late as the eighties, constraints which often led to absurd or highly improbable situations: Bertha had been Philip Vanstone's wife, and Laurence Bloomfield was a doctor, yet he could marry her without realizing this fact. The only freedom left to Gissing, though it was not without possible consequences for his income, was to kill off as many characters as he wished. He later noted this paradox with bitterness in refusing to deal with the character of "Nancy, or of other lost creatures appearing in Dickens":

> The Emperor Augustus, we are told, objected to the presence of women at the public games when athletes appeared unclad; but he saw nothing improper in their watching the death combats of gladiators. May we not find a parallel to this in the English censorship? To exhibit the actual course of things in a story of lawless (nay, or of lawful) love is utterly forbidden; on the other hand, a novelist may indulge in ghastly bloodshed to any extent of which his stomach is capable. Dickens, the great writer, even appears on a public platform and recites with terrible power the murder of a prostitute by a burglar, yet no voice is raised in protest. Gore is perfectly decent;

but the secrets of an impassioned heart are too shameful to come before us even in a whisper.[65]

In mock moralism he allows death to descend upon the main actors of the drama: Vanstone pays for abandoning his wife and wringing money from a stranger; Laurence, by throwing himself into the canal, expiates his crime, and the *coup de grâce* administered to Bertha is her just penalty for her sin of omission—and her polyandry. As for old Mrs. Bloomfield, we leave her in a state of blessed incomprehension.

One must, of course, expect certain deficiencies in technique and style from a budding novelist of twenty-two. We can hardly blame him for taking up the buttonholing manner of a Thackeray and addressing the reader directly, for greater men than he had used that trick profusely; Gissing was following a practice which he condemned a few years later. Perhaps a more serious defect lies in his awkward justifications of his authorial interpolations like that in the last paragraph, where it is said that Vanstone apparently confided his secret to no one, "doubtless wishing to reap all the profit himself." There are also some graceless split infinitives and a disquieting recurrence of the phrase "at length," but it may be assumed that Gissing would have corrected these minor blemishes in the proofs had the manuscript been published. The true signs of immaturity are elsewhere, notably in his emulation of often second-rate passages in the works of older writers.

But what if, after all, the clocklike progression of the plot, the summary psychology, the hackneyed situations, and the propitiatory bloodshed at the end were a satire or a pastiche of the cheap novelette of the day? Gissing did threaten to write a volume to be entitled *A Highly Respectable Story,* in which he would ridicule the taste of the critics and the public, this as a sequel to the offensive and never published *Mrs. Grundy's Enemies.*[66] If the notion that this is a parody could be entertained, it would be the saving grace of a very amateurish piece of writing astounding after the fair promise of *Workers in the Dawn,* but this assumption is rather far-fetched, and it is perhaps

[65] *Charles Dickens: A Critical Study,* pp. 158–59.
[66] See his letter to Algernon of February 14, 1883, in *LMF,* p. 123.

safer to see "All for Love" merely as a somewhat unexpected but quite illuminating step in the author's early career.

VI: "The Last Half-Crown"

"The Last Half-Crown" possesses a host of features highly characteristic of Gissing's earlier work. It is a slender tale told with grim earnestness in a moment of despair, or at least in a moment when he tried to recapture the sense of his own hopelessness shortly after his return from America.

The setting of the story is drawn from Gissing's own life. From the end of 1877 to September, 1878, he lived at 22 Colville Place, a mean lane that was destroyed by bombing during World War II. The locality and its atmosphere are described in *Henry Ryecroft* (Spring X):

> I see that alley hidden on the west side of Tottenham Court Road, where, after living in a back bedroom on the top floor, I had to exchange for the front cellar; there was a difference, if I remember rightly, of sixpence a week, and sixpence, in those days, was a very great consideration—why, it meant a couple of meals. (I once *found* sixpence in the street, and had an exultation which is vivid in me at this moment.) The front cellar was stone-floored; its furniture was a table, a chair, a wash-stand, and a bed; the window, which of course had never been cleaned since it was put in, received light through a flat grating in the alley above. Here I lived; here *I wrote*. Yes, "literary work" was done at that filthy deal table, on which, by the bye, lay my Homer, my Shakespeare, and the few other books I then possessed. At night, as I lay in bed, I used to hear the tramp, tramp of a *posse* of policemen who passed along the alley on their way to relieve guard; their heavy feet sometimes sounded on the grating above my window.

The resemblances are striking. Gissing made his own two successive lodgings at the same address as the homes of Harold Sansom and Mrs. Wilson and Lizzie. The furniture in Harold's garret is as rudimentary as that in Ryecroft's cellar, and the situation of the basements is identical. The light of day filtered into them through a dirty window separated from the pavement by a grating.

The hero's character and predicament also resemble those of the novelist. Gissing's stay in Colville Place was a time of starvation, of ill health, of physical and material unease. He had not come to live there "of his own free will," and his childhood at Wakefield before his father's death had offered him "the comforts of a very different home." Behind "the miserable train of circumstances," one catches an echo of the author's own disgrace and scant repentance. He, too, forced himself to write when his ill-nourished brain was paralyzed by material cares and feared that, had an employer been tempted to engage him, his threadbare clothes would do him a disservice.[67] Just as Harold took long, solitary walks in London, Gissing haunted the city streets to find suitable material for his novel in progress.[68] He occasionally did odd jobs for the secretary of a hospital and, goaded by necessity, made "desperate efforts to write something on his return." Late at night, when he had finished his writing, he sought to forget his misery by taking down from his row of books a volume of Gibbon's *Decline and Fall of the Roman Empire* (a prize from his Manchester days) or a battered copy of Horace. He was friendless as his hero—he had not yet met Eduard Bertz, and Morley Roberts, his former college friend, was wandering in the Australian bush.

The despair which is said to have driven him to the verge of suicide at Niagara Falls frequently took hold of him at Colville Place. His brother William, whose own situation was unenviable, did his best to cheer him up, but George's spirits were generally as low as Harold Sansom's. "I have given up all hope of anything but starvation," he lamented in July, 1878.[69] Soon, however, his financial predicament was eased for a while. On his father's death, his share of a trust fund had been thrown into chancery, and a sum of about three hundred pounds fell to him on coming of age.

Other autobiographical notes are sounded in "The Last Half-Crown." First, the exultation recalled by Gissing at finding sixpence in the street suggested his plot to him.[70] Second, he endowed his hero with a quality which he often revealed in his own life: a generosity that was the result of shyness and the fear of offending others. One

---

[67] "Am in a perfectly doleful state for clothes. Even should any good position turn up, I fear I shall be absolutely debarred from obtaining it by my disreputable appearance" (to Algernon, February 28, 1878, Berg Collection).

[68] See William's letter to George, June 16, 1878: "It must be very interesting examining the holes of London, as long as you don't catch a fever" (*LMF*, p. 31).

[69] To Algernon, July 24, 1878, *LMF*, p. 32.

[70] See *Henry Ryecroft*, Spring X, and, in the same volume, the anecdote of the child who cried because he had lost sixpence (Spring III).

feels quite sure, in the light of his attitude toward Algernon after the latter determined to earn his living by his pen or toward Plitt in Paris and Naples, that he would have acted like Harold under similar conditions, probably cursing himself all the while for his own weakness. There were truths which he could not bring himself to tell.

Crude as the story may appear, it is a distinct improvement upon the American tales, in which, as a rule, he seemed more concerned with the plot than with the characters and made a shameless use of coincidences and fantastic devices to bring about the denouement. Social agencies take the place of arbitrary fate. There is nothing incongruous in the narrative; we can carp at the tinge of staginess and sentimentality, but the characters themselves are perfectly lifelike, and, if the young writer may appear to some readers to have too much of a Chatterton in him, he is, after all, only the slightly too obvious dramatization of the author himself. Harold acknowledges his defeat, from which Gissing was saved by the exhortations of his brothers. The ending is foreshadowed several times unambiguously. Harold is, we feel from the outset, one of "those of more delicate mould [who] are soon driven to strange extremities," and when he asks Mrs. Wilson to tell the milkman not to leave any milk for him, the story is as good as over. Indeed, his Christian name, reminiscent of Byron's romantic youth who "almost long'd for woe, / And e'en for change of scene would seek the shades below," marks him for a tragic life. The protagonist of the third short story in the present volume bears the same name, as does Biffen, the eccentric novelist in *New Grub Street*, who, a penniless writer like Harold, poisons himself on Putney Hill. His compassion, associated as it is with sexual emotion, is of the kind which led Gissing to disaster at Manchester.

Lizzie's presence accounts for the sentimental note in the narrative. She is the lineal descendant of Marion Hyde, the fair cripple in "The Warden's Daughter," whose idealization is carried even further. Her nascent love for Harold, also born of pity, is developed later, in Gissing's last proletarian novel, in the character of Jane Snowdon, a poor working-class girl who looks up to Sidney Kirkwood with speechless admiration and tenderness.

The two characters of Mrs. Wilson and Mrs. Higgs, and indeed Lizzie's sentimentality, have a strong Dickensian flavour about them.

Mrs. Wilson has the roundabout Cockney way of getting to the point of a story and joyfully mutilates the English tongue. As for Mrs. Higgs, she is a diminutive replica of the rapacious, evil-tongued Mrs. Pettindund in *Workers in the Dawn* and suggests the picturesque though sinister world of landladies so copiously developed in Gissing's later novels and stories. Her talent for grim humor is quite unconscious, and she assumes the melodramatic part of the villain: but for her insistence on being paid the week's rent in advance, Harold's suicide might have been prevented.

Money, the possession or lack of it, is in the last analysis the only theme of "The Last Half-Crown," as it is in *Demos, New Grub Street*, and *Born in Exile*. Even in Wakefield when his father's shop fed and clothed the seven members of his family, Gissing had been deeply impressed by the tyranny of cash. One day his father borrowed a life of Dürer from a book club, and when the time came for returning it, he read on his son's face the regret that the volume had to be sent away and deplored the fact that he could not afford to buy it. Over twenty-five years later his son put down this anecdote, concluding with the memory of his own bashful apology for appearing to ask his father to buy the volume.[71]

Gissing's indignant protest against Harold Sansom's abject poverty might have been rounded off nicely with this passionate comment on the situation of Emily Hood in *A Life's Morning*, at the end of chapter 5:

One would not murmur at the kindly order of life, whereby passion gives place to gentle habitudes, and the fiery soul of youth tames itself to comely gravity; but that love and joy, the delights of eager sense and of hallowed aspiration, should be smothered in the foul dust of a brute combat for bread, that the stinted energies of early years should change themselves to the blasted hopes of failing manhood in a world made ill by human perverseness, this is not easily—it may be, not well—borne with patience. Put money in thy purse; and again, put money in thy purse; for, as the world is ordered, to lack current coin is to lack the privileges of humanity, and indigence is the death of the soul.

Or again, one recalls this heart-felt sentence in *Henry Ryecroft* (Spring V): "When I think of all the sorrow and the barrenness that

[71] The story is taken from a notebook held by the Yale University Library, "Reminiscences of my Father." The entry was made in 1896.

has been wrought in my life by want of a few more pounds per annum than I was able to earn, I stand aghast at money's significance." Poverty among the "ignobly decent" was in those days associated with an oppressive sense of respectability. Harold is unable to leave the house until nightfall on account of his threadbare clothes, and, in a now almost incredible tragedy, Mr. Hood, in *A Life's Morning*, after his hat is blown away in a train, thinks it impossible to walk in town without one, steals some money from his employer to buy a new one, and precipitates a series of disasters, culminating in his suicide. Mr. Hood, highly self-conscious, fears that his bare head will make some people sneer, and "the sneer would have cut him like a knife."

In a more general way, the evocation of the London crowd, with the typical classical allusion to "the beasts at Ephesus," anticipates the well-known bank holiday scene in *The Nether World* (chap. 12):

It is a great review of the People. On the whole how respectable they are, how sober, how deadly dull! See how worn-out the poor girls are becoming, how they gape, what listless eyes most of them have! The stoop in the shoulders so universal among them merely means over-toil in the workroom. Not one in a thousand shows the elements of taste in dress; vulgarity and worse glares in all but every costume. Observe the middle-aged women; it would be small surprise that their good looks had vanished, but whence comes it they are animal, repulsive, absolutely vicious in ugliness? Mark the men in their turn: four in every six have visages so deformed by ill-health that they excite disgust; their hair is cut down to within half an inch of the scalp; their legs are twisted out of shape by evil conditions of life from birth upwards. Whenever a youth and a girl come along arm-in-arm, how flagrantly shows the man's coarseness! They are pretty, so many of these girls, delicate of feature, graceful did but their slavery allow them natural development; and the heart sinks as one sees them side by side with the men who are to be their husbands.

Yet the similarity in subject matter and style conceals one essential difference. In "The Last Half-Crown" Gissing speaks as one in sympathy with the sufferings of the people, indeed, as one of them. By the time he wrote *The Nether World*, though Nell's death did temporarily modify his new attitude, he had come to realize that his aspirations and intellectual sufferings had little in common with those of the masses. He had disassociated himself from demos. No longer could he address a socialist audience in a London working-class club on "Faith and Reason" or "The State Church from a Rationalist's Point of View," not because his opinions on these topics were very much altered but because he had grown to despair of the people. He had made the long intellectual journey from the enthusiastic altruism of Arthur Golding in *Workers in the Dawn* to the argumentative skepticism of Osmond Waymark in *The Unclassed*. The following comment may safely be read as Gissing's confession:

> I often amuse myself with taking to pieces my former self. I was not a conscious hypocrite in those days of violent radicalism, working-man's club lecturing, and the like; the fault was that I understood myself as yet so imperfectly. That zeal on behalf of the suffering masses was nothing more nor less than disguised zeal on behalf of my own starved passions. I was poor and desperate, life had no pleasures, the future seemed hopeless, yet I was overflowing with vehement desires, every nerve in me was a hunger which cried to be appeased. I identified myself with the poor and ignorant; I did not make their cause my own, but my own cause theirs.[72]

VII: "Cain and Abel"

In his efforts to get a foothold in the English literary world, Gissing inevitably bethought himself of his experiences in Chicago, when his only income derived from the fees he received for his short stories in the local press. In a fair number of these, which he had written under the pressures of time and hunger, he had chosen thrilling themes, his readers being more likely to be captivated by them than by the social indignation that was beginning to seethe in him. The shrillest note in this high-pitched series was struck in the Dr. Vargrave trilogy, composed of "The Death-Clock," "The Serpent Charm," and "Dead and Alive," and the better-known "Brownie." Looking back after three years, Gissing could not place these stories in the front rank of his achievements, yet he could not altogether dismiss the possibility of using themes of which the British reading public, like its American counterpart, never seemed to tire. Was he to revise all his stories, as he had done with "An Artist's Child," a considerably expanded version of which appeared in *Tinsley's Magazine* for January, 1878, and try to sell them again to the more exacting English editors? The writing of two novels—one perhaps already

[72] Chap. 25.

committed to the flames, the other going the round of London publishers—had made him very critical of his early work. His artistic
sense assured him that his American tales would not stand revision
and that he must find new subjects, invent new stories altogether.

Had Gissing been asked at the end of his life what had suggested
the idea of "Cain and Abel," he would probably have replied that,
being short of inspiration, he turned to the Bible and spun out a
Poesque story from Genesis, chapter 3. In saying this, he would, I
think, have been quite sincere. However, at the time it was by no
means natural and spontaneous for young Gissing to look for a subject in the Bible, a book he had never been encouraged to read. His
use of the story of Abel and Cain has some psychological interest
because, together with some of his other tales, it shows how, in the
years immediately following his dramatic expulsion from Owens
College, his mind fastened on "situations"—in the theatrical sense of
the word—illustrative of injustice and the cruelty of fate. If, by an
effort of will, he succeeded in putting aside the theme of injustice, as
in "All for Love," he fell back on that of violence. In "Cain and
Abel" we find the two associated. In an atmosphere of diabolical
machinations (one of the few settings in which Gissing's mental
faculties could function easily at the time), he imagines himself
within the four walls of a prison cell. Here, as in his more mature
fiction, man appears as a captive. Heredity, family surroundings,
education, social limitations—wherever he looks, some obstacle con-
fronts him. However, one has the impression that, after his obsession
had provided the outline of the tale, Gissing rather enjoyed developing
the plot. As he wrote he must have become decreasingly committed to
his gloomy view, and I venture to guess that the work of composition
acted on him as a catharsis. In the evening of January 2, 1880, he
could stand back from his manuscript with the half-amused look of
the reader who sees through the writer's intentions and technique but
nonetheless appreciates the effect produced.

Naturally, the psychological analysis and the verisimilitude of
the action are subordinated to the main aim, the creation of an atmosphere. The dramatis personae have no human complexity, and none
is intended. Eli Charnock (Gissing learned early the trick of con-
veying a character's personality through his name) is motivated only

by systematic ill-will and a gratuitous desire for revenge upon his sister-in-law and her son Cain. He is a caricature, devoid of any redeeming feature. Abel appears to be nothing more than a replica of his uncle, and the two women are content to submit to man and fate. Psychological simplification could hardly go further. In this assault of wickedness and trickery upon meekness and innocence, Gissing, as in "All for Love," sees to it that morality gets its due. He does make the shadowy, vacillating heroine sacrifice her honor, but he hastens to punish all the parties involved in the rather unnatural mischief. Cain Charnock is one more of the heroes, so common in the author's early work, whose guilt is only apparent. However— a proof of temporary disengagement—there is a difference between Cain and, say, Aymer Preston in "The Warden's Daughter" or Joseph Yates in "Joseph Yates' Temptation." The storyteller explains rather than denounces. He would seem to have realized that exposition can be achieved without its alluring adjunct, indignation.

The story is almost completely free of autobiographical elements. One may wonder whether the description of Cain's father as "a fairly well-to-do tradesman" and "a man of kindly disposition and some intellectual pretensions" does not have some kinship with Gissing's own father. Thomas Gissing's wealth was modest enough, but his intellectual capacities as a pharmaceutical chemist, botanist, and poet commanded respect in Wakefield. He transmitted his curiosity for the things of the mind to his eldest son, who in turn often attributed it to his protagonists when they were sympathetic (Mr. Charnock, like Cain, lacks this attribute). It is also worth noting that Cain uses language concerning women which Gissing never completely discarded even when brutal experience had taught him that such perfection rarely walks the earth. "So pure and noble a being," says Cain of Winifred. "Their Pretty Way" shows the writer in another mood, but Gabrielle Fleury, his last companion, restored for a time his capacity for idealization, as is clearly shown in *The Crown of Life*.

"Cain and Abel" presents some situations which the author, here and in some later stories, took pleasure in stigmatizing: martyred childhood, the dispute over a child's right to education (which brings about a conflict between Cain and his mother reminiscent of David

Copperfield's frustration in expressing his love for his mother after her marriage to Murdstone), the helplessness of the poorly educated Victorian widow, the search for solace in debauch (depicted at some length in *Workers in the Dawn*), and parental refusal to let children marry according to their inclination. The hopeless love of Cain and Winifred presages the impossible union of Harold Cuthbertson and Bertha Lashmore in "The Quarry on the Heath."

Gissing was gradually overcoming the more obvious problems of his art and acquiring some finesse. The tale is well told and shows a capacity for terseness when terseness is required either for stylistic reasons or because of the dramatic turn taken by the action. The episodes unfold smoothly, with just an occasional authorial intervention, which, by warning of the new phase to come, arouses the reader's interest. The use of the first person singular, which Gissing soon dropped and did not resume until the end of his career, gives a welcome conviction and urgency to the tale, a freshness, in spite of the subject, comparable to that of two other stories of the same period, "My First Rehearsal" and "My Clerical Rival."

In view of the mediocrity of the stories published in the popular magazines of the time, it is surprising to find that none of those Gissing wrote at 5 Hanover Street were accepted. He could, as the occasion demanded, lose all self-confidence or show indomitable perseverance: perhaps here he gave up the struggle too easily. In Chicago he had, with much poorer stories, shown greater persistence and obstinacy in attempting to sell them, doubtless because his physical survival was at stake. Now, despite his frequent references to the specter of starvation, he had the income from his private tuition to live on, and it was still possible that *Workers in the Dawn* would prove a success.

As an experiment in suspense, "Cain and Abel" evinces some power. The flashback, in particular, avoids a beginning which might have been laborious and lengthy, yet does not dissipate our interest because we nevertheless have to wait until the end of the story to discover the circumstances of the crime announced in the title itself. There are echoes here of some tales by Poe, and the motto of "MS Found in a Bottle" may well have given him the idea of the subject.

Poe quotes two lines from Quinault: "Qui n'a plus qu'un moment à
vivre / N'a plus rien à dissimuler" ("he who has but a moment to live
no longer has anything to dissemble"). And Gissing may have had in
mind the beginning of "The Pit and the Pendulum": "The sentence
—the dread sentence of death—was the last of distinct accentuation
which reached my ears." The rhythm of Poe's periods lingers in the
opening paragraphs of "Cain and Abel," harmonious and majestic,
fraught with impending woe. From the first we are enveloped in an
atmosphere of mystery and irrevocable fatality which is quite different from that in "The Last Half-Crown"; thanks to his model Gissing
does not fall into the trap of self-pity. He has no time for meditation
on his hero's unjust treatment. Indeed, the phrase "yet condemned
justly," which closes the first sentence, has the value of a promise
to the reader. We shall have a straightforward narrative and "circumstantial evidence," and moral undertones shall be discreet.
Neither the narrator nor the hero hesitates. We know that we are
heading for catastrophe.

There is another suggestion of Poe in the frequent allusions to
the prisoner's dreadful past and equally horrible future. The narrow
cage of the present allows only visions of either. We are caught between horror and incomprehension. The epithets belong to Poe's reg-
ister: phrases such as "overmastering dread," "the unutterable degradation of my trial," and "some fearful and inexplicable destiny"
might have been borrowed en bloc from the *Tales of Mystery and
Imagination*. Only after the initial paragraphs does Gissing seem
more independent of his model because he then has his own story
to tell.

It is to be feared that readers who know Gissing only through
New Grub Street or *Henry Ryecroft* will not easily see the promise
of great literary talent in "Cain and Abel." They will perhaps discover in it little more than a deliberate quest for the sensational.
The quest is indubitably there, but beyond the experimentation and
imitation, the adventure bordering on the penny dreadful, there lies
the belief Gissing expressed at the height of his career: "If I hold
any religion at all, it is *Manichaeism*." At twenty-two his illustration
of this creed was spectacular and dramatic; at forty-four when he

47

revised *Henry Ryecroft,* he was content to let his thoughts wander in search of manifestations of it in literature or in nature, in the Greek dramatists or in the scenery during a solitary walk.

VIII: "The Quarry on the Heath"

Whereas "The Last Half-Crown" did not claim to be more than a vignette and "Cain and Abel" was prudently imitative, "The Quarry on the Heath" reveals more ambition and greater skill. This time Gissing places his action within a wider framework than in "The Last Half-Crown" and again shuns the strictly chronological narrative. He makes a few necessary incursions into the past of his characters and manages to focus on a restricted period of time, drawing some dramatic effects from this concentration. As in "Cain and Abel," the narrative is never unbalanced, and, even if the last paragraph looks somewhat like an after-thought designed to placate Mrs. Grundy, it does not disturb the over-all impression of harmony. The strange atmosphere produced by the opening pages, which is not unlike our first glimpse of *The Mayor of Casterbridge*, immediately engages the reader's interest.

In an indirect way, the story, like "All for Love," demonstrates how the artist's choice of his subject came up against moral taboos. True, Gissing had not yet abandoned his questionable taste for melo-drama,[73] but he would not have selected such a subject had he been free to depict life as he saw it. Adultery was what he meant to study, and since neither public nor publishers would allow its treatment in a novel (he had ignored the prohibition in "Cain and Abel," per-haps to his own disadvantage), he was, paradoxically, led to turn to a far more exceptional and abnormal case which had the apparently saving grace that the characters knew nothing of their sin. Incestuous love was made artistically tolerable to the average reader by the fact that Harold Cuthbertson and Bertha Lashmore were ignorant of

[73] Perhaps he never shed it altogether, as I have suggested above in referring to *The Town Traveller,* but other examples likely to have been inspired by contem-porary news items, as was the plot of *The Mayor of Casterbridge,* crop up here and there in his major novels: Mrs. Damerel and her underhanded doings in *In the Year of Jubilee,* for example, or the rather ambiguous situation of Mrs. Borisoff in *The Crown of Life.*

their true connection. Gissing repeatedly complained[74] that the English novelist of his day was handicapped by the hypocrisy prevalent in his country, and one may imagine his vituperation of moralists of all kinds as he developed the plot of "The Quarry on the Heath."

As the narrative moves along, one naturally sees relationships between this or that moment or attitude and other moments or attitudes in the published works. For the general theme—expressed in one of the canceled titles, "Visited upon the Children"—Gissing relied on his first published short story, "The Sins of the Fathers." There the motivation was of the weakest. A well-to-do English cotton spinner, Mr. Vincent, treacherously pretends to give his assent to his son's marriage to a girl of the lower class named Laura Lindon on condition that Leonard Vincent go to America and earn his living there until he attains his majority. He leaves for the United States, and his fiancée comes to live with his parents. After some time his father has a forged letter sent Laura in which her fiancé asserts that he has lost all affection for her. The frantic Laura leaves the Vincents' house, and Leonard is informed by his father that she has been taken ill and has died. She reappears some years later in America, where Leonard has married in the interim, and, on learning his situation, drags him to a river in which they both perish by drowning. The last sentence points the moral of the story: "The thick snow soon made the river once more a smooth white surface, and the hidden depths bore witness to the edict that the sins of the fathers shall be visited upon the children."[75] Although the two narratives differ sufficiently in outline, at least two particulars have survived in "The Quarry on the Heath." Both Harold and Leonard, like Gissing in Waltham, are schoolteachers, and they die the same death—snowy ice yields under their weight and they sink into the frozen depths.

[74] Beside the examples given in Section V above, one may recall Gissing's attack on prudery in the *Pall Mall Gazette* of December 15, 1884, or the following passage in a letter to Thomas Hardy dated June 30, 1886: "In literature my interests begin and end; I hope to make my life and all its acquirements subservient to my ideal of artistic creation. . . . The misery of it is that, writing for English people, one may not be thorough; reticences and superficialities have so often to fill places where one is willing to put in honest work" (University of California at Los Angeles Library).

[75] *The Sins of the Fathers and Other Tales*, p. 31.

Other material elements were transferred to *A Life's Morning*. The quarry was a feature of the local topography of the novelist's home town (Wakefield became Dunfield in the novel) and was the scene of James Hood's death, as it was of Harold Cuthbertson's. Indeed, the whole atmosphere of Dunfield and of the neighboring villages cannot be distinguished from that of Wastell Heath, which is really a first version of Banbrigg in the book (Agbrigg, in fact). The following extracts from chapter 5, "The Shadow of Home," amply demonstrate the point:

The house which was the end of Emily's journey was situated two miles outside the town of Dunfield, on the high road going southward, just before it enters upon a rising tract of common land known as the Heath. It was one of a row of two-storied dwellings, built of glazed brick, each with a wide projecting window on the right hand of the front door, and with a patch of garden railed in from the road, the row being part of a straggling colony which is called Banbrigg. Immediately opposite these houses stood an ecclesiastical edifice of depressing appearance, stone-built, wholly without ornament, presenting a corner to the highway, a chapel-of-ease for worshippers unable to go as far as Dunfield. . . . There was a public-house, or rather, as it frankly styled itself in large letters on the window, a dram-shop. . . . At no season, and under no advantage of sky, was Banbrigg a delectable abode. Though within easy reach of country which was not without rural aspects, it was marked too unmistakably with the squalor of a manufacturing district. . . . The stretch of road between it and the bridge by which the river was crossed into Dunfield had in its long, hard ugliness something dispiriting. Though hedges bordered it here and there, they were stunted and grimed. . . . . The Heath formed the long side of a slowly rising hill; at the foot the road divided itself into two branches, and the dusty tracks climbed at a wide angle with each other. The one which Emily and her father pursued led up to stone quarries, which had been for a long time in working, and, skirting these, to the level ground above them, which was the end of the region of furze and bracken. . . . Over all hung a canopy of foul vapour, heavy, pestiferous. Take in your fingers a spray from one of the trees even here on the Heath, and its touch left a soil.

In chapter 13, when the body of Emily's father is discovered by Dagworthy's dog, there even occurs the mention of a little grass-bordered pool, which was, rather needlessly, carried over from the description in "The Quarry on the Heath." Similarly, the delirium of the heroine recurs in the longer story. One can also see how Gissing passed from one story of frustrated love to another (for *A Life's Morning* was at first intended to end tragically) through an intermediate stage marked by *Pastures New*, the sketch of a novel outlined by George for his brother Algernon. The broad lines of the narrative are described in a letter of October 31, 1883. The novel was meant to relate the experiences of a Wakefield girl whom her parents wanted to marry to some stupid young man of the town who was on the point of being chosen mayor, although her heart was drawn to a more intellectual young fellow with advanced ideas. That the story was to have a happy ending is merely a concession to Algernon, for when George developed it for his own use, only the threat of starvation induced him to rewrite the last chapters after James Payn, manuscript reader for Smith, Elder, had made a happy ending the condition for his acceptance.

On the plane of characterization, some features of "The Quarry on the Heath" are also used in subsequent novels. Mrs. Lashmore, a passive woman who is cowed in her husband's presence, foreshadows both the motherly, poverty-stricken Mrs. Hood in *A Life's Morning* and Mrs. Alfred Yule in *New Grub Street*. The latter's husband cuts the same intolerant, impatient, tyrannical figure as does Reverend Lashmore in the short story. Altered to Lashmar, this name reappears in *Our Friend the Charlatan*, where the hero's father, another skeptical clergyman, is more akin to Reverend Norman in *Workers in the Dawn* or Reverend Wyvern in *Demos* than to Bertha's diabolical scarecrow of a parent.

The tale contains some of Gissing's favorite tricks. Bertha's and Harold's mutual ignorance of their blood relationship is but a tragic variant of a theme used repeatedly in the early short stories, that of misapprehension. In "A Terrible Mistake," written in Gissing's Chicago period, two friends are in love with two sisters but imagine that they are each attached to the same girl. In "My Clerical Rival" the hero eventually discovers that his supposed rival, a curate with highly temporal interests, is courting his sweetheart's affluent widowed mother, and the leading character of "An Heiress on Condition" assumes a double identity to increase the difficulty he experiences in winning his fair cousin's hand. Reverend Lashmore's casual overhearing of the lovers suggests the similar scene in *Thyrza*, and death by drowning recurs so frequently in the early writings as to suggest an obsession.[76] Gissing takes care to hint at it when he brings together the clergyman and the young people for the first time. Bertha's protest that her father has no right to part her from Harold is followed by the symbolic splash of a piece of stone or earth into the pool. Gissing endeavors, less awkwardly than in the American stories, such as "Brownie," to create a somber, violent atmosphere and strikes a lurid note from the very first line of the opening description. If anything, the characters are almost too closely in harmony with their surroundings. Gissing shows thereby how much he disliked his native town and the phenomenon it exemplified—industrialism—which he vehemently attacked in three successive novels, *Isabel Clarendon*, *A Life's Morning*, and *Demos*. At the same time, it is difficult to rule out the influence of Emily Brontë's pictures of Yorkshire life. Gissing had read *Wuthering Heights* at an early age and, even though it may have been unconscious, tried to catch something of its tormented, painful atmosphere, from which his melodramatic strain is partially derived.

Technically, "The Quarry on the Heath" helps one to understand how Gissing passed from the blood-curdling tales published in the American press to his mature work. The behavior of the actors of this drama is more human and their conduct is made psychologically more plausible, but Gissing also has to contend with the habits he had formed in the construction of three-deckers, which prompt him to explore the antecedents of the characters at unnecessary length. The crispness in an O. Henry story like "The Cop and the Anthem" or in a Hubert Crackanthorpe story like "Saint-Pé" he rarely attained, but it is only just to add that he did not attempt to make his stories crisp. He preferred a somewhat flat, unsensational ending typical of most events in human life to a clever and unexpected conclusion.

The rough draft of "The Quarry on the Heath" gives us a fairly clear idea of Gissing at work. To all appearances the first page was the hardest. Should he start with a description of the village, or immediately introduce his characters? He modified some expressions, tried

[76] Another device, here merely embryonic, used at full length for Richard Mutimer in *Demos*, is to reveal a man's character through the books on his shelves: "Mr. Lashmore's library consisted of nothing but works of controversial theology, in literature he took no interest whatever."

to make the details more coherent, and removed an occasional trace of hostility toward Reverend Lashmore, which smacked of awkward authorial intrusion. Such sentences as "Let us hope Mr. Lashmore was not dwelling upon the images of a future world," with their clumsy irony, were wisely deleted in the final version, and the physical description of the lovers and account of their surprise was better organized.

The changes vary from one word to an entire paragraph in length. In magnitude they range from minor stylistic alterations (see, for example, footnotes 12 and 70), sometimes merely to correct a slip (see footnote 14) and in two cases a particularly infelicitous phrasing (see footnotes 30 and 80), to substitutions which seriously alter the course of the narrative. In the first version a fire was to be lit in Mr. Lashmore's room and all the letters were to be burned, but Gissing, who must have begun to write before working out all the details of the plot, would thus have been deprived of a ready means of convincing Harold of his parentage at the crucial moment. He also canceled various signs of emotion (see footnotes 33, 34, and 38) and touched up a few passages in the dialogue which were not in harmony with the character of the speaker: the clergyman's hospitable offer of a room in his house (footnote 54) was as out of tune as Cuthbertson's insolent retort in the hut (footnote 20). The change in Mr. Lashmore's age from fifty to forty-five, making him even younger at the time of his fault, adds plausibility to his behavior as a young man.

These characteristic examples taken from a manuscript for which, unlike most of Gissing's novels, we have the early drafts, indicate that whatever literary skill he still had to acquire, he was craftsmanlike in his approach. The difference between the first and second drafts indicates a great capacity for refinement.

IX: "The Lady of the Dedication"

In "The Last Half-Crown" Gissing timidly ventured into the domain of the writer's life. With "The Lady of the Dedication" he took a new step toward his novelist's novel, *New Grub Street*. By the time that he wrote this short story he had gained some experience of the publishing world, from a distance; he had also discussed his own position as an impecunious writer many a time with companions like Morley Roberts and Eduard Bertz, and, if we judge from the manner and conclusion of his narrative, the youthful optimism of his schooldays had not yet spent itself.

Robert Adler strikes one as a reflection of the author in reality and in his dreams. The vague, yet passionate, reference to Adler's past has an unmistakably apologetic flavor: "Never mind how a young man of education and talents came to be living thus from hand to mouth. It was not exactly his own fault, unless we may impute to a man as a crime the possession of a restless heart and impetuous qualities little consistent with prudence." Gissing, too, had grown quite accustomed to rejection of his manuscripts, but he had so far failed to score his first success against the "great big stupid" (he liked this phrase of Thackeray's and used it again in *Henry Ryecroft*). That came with *Demos,* by which time he could look back on his and Adler's "lodging-house in the neighborhood of Tottenham Court Road" from the standpoint of comparative security. He is not known to have resorted to the pawnshop in order to eat, but as late as 1890, some eight years after this story was written, he had to sell books off his shelves to survive until he could negotiate *New Grub Street.* He did not imagine he would experience such financial difficulties after his novel on socialism had made its mark.

In "The Lady of the Dedication," for once, he chooses to look at literary life with hope. The landlady and the prospect of the week's rent to pay, the loss of a poorly paid job, the overcoat in the pawnshop, the "ragged regiment" of books (which, like the artist's derisive scorn for the public, crops up anew in the reminiscences of Henry Ryecroft) are all present, as they are in that gloomy picture of literary bohemia, but a heaven-sent check and the promise of effective patronage relegate all embarrassments to the background. There are also signs that Gissing was thinking of the novelist's unfortunate dependence upon the commercial coalition of publishers and lending libraries. He dreamed of the day when sheer financial necessity would no longer compel him to spin out three-deckers—when, like Robert Adler, he could fill one volume and be successful. The sum received by his hero—fifteen pounds paid outright—also illustrates a problem which oppressed him for years. Not until 1892 was he able to use the royalty system, the only arrangement that was fair to both author and publisher. Until then his carking financial cares forced him to get the maximum out of his manuscripts immediately. Despite all these shadows, which were present for a decade, it is a jocose Gissing that we have in "The Lady of the Dedication." When he tried his hand again at light writing with *The Paying Guest* (1895), he did so with the outlook of middle age and was so displeased by the publisher's puff of the book that he promised himself never again to pander to the public taste for humor.[77] His own struggle for life had by then suppressed almost all his capacity for joyousness.

The gentle satire of Mr. Swanwick, the magazine editor, does not fully reflect Gissing's resentment at the treatment he had received from specimens of that tribe. Swanwick has never experienced the squalor and bitterness of Grub Street; he presents a benevolent, smiling face to the good-natured, yet incisive, criticisms of his wife. He spends only a moderate amount of time reading the manuscripts submitted to him and refuses to allow himself to be ruled by his spouse's sentimental generosity. He leads a life which young Gissing, from his garret or basement, viewed as nothing short of ideal but which he depicted in quite another light in *New Grub Street*. Mrs. Swanwick, on her side, embodies some of the qualities he associated with his ideal of womanhood and to a large extent found in his own life with Gabrielle Fleury. The editor's wife possesses the virtues of an able housekeeper while, on the intellectual plane, she offers her husband worthy company. No strife emanates from the kitchen, material things in the household are taken as a matter of course, and the children know how to behave themselves. Mrs. Swanwick rules almost unseen over her home; with everyone she shows a gentleness of manner and address to which Gissing was very sensitive; she would have soothed the wounds of Edwin Reardon or Godwin Peak. Good, cultured, intelligent, tender-hearted, she is a first sketch of Stella Westlake in *Demos*. Of course, she partakes too much of the good fairy to be absolutely convincing; in creating her, Gissing was indulging in wishful thinking—a weakness which

[77] He was faithful to his promise, unless *The Town Traveller*, written with a view to serialization but published only in book form, is considered as an exception.

his infernal life with Nell makes either astonishing or understandable, depending upon one's point of view.

The presentation of Ellen is of a piece with that of Mrs. Swanwick. Given her humble origin and her past work in a factory, her earnest desire for self-improvement has something remarkable about it. Late in his life, Gissing would look upon such an idealization with an indulgent smile, but in 1882 he was deadly serious. Though his failure to redeem Nell had long been acknowledged by both parties (had he not clearly foretold it through Carrie Mitchell in *Workers in the Dawn*?), he had not yet abandoned the dream of raising a working-class girl to his level of culture by his sheer intellectual force.

With women he was a born teacher; he could not lay books aside when making love. He read "The Pied Piper of Hamelin" to Edith Underwood in 1890 and Tennyson, Browning, and Poe to Gabrielle Fleury in 1898. In his books he continued to waver between his early faith in educating lower-class girls and belief in the futility of making such an attempt. *The Unclassed*, his next completed novel after "The Lady of the Dedication," shows the two trends side by side: Osmond Waymark succeeds in winning Ida Starr from the life of the streets, but Julian Casti is dragged down to ruin by his cousin Harriet Smales, whom he has endeavored to save. In "The Lady of the Dedication" Ellen Lake shares many attractions with Thyrza Trent, Gissing's heroine of the working class. They have the same charm, the same sensitivity, the same delicacy, the same taste for poetry. Their idealization forms a singular contrast with the impossible females, mostly of the middle classes, with whom his novels and short stories of the eighteen nineties are teeming. It is a far cry from the sweet, modest, pliable Ellen Lake to such vulgar and cantankerous creatures as the French sisters of *In the Year of Jubilee*.

Ellen helps us to realize to what extent Gissing associated pity with sexual emotion in his late teens and early twenties. Given this temperament, he was doomed to make a disastrous marriage. With a girl like Ellen Lake he would have been happy—at least for a while—but she is too much of a conglomerate of incompatible elements to have a counterpart in real life. In Edith Underwood, his second wife, he at first thought he had found the qualities he describes here, but matrimony revealed a character which was fundamentally bitter and rampageous, and she soon grew impatient with her husband's attempts to educate her. Yet in the days of his courtship he could have used to her (and perhaps did[78]) the very words of Robert Adler: "Without you the book would never have been written." And this would have been the literal truth: for months he had been wasting his time and losing his patience over a series of false starts, but once he met Edith inspiration descended again upon his discouraged, tormented brain, and he wrote *New Grub Street* at one stretch.

The presence of children in this early piece of fiction requires some comment. As a rule, children played next to no part in Gissing's writings until he himself became a father and was seriously concerned with his sons' education. The problem is examined for the first time in *In the Year of Jubilee* and more fully in *The Whirlpool*, but the actual turning point was probably represented by Reardon's son in *New Grub Street*. Hitherto his attitude, dictated by despair, might have been taken by the uninitiated for cruelty or cynicism. Thus, for instance, he wrote of the Hoods in *A Life's Morning*: "After Emily, two children were successively born; fate was kind to them, and neither survived infancy."[79] In "The Lady of the Dedication" the presence of children does not represent a burden incompatible with a leisurely style of life, and it is characteristic that they are associated with learning. We are allowed only a glimpse of Godfrey, but it can safely be asserted that Gissing remembered him in *Isabel Clarendon* when he created Master Percy, the son of Reverend Vissian. The rector's little boy, who is the same age as young Godfrey, offers a more fully developed portrait of an intelligent, quick-witted, well-bred, sympathetic child. This is how Gissing describes the boy's relations with the retiring, book-loving Kingcote, the anti-hero of the novel:

When he had tea with his friend everything tasted to him quite differently from the flavours of home; the mere bread became cake—he munched dry pieces with a strange relish, and the milk did not come from ordinary cows. But his great delight was when, after such a meal, he settled himself

---

[78] Alfred Gissing, the author's son, assures me that this correspondence, which, for material reasons, cannot have been very bulky, has been destroyed.

[79] P. 77 (London: Home & Van Thal, 1947).

on his uncomfortable chair and saw Kingcote preparing to read to him. Often the reading was of English poetry, and that was enjoyable; but better still was when the wizard took down one of those books of which the mere character suggested magic lore—a German book, and, turning it into free English, read a tale of Tieck, or Musäus, or Grimm, or Bechstein, or Hauff. Then did the child's face glow with attention, his features become elf-like with the stirring of phantasy; and, when Kingcote ceased, he would move with a deep sigh and peer curiously about the room. He would beg to be allowed to look at these volumes for himself, touching the pages with delicate fingers, spelling here and there a word and asking its meaning. There was a book of German ballads, plentifully illustrated, and over these pictures the boy was never tired of musing. Percy Vissian owed not a little to his friend for these afternoons at Wood End.[80]

Godfrey's congenial performance, like the doings of Master Percy in the book, imparts a certain light-hearted freshness to the narrative. The homes of the Swanwicks and the Vissians were drawn from those which Gissing occasionally came across among his acquaintances but which he was unable to create in his own life. In describing them he wrung from his brain whatever joy his life in modern Grub Street had not annihilated. While in America, at his darkest hour, he had summoned enough detachment to dash off a sprightly tale entitled "An English Coast-Picture,"[81] which had won him some praise. Had he reached the cool-headed objectivity of that perfect abstraction, the realistic novelist? He would now and then fancy that he had. The good-humored bantering tone of "The Lady of the Dedication" at least seems to show that he had not yet taken a totally somber view of his dependence upon editors; the chimerical vision,[82] expressed in fervid, amorous notes, of the young writer laying literary wreaths of laurels at the feet of his humbly born hero-worshiping lady is one of the last resurgences of his native optimism. With few qualifications, the words Gissing wrote in his Preface to the second edition of *The Unclassed* apply to this story: "It will be recognised as the work of a very young man, who dealt in a romantic spirit with the gloomier facts of life"—to which he added, from the

[80] Vol. 1, pp. 188–89.
[81] *Appleton's Journal*, July, 1877, pp. 73–78.
[82] The initials of Adler's beloved "E.E.L.," by inevitably recalling those of Letitia Landon, the once famous "L.E.L.," emphasize the romantic note of the love story.

vantage point of middle age, "Romance has no moral, and youth may be pardoned its idealism."[83]

X: "Mutimer's Choice"

The next story in chronological order affords as convincing an example of self-effacement as can be found in Gissing's early work. This is so for the very simple reason that here he was not tempted to attribute his own feelings to any of his characters. In "The Last Half-Crown" and "The Lady of the Dedication" he was to a large extent drawing upon his own experience as a literary tyro; in "The Quarry on the Heath" his imagination had worked on a situation which his sympathy for unfortunate lovers and his hatred of tyranny—and that of the parson in particular—made vivid in his mind. With "Mutimer's Choice" he set aside his own biography and selected a subject requiring observation as much as imagination. As the protagonist's surname indicates, we are moving toward *Demos*, with its multifarious scenes from the life of the people. The presence of the novelist in search of material, notebook and pencil in hand, is felt through many details which bespeak an intimate knowledge of the type of characters described. James Mutimer and Bill Snowdon (a name which reappears in *The Nether World*) are artisans worthy to figure in his proletarian novels; they are seen not from the perspective of a West End drawing room but from the back lanes of Lambeth or Islington.

Throughout the story Gissing watches his characters with unflagging attention, much as the ill-assorted married pair watch each other irritably in the opening scene. He carefully notes every position, every gesture, and by the end of the first page, before the dialogue between husband and wife has begun, the reader is prepared for a domestic explosion in the oppressive atmosphere of their suburban working-class home. As he did later in *Thyrza*, he invests the ringing of the nearby church bells with symbolic significance and proceeds to show the angry couple in attitudes no less symbolic. James Mutimer, the thirty-five-year-old, thoughtful, honest workingman, broods over his matrimonial misery, his head resting on his hand;

[83] Preface to the 1895 edition published by Lawrence and Bullen, p. v.

his impatient, unsatisfied, pretty young wife nervously chafes by the fireside, intent on waging marital warfare. He is trying to sort out the tangle of his gloomy thoughts; she is angry at her dependence and defiantly dreams of another style of life.

Mutimer is one of the types which roused Gissing's sympathy. Such a man, hard-working, alive to the monotony of his role in the world, is doomed to be unhappy. His intelligence, undeveloped because of lack of opportunity, yet a highly redeeming feature in the author's eyes, is always a handicap in a world where social barriers are well-nigh impassable. Mutimer, with his introverted turn of mind, his clear consciousness of his own temperamental limitations, his acceptance of his fate, belongs in the gallery of Gissing's passive heroes. One sees in him the qualities that go to make those two pathetic figures in *Thyrza* and *The Nether World*, Gilbert Grail and Sidney Kirkwood, though their intellectual attainments are altogether denied him. He is in all respects but that more akin to them than to his namesake, Richard Mutimer in *Demos*. Of Richard he has only the physique, whereas, like Grail and Kirkwood, he is predisposed to disaster. He is deeply convinced of the futility of revolt against circumstances, of which he is a victim in the objective, not the ironical, sense of the phrase. Grail gives up all hope of love and of rising in society; Kirkwood's overpowering sense of personal duty makes him marry the vitriolized, repentant Clara in preference to Jane Snowdon, whose wealth he cannot bring himself to share; similarly, James Mutimer chooses death over life as a cripple with a wife who does not love him and who would soon learn to loathe him. His self-abnegation goes even farther than the renunciation of Grail or Kirkwood; he paves the way for the happiness of the two persons who will remain when his refusal to allow amputation of his leg has had its fatal result. Additional interest attaches to Mutimer's heroic sacrifice in that it represents a case of jealousy overcome. Instances of jealousy are common in Gissing's works, from the painter Gresham in *Workers in the Dawn* to the traitor Marcian in *Veranilda*,[84] but

[84] Other cases are Harriet Smales (*The Unclassed*), Kingcote (*Isabel Clarendon*), Beatrice Redwing (*A Life's Morning*), Miriam Baske (*The Emancipated*) Alfred Yule (*New Grub Street*), Eustace Glazzard (*Denzil Quarrier*), Widdowson (*The Odd Women*), Jessica Morgan (*In the Year of Jubilee*), Alma Rolfe (*The Whirlpool*), and Olga Hannaford (*The Crown of Life*).

few of his envious characters subdue their feelings, and none do so
to this extent. Mutimer has the low vitality of Bernard Kingcote and
would hardly have behaved differently if he had read "The Hope
of Pessimism."

His wife Bella (a name redolent of artificiality and cheapness)
would not be out of place among the intolerable females of *In the
Year of Jubilee*. She suffers from the common folly of aping one's
betters in dress. Fortified by her bad taste, she longs to spend the
money that she does not possess and covets the first bauble that her
eye falls upon. Bill Snowdon's resources will, we feel, be drained like
Mutimer's to assuage his wife's petty vanities. She is a type which
Gissing, in his middle age, despaired of educating. It appears again
with great force in Alice Mutimer of *Demos* and with more humor
in *The Town Traveller*. Gissing had a deep and—thanks to his first
wife—direct knowledge of the psychology of working-class women.
In Nell he had studied duplicity from the life, dictated by her urge
to drink as it is in "Mutimer's Choice" by Bella's desire to outshine
her neighbors. By dint of well-chosen descriptive details, Gissing
manages to convey Bella's animality. She eventually recoils from her
husband physically while she is being drawn to Bill Snowdon. One
may guess that she would have done her best to hasten poor Mutimer's
end if he had not robbed her of this pleasure, for she hears of the
accident coolly enough to make one think her capable of lending fate
a hand.

Snowdon (who has nothing in common with his namesakes in
The Nether World) behaves generously toward Mutimer and his
wife. Bella's lie, while flattering his male self-esteem, should put him
on his guard, but we doubt that he will escape her clutches. He is a
man likely to be deluded by appearances and to suffer the domestic
hell endured by Arthur Peachey in the shrewish world of *In the Year
of Jubilee*. However, within the time limits of this narrative, he resembles more closely the good-natured Daniel Dabbs of *Demos*.

Two elements of the story were used in subsequent novels. In
Demos, it will be remembered after the fiasco of his socialist venture,
Richard Mutimer received the support of an anonymous young man
who pressed him to accept five hundred pounds so that he might
"continue by means of public lecturing to spread the gospel of

emancipation." This young man to all appearances had an accident like that of James Mutimer, since he is without the use of his
limbs.[85] On the other hand, the situation between the three leading
characters is repeated though on a different social level, with the
Reardons and Jasper Milvain in *New Grub Street*. Amy Reardon, like
Bella, is dissatisfied with her husband's earnings and has come to
regret having married him because she cannot bear poverty. "He had
won the world's greatest prize—a woman's love—but could not retain
it because his pockets were empty." She is "attracted by Jasper Milvain's energy and promise of success. He [Reardon] had no ignoble
suspicions of Amy, but it was impossible for him not to see that she
habitually contrasted the young journalist, who laughingly made his
way among men, with her grave, dispirited husband. . . . She enjoyed
Milvain's conversation, it put her into a good humour; she liked him
personally, and there could be no doubt that she had observed a
jealous tendency in Reardon's attitude to his former friend—always
a harmful suggestion to a woman."[86] Like Bill Snowdon, Milvain
is innocent and takes no special pains to excite envy and to gain the
love of his friend's wife. He too will win in the end. The comparison
can even be carried further: the home of Bella's mother, mentioned in
passing as a potential refuge, will become, *mutatis mutandis,* the retreat of Amy when, at the end of the same chapter, she leaves her
husband for good. Also, when we enter into Reardon's bitter medita-
tions, "the bells of St. Marylebone began to clang for afternoon service." They call up no more pleasant thoughts than those of St. Mary's
of Battersea. Reardon "marvelled that there were people who could
imagine it a duty or find it a solace to go and sit in that twilight church
and listen to the droning of prayers. He thought of the wretched
millions of mankind to whom life is so barren that they must needs
believe in a recompense beyond the grave."[87]

With "Mutimer's Choice" Gissing took a great step toward the
mastery and skill of his best short stories of the eighteen nineties.
Whatever traces of immaturity the previous pieces revealed are now
gone. The omniscient author has almost disappeared; he keeps in the

[85] Vol. 3, pp. 97–99.
[86] *Ibid.*, pp. 107–8.
[87] *Ibid.*, p. 106.

background and has the threads of his narrative well in hand. Perhaps the character analysis that follows the first scene could have been shortened without any damaging effect, but Gissing has shaken off the remnants of the three-decker technique which still encumbered "The Lady of the Dedication." He no longer finds it necessary to expand upon the protagonist's antecedents; he merely relates the episodes that matter, making an efficient use of physical description and dialogue. He does not resort to unlikely incidents to make his plot advance; the ending is reached with a commendable economy of means and with a discretion and studied gravity characteristic of his most valuable efforts in short fiction.

XI: *"Their Pretty Way"*

Whether "Mutimer's Choice" was submitted for publication and rejected or was consigned to obscurity by its author immediately after it was completed cannot be determined. It is certain that it was the last short story Gissing wrote in the eighties. For the next seven years he turned out novel after novel and did little, if anything, for the magazines. For one thing, he had become convinced that he did not possess the special knack required by that genre (similarly, he thought that he would never succeed in the serial form), and, moreover, he feared that he might endanger his rising reputation by stooping to this branch of journalism. However, a visit to Glastonbury inspired him to use the sleepy old town as the setting of a tale. *Blackwood's Magazine* printed the story[88] and paid Gissing generously. Henceforth, for financial and other reasons, he availed himself of the growing demand for such fiction. The years 1893–1895 in particular were devoted largely to short stories and sketches, and the last piece printed in the present collection is a good example of the qualities of his art in the mid-nineties. That it was apparently not published in his lifetime does not reflect upon its value—indeed, it outdoes in interest and piquancy some of the sketches in *Human Odds and Ends*.

The locale of "Their Pretty Way" had been Gissing's home for little more than a year. It was not the very suburban town of Brixton itself that had attracted him, of course, but the new public library,

[88] "A Victim of Circumstances," January, 1893, pp. 69–86.

the founding of which had been reported in the newspapers. There he found a newly middle-class population, often trying to live above its means and conspicuous by the vulgarity of its tastes. He quickly turned this environment to literary use. He had been settled in Brixton for hardly a fortnight when the place gave him the idea of a novel which he called "Miss Lord of Camberwell"—it became *In the Year of Jubilee*—closely followed by a series of short stories more or less inspired by his surroundings. "Their Pretty Way" in particular reflects the characteristics of the time and place. Though the point must not be overemphasized, Gissing even recalled in it some personal experiences reported in his diary. After leaving Exeter he went to Brixton alone to find and set up an apartment, and his expenses, which he thought extravagant, included items which appear in his story: he spent some six or seven pounds for new furniture for the drawing room, and, along with the necessary carpets, curtains, and linoleum, invested a few precious shillings in "a geranium, [a] fuchsia and some leafy green plant."[89] Some of these purchases were prompted by his desire to mollify his wife. Always haunted by the fear of the future, he felt he was spending more than he could afford, and was rewarded for his propitiatory offerings no more than was Joseph Rush in the story. Discontent renews itself indefinitely, and Edith was soon carping and grumbling with fresh vigor, so that Gissing did not need to seek far for a subject. Furthermore, his neighbors, whom he was content to see from a distance, must have provided him with useful material. The first chapters of *In the Year of Jubilee*, which was written before "Their Pretty Way," show to what excellent account he put them.

The main theme here is the destructiveness of social pretense, for which Gissing held a certain type of woman responsible. Females like Elizabeth Wager and Theresa Rush have a semblance of education which makes them more dangerous to themselves and others than would unpretentious ignorance. In a choice between them and Henry Ryecroft's dutiful housekeeper, with her blessed simplicity of mind and manners, Gissing's preference for the lesser evil is obvious. These products of a suburban civilization are endowed with some of the worse defects of their sex: vanity and jealousy prompt them to com-

[89] Diary, June 17, 1893.

pete with each other about childish matters; they will not forget the neighbor who has had a new carpet delivered or a new dress made. To make their husbands provide the money for their follies, they exert all kinds of pressure, ranging from sullenness to fury. They are attentive to the thousandth echo of an offensive or even a critical remark. They are inclined to imagine themselves martyrs whenever they are denied a bauble; they accuse their husbands of tyranny when the simple truth is that their own whims rule the household. They are incapable of spending their time in an intelligent and profitable way: their hours of leisure are spent in gossip or in futile quarrels with the servant in the basement.

Gissing knew them all too well, these half-educated females who were as incapable of keeping their homes in order as their tempers in check. His own wife shared both their domestic ineptitude and their ill-humor. While working at his desk he was often disturbed by an uproar coming from the lower part of the house, whereupon he had no choice but to go downstairs and try to restore peace. "Their Pretty Way" reflects this irksome preoccupation with the servant question. Incompetent to carry out even the humble tasks required, moved to revolt by Edith's nagging, poorly paid for their services, Gissing's maids succeeded each other at an alarming rate. The system was unsatisfactory to employer and servant alike, but it persisted until time and the changes brought about by two world wars put an end to it.

By the time the story ends, Henry Wager has realized a dream which was Gissing's for some years   to establish for his wife boundaries that cannot safely be transgressed. This is one more instance of the phenomenon which has been noted with regard to Laurence's murder of the blackguard Vanstone in "All for Love." However, the comparison which seems more appropriate is found in a short story completed on October 13, 1894, that is, about a week after "Their Pretty Way." Its form is rather original: it consists of a long narrative to a friend by a man who was rumored to have behaved brutally to his wife. The title—"The Tyrant's Apology"[90]—should be interpreted as "the tyrant's self-apology" and (which Gissing's readers could not know) the author's own apology for the so-called tyrant.

[90] *The English Illustrated Magazine*, July, 1895, pp. 297–304, reprinted in *A Victim of Circumstances*, pp. 239–54.

The "tyrant" presents his defense to one of his wife's former suitors; the latter, after the interview, must have been freed of all his regrets, if any, at having been rejected. Jenny's husband describes at some length the domestic hell he underwent until he made his will law. Jenny is the same sort of woman as Theresa Rush in "Their Pretty Way," and she eventually suffers the treatment inflicted by Wager upon his wife. With the anger of a man who has been done a grave injustice, the pseudo-tyrant passes in review the stages of his married life—his useless concessions to Jenny's caprices, the financial crisis her extravagance brought about, the meaningless social relationships she has led him into. Now, through sheer determination, he has put an end to this nonsense. He has adopted toward the whole world and his wife the only policy he should ever have had, that of firm resolution and vigorous common sense. He refuses to listen to her eccentric pro- posals, to let himself be surrounded by an atmosphere of stupidity, to mingle with a crowd that has, to quote Carlyle, "no more brains than a rabbit." And, most difficult of all, he will smile away any incitement to quarrel. The conclusion of the short story adequately sums up the tyrant's attitude, of which Gissing fully approved, re- garding the best remedy for snobbery and childish rebellion in wives:

"I have recovered self-respect, and I am master in my own house. It may take years of steady ruling before Jenny gives up all hope of a return to the fashionable life. At present she is trying sentimental hypocrisy; but it's no use.
Her rights as an individual? Humbug! She is not an individual; it's the rarest thing to meet a woman who is.
If the life becomes intolerable to her? The door is always open, and an allowance at her disposal."

James Mutimer might have spoken thus to Bill Snowdon in the previous tale had he "the will to live."

"Their Pretty Way," like "The Tyrant's Apology,"[91] reveals

---

[91] The theme of the strong man who brings his frivolous, irresponsible wife under control had already been treated in "The Honeymoon," a short story written from December 14 to 16, 1893, and published in *The English Illustrated Magazine,* June, 1894, pp. 895–904. Waldron, a journalist of thirty-three, persuades his young wife to renounce the publication of a three-volume novel that she had written be- fore her marriage and had even had accepted by a publisher. Using a method com- parable to that of the nameless "tyrannical" husband, Waldron tames Phyllis' in- clination to revolt. The story was included in *A Victim of Circumstances,* pp. 147– 64.

Gissing at his most anti-feminist. In the course of his life he wavered
between the idealism inherent in his nature and the harsh realism
prompted by his struggle for existence amid uncongenial surroundings. Anti-feminism was his temporary response to the problem of
feminine emancipation. The narrative makes it clear that the experiment of the two married pairs in sharing a house, however unprac-
tical, falls through because of the pointless rivalry between Mrs.
Wager and Mrs. Rush. Had it been for the men, it is probable that no
quarrel would have broken out. Wager and Rush tend to see their
shrill-voiced, peevish consorts as belonging to a different human
species, with whose affairs one should interfere as little as possible.
They each fall into the traps laid by female animosity, but their tem-
peraments lead them in opposite directions. Wager, the chop merchant, gains the upper hand, whereas Rush, the cashier, embezzles to
satisfy his wife's vanities. The conclusion underlines the division of
the characters according to their sex in a manner apt to cut a feminist
to the heart. One thinks of Sir Austin Feverel's aphorism in Mere-
dith's novel: "I expect that woman will be the last thing civilized by
man." To a pessimist in the nineties, the image of the average female
suburbanite might well invite agreement with that deceived baronet,
rather than with his more generous creator. But what verges on
tragedy for the actors often looks irresistibly comic to the spec-
tator.

As always in Gissing's works, embezzlement is presented as an
excusable offense. In his opinion, Joseph Rush is reprehensible for,
at worst, his weakness of character, and it is his wife who should
bear the onus of the act. One cannot help thinking that Gissing was
brooding over his own past and could not bring himself to admit the
guilt which had been imputed to him. He repeatedly exploited the
theme in his early American short stories[92] and again resorted to it

---

[92] See "Too Dearly Bought" in *The Sins of the Fathers and Other Tales*,
pp. 91–124. Tim Ridley, a cobbler by trade, steals ten pounds from a friendly cus-
tomer to enable his own granddaughter to realize her dream of going to the
country. Gissing's defense of Ridley's act is of great psychological interest:
"Hitherto Ridley had ever been a scrupulously honest man, not only through fear
of the laws, but in consequence of moral conviction. His nature was susceptible
of every good impulse, and before that day he had never known what it was to
harbor for a moment a thought of a temptation which conflicted with his firmly
rooted notions of right and wrong. For his own sake only he would never have

for the plot of *A Life's Morning*. It would seem that fictional condemnation of robbery was for him a psychological impossibility. His conscience would not allow him to denounce a behavior which, in his own case, had originated in indignation at the injustice of society and in generosity toward one of its victims. Henry Wager, in "Their Pretty Way," is a character who fulfills the author's sense of justice. His discreet, efficient intervention is contrasted with the sometimes spectacular and misdirected charity of the age and offers us Gissing's notion of worthy human conduct. Wager assuredly deserves a place among the group of Englishmen who alone allowed the worn-out Henry Ryecroft, at the end of his life, not to despair of the future of England.[93] Wager may be only a chop merchant, but he has "the intelligence of the heart."

This short story exhibits one of the most winning elements of Gissing's later style—his subtle use of irony, reminiscent of Samuel Butler, whose works he esteemed. The short-lived idyll between the two wives succeeds "the buoyancy of prenuptial days"; their vapid craving for novelty ("their names being Elizabeth and Theresa, they decided to call each other Muriel and May"); the quick deterioration of the initial "ideal harmonies"—all are depicted with commendable restraint. They testify to a talent for social comedy which, though not his greatest strength as a writer, deserves recognition and analysis. *The Paying Guest* and *The Town Traveller*, which have been deprecated by modern critics, would, if studied from that standpoint, yield a greater harvest than one might expect from a period piece. Of course, Gissing's major claim to recognition does not lie here, but social comedy represents a not unimportant aspect of the work of a writer who is more complex than is generally acknowledged.

---

dreamt of committing the theft, even had the opportunity and the sum to be gained been increased manifold. It was the essential goodness of his heart that, by so forcibly presenting to him the excellence of the end to be attained, blinded him for the moment to the true nature of the means. 'Nemo repente fuit turpissimus,' and Ridley's action, viewed in its true light, had very much to mitigate its turpitude" (p. 106). Other examples of robbery condoned occur in "The Warden's Daughter," "Twenty Pounds," and "Joseph Yates' Temptation," all reprinted in *Brownie*, pp. 41–71.

[93] Winter XXV.

XII: Conclusion

The miscellaneous character of the essays and stories gathered in this volume makes a general conclusion almost impossible. The variety of outlook is too great for any single critical approach to encompass all their aspects. Yet they cannot be dismissed as so many fragments among Gissing's literary output. If they present no unity among themselves, they reinforce the unity of the published works. Their interest lies on two planes, that of the ideas and that of the art they embody.

With the exception of "All for Love," which is not a characteristic story and which seems to be the product of the novelist's vexation at the difficulties he encountered in placing *Workers in the Dawn* with a publisher, the short stories and essays show Gissing growing less and less committed. In "The Last Half-Crown" or in the philosophical essay there is a personal fervor bordering on anger, which is far from the notion of art for art's sake with which he toyed for a time in the eighties. But as the years went by, his emotional and philosophical distance from his subject matter increased, and the swings of the pendulum between youthful optimism and despair gradually lost their momentum. He was moving slowly toward the defensive and mildly disillusioned attitude of his last heroes, Ryecroft, Will Warburton, and Basil in *Veranilda*. His manner, as well as his matter, reflects his increasing detachment. Whatever he may have believed to be his capacity to withdraw from personal involvement after reading Schopenhauer, he was still far from pure objectivity; he was still doing much more than merely recording and reporting. Yet as early as "Mutimer's Choice," his artistic consciousness was being refined, passion was being replaced by irony, and he had acquired the basic tools of his art.

Gissing was not a born artist, though his literary precocity compels astonishment. He had an extraordinary curiosity about the things of the mind, the intellect, from an early age; nevertheless, although he turned to literary expression spontaneously, first as a youth in college, then as a starveling journalist in America, his works were always as much, if not more, the result of determination powerfully sustained by interest as of a genius for literature. This is not to belittle his contribution to English letters. His writings have no exact counter-part, even though his descriptions of destitution and misery at times recall the poetry of George Crabbe or the novels of his contemporary, Mark Rutherford. His literary position now seems secure. Shortly after his death, Thomas Seccombe, who followed his career with particular attention, wrote in his introductory survey to *The House of Cobwebs* that Gissing would "sup late."[94] If Seccombe meant thereby that his merits would eventually be acknowledged by the general reading public, Gissing is likely never to sup at all. However, if we are to understand that it would take time for his place in the cavalcade of the English novel to be assured, the prophecy—judging from the steady stream of publications on his life and works—is well-nigh fulfilled. The contents of the present collection may be nothing more than delicacies to the connoisseur, yet it is hoped that they will bring new readers to his major works, for these offer not only a panoramic picture of late nineteenth-century England but also the comments of an intelligent man on human nature. Gissing's novels, seen in that light, never fail to transcend the ephemeral.

[94] P. liii.

Selected Bibliography

THE FOLLOWING BIBLIOGRAPHY, with the exception of the list of Gissing's works published in book form, is drastically selective. I have been content to mention the books and articles I have found most useful for this study. Readers will find in the Introduction and the footnotes appended to it references to writings by or on Gissing which have been hitherto overlooked or neglected by scholars and which I have not thought it necessary to list here.

Gissing's Works

Workers in the Dawn. 3 vols. London: Remington and Co. 1880.
The Unclassed. 3 vols. London: Chapman and Hall. 1884.
Demos. 3 vols. London: Smith, Elder. 1886.
Isabel Clarendon. 2 vols. London: Chapman and Hall. 1886.
Thyrza. 3 vols. London: Smith, Elder. 1887.
A Life's Morning. 3 vols. London: Smith, Elder. 1888.
The Nether World. 3 vols. London: Smith, Elder. 1889.
The Emancipated. 3 vols. London: Bentley and Son. 1890.
New Grub Street. 3 vols. London: Smith, Elder. 1891.
Born in Exile. 3 vols. London: A. and C. Black. 1892.
Denzil Quarrier. London: Lawrence and Bullen. 1892.
The Odd Women. 3 vols. London: Lawrence and Bullen. 1893.
In the Year of Jubilee. 3 vols. London: Lawrence and Bullen. 1894.
Eve's Ransom. London: Lawrence and Bullen. 1895.
Sleeping Fires. London: Fisher, Unwin. 1895.
The Paying Guest. London: Cassell and Co. 1895.
The Whirlpool. London: Lawrence and Bullen. 1897.
Human Odds and Ends. London: Lawrence and Bullen. 1898. (short stories).
Charles Dickens: A Critical Study. London: Blackie and Son. 1898.
The Town Traveller. London: Methuen and Co. 1898.
The Crown of Life. London: Methuen and Co. 1899.
By the Ionian Sea. London: Chapman and Hall. 1901.
Our Friend the Charlatan. London: Chapman and Hall. 1901.
Forster's *Life* of Charles Dickens, revised and abridged. London: Chapman and Hall. 1903.
The Private Papers of Henry Ryecroft. London: Constable and Co. 1903.
Veranilda. London: Constable and Co. 1904.

Will Warburton. London: Constable and Co. 1905.
The House of Cobwebs. With an introductory survey by Thomas Seccombe. London: Constable and Co. 1906. (short stories).
The Sins of the Fathers and Other Tales. With an introduction by Vincent Starrett. Chicago: Pascal Covici. 1924.
Critical Studies of the Works of Charles Dickens. With an introduction and bibliography by Temple Scott. New York: Greenberg. 1924.
The Immortal Dickens. London: Cecil Palmer. 1925.
A Victim of Circumstances. With an introduction by A. C. Gissing. London: Constable and Co. 1927. (short stories).
Selections, Autobiographical and Imaginative from the Works of George Gissing. Ed. A. C. Gissing. Introduction by Virginia Woolf. London: Jonathan Cape. 1929.
Brownie. With introductions by G. E. Hastings, V. Starrett, and T. O. Mabbott. New York: Columbia University Press. 1931. (short stories).
Stories and Sketches. With an introduction by A. C. Gissing. London: Michael Joseph. 1938.
George Gissing's Commonplace Book. Ed. Jacob Korg. New York: The New York Public Library. 1962.
Notes on Social Democracy. With an introduction by Jacob Korg. Enitharmon Gissing Series, no. 1. London: Enitharmon Press, 1968.

Letters

Letters to Edward Clodd from George Gissing. Printed for private circulation. 1914.
Letters to an Editor [C. K. Shorter]. Printed for private circulation. 1915.
Letters of George Gissing to Members of His Family. Ed. Algernon and Ellen Gissing. London: Constable and Co. 1927.
George Gissing and H. G. Wells, Their Friendship and Correspondence. Ed. Royal A. Gettmann. Urbana: University of Illinois Press. 1961.
The Letters of George Gissing to Eduard Bertz, 1887–1903. Ed. Arthur C. Young. New Brunswick, N.J.: Rutgers University Press. 1961.
The Letters of George Gissing to Gabrielle Fleury. Ed. Pierre Coustillas. New York: The New York Public Library. 1964.

Critical and Related Material

Comte, Auguste. *Cours de Philosophie Positive*. 6 vols. Paris: Rouen frères. 1830–42.
Copleston, Frederick. *Arthur Schopenhauer, Philosopher of Pessimism*. London: Burns Oates and Washbourne. 1946.
Coustillas, Pierre. *Collected Articles on George Gissing*. New York: Barnes and Noble. 1968.

Cresson, André. *Auguste Comte. Sa vie, son oeuvre, sa philosophie*. Paris: Presses Universitaires de France. 1957.

Francis, C. J. "Gissing and Schopenhauer," *Nineteenth Century Fiction*, June, 1960, pp. 53–63.

Gardiner, Patrick. *Schopenhauer*. Baltimore: Penguin Books. 1963.

Goodale, Ralph. "Schopenhauer and Pessimism in Nineteenth Century English Literature," *PMLA*, March, 1932, pp. 241–61.

Korg, Jacob. *George Gissing, a Critical Biography*. Seattle: University of Washington Press. 1963.

Roberts, Morley. *The Private Life of Henry Maitland*. London: Eveleigh Nash. 1912.

Schopenhauer, Arthur. *The World as Will and Idea*. Trans. R. B. Haldane and J. Kemp. 3 vols. London: Routledge and Kegan Paul. 1883–86.

Spencer, W. T. *Forty Years in My Bookshop*. London: Constable and Co. 1923.

Sully, James. *Pessimism, A History and a Criticism*. London: Kegan Paul and Co. 1891.

The Hope of Pessimism

UNLIKE THE OTHER writings in the present volume, "The Hope of Pessimism" has long been known to be in existence. In *Letters of George Gissing to Members of His Family* the following excerpt from a note George addressed to his brother Algernon on October 6, 1882, gave as much as has hitherto been revealed about the essay, apart from the summary and brief comments by Jacob Korg in his *Critical Biography*: "The pessimistic article is finished, but I shall not even try to get it published, seeing that it has developed into nothing more nor less than an attack on Positivism. So far has my intellectual development brought me. There is little hope that the *Nineteenth [Century]* or the *Fortnightly [Review]* would accept the thing, but, if they did, I should feel uncomfortable at the thought of Harrison reading it."

Since at that date he was already "struggling bitterly with the old foe," i.e., his quarterly contribution to Turgenev's review, he must have completed this twenty-eight-page manuscript in the very first days of October, 1882. Doubtless Gissing's letter to Algernon for September 20 also refers to it, but only a short extract from it has been printed and the whereabouts of the original are not known. I incline to think that he finally turned to his essay only after that date, when he had received a note from Smith, Elder and Company rejecting the manuscript of his new novel, *Mrs. Grundy's Enemies,* because it was "too painful to please the ordinary novel reader and treats of scenes that can never attract the subscribers to Mr. Mudie's Library."*

"The Hope of Pessimism" was written at 17 Oakley Crescent (now Oakley Gardens), Chelsea, where Gissing had moved on September 6. As the manuscript was never submitted to any editor, it does not bear the author's address. It was probably the first of his writings to have his new authorial signature, which omits his second Christian name.

* *LMF,* p. 119.

INCE MAN BEGAN to reflect on the ultimate problems of his existence, deep-pondering minds have found an unfailing source of wonder in the unconscious optimism of humanity. The strange spectacle of generations of beings endowed with discourse of reason, looking before and after, yet permitting themselves to be lured on through all woes of existence by merest *ignes fatui*; never blest, but always to be so; forthwith forgetting the bitterness of the aftertaste of one joy when another arises to tempt them; each in practice thinking all men mortal but himself, and, as often as not, urging to quicker flight the hours which stand between him and his end;—this makes wise men marvel; over this, now as of old, your Heraclitus shed tears, whilst your Democritus fall a-laughing. Hence, too, the founders of religions, men who saw through the outward show of things and were fired with zeal to deliver their fellows from the bondage of the apparent. The aspiration after the knowledge of a perfect God derives its strength from a recognition of man's own imperfection; the longing for a future life is the hope of recompense hereafter for the miserable failure of existence on earth. To the chosen few these truths are ever in sight; the world at large only accepts them under constraint. The mass of men are, for the greater portion of their time, under the dominion of blind instinct, the instinct which whispers that they must cleave to life as to their dearest possession. In their reflective moments they will fully acknowledge the vanity of all that they pursue; but, though ever their every-day discourse abounds in proverbs and quotations testifying to the hardship of the human lot, they continue to be in practice victims of their delusions. For them Hope still thrones in the glory of each day's dawn; reflection is a labour all the less frequently and reluctantly performed that it is believed to be a duty; the strange comedy goes on now as ever for him who has eyes to see it, and man still plays such tricks before high heaven as may make us weep if we are lachrymose, laugh if our elements so dispose us.

Optimism is of course a term of varying application. That unconscious optimism of which I speak has reference merely to the life of the present world. Take your average European in his rare moments of introspection, and he is an optimist in a wider sense of the word, this time consciously so, inasmuch as he would most probably confess a faith which endows the human spirit with a heritage of eternal blessedness beyond the grave. By the same operation his standpoint relative to worldly life is entirely altered; in this respect he is now a pessimist, that which was previously his good he repudiates as evil. His favourite utterances are mere condemnations of all which he before set himself more persistently to pursue, the earth is a vale of tears, an abode of misery, a furnace through which his soul has to pass that its righteousness may be tested. With Sir Thomas Browne he says of the world, "I count it not an inn, but an hospital; a place not to live in, but to die in." This is the view of him who adheres to pure Christianity, which in its essence is pessimistic. Optimistic religions there have been: the religion of Hellas, Judaism, Islam. An optimist, moreover, both for the world and that to come, is your modern rationalistic Christian, who, by the adulteration of his creed, seeks to find the kingdom of God already upon earth, and maintains that all which is, is good. The difference is not great between him and the Pantheist, for whom the world is divine, and his faith consequently one of cheerful interpretations.

One other scheme for the conduct of life on optimistic principles it has remained for our own times to develop, and the circumstance of its having sought establishment under the form and title of a religion recommends it to the attention of all who, awake to the fact that old faiths are failing us, passing away without hope of restoration to the hearts and consciences of men, look darkly wondering into the world's future, and speculate anxiously as to the effect upon men's every-day life of intellectual conditions so different from those under which modern civilization grew to consistency. In the Religion of Humanity we are presented with a creed essentially optimistic. Here there is no comparison instituted between the imperfection of the present world and the glory of one which is to come; on the contrary, the unconscious optimism of the average man is embraced as a philosophical sufficiency, the scientific doctrine of evolution is made to yield a principle of beatitude, and the very agonies of existence are turned to the service of an all-hoping, all-enduring faith.

Founding itself, as it does, on the solid-seeming accretions of human knowledge, seeking its guarantee in the most obvious tendencies of what we call modern progress, declaring itself tolerant with

77

the tolerance of scientific investigation, making its supreme appeal to what has ever been confessed the noblest of man's instincts, that of self-forgetfulness in devotion to others' good,—this agnostic optimism with justice proclaims itself the first serious attempt to replace the old supernatural faiths by a religion consonant with the new intellectual attitude, and as such demands serious and reverent investigation of its authority. A religion, as the word has hitherto been understood, must serve a twofold purpose; it must, on the one hand, supply an explanation of being, on the other, present a guarantee for human morality. Hitherto, moreover, it has been deemed essential that it should perform these offices in the strength of supernatural revelation, otherwise it lost its title of religion, and became mere philosophy. The new faith would abolish the distinction, confessing that religion in the old sense is no longer within our reach, and that philosophy must needs assume the diviner garb and utter its earthly wisdom from the seat of the vanished oracles. The twofold service is still to be performed, but in a different way. For it is assumed that, in discarding supernaturalism, we have learned the truth that knowledge of the absolute is incompatible with the conditions of our being. Hence, when we ask for an explanation of the universe, we are referred to the book of Science, in other words bidden to study the co-ordination of the facts of human consciousness, beyond which we cannot go. And when we seek the sanction for the ethical system propounded to us, we are answered partly by deduction from the apparent course of social development, partly by an appeal to those sentiments of good and evil which we must be content to regard, and speak of, as intuitive. Thus, in the new religion, man is the beginning and the end; in himself is precept and sanction; moreover, in himself is the reward.

For, with reward we can by no means dispense, any more than our intellect is capable of getting outside the relationship of cause and effect. Refine your reward until, to gross perceptions, it assumes the character of a punishment, none the less it is there, set up before you, made the object of your pursuit. An agnostic philosophy developing itself into religion can, in the nature of things, present but one reward, and that the simplest of all, being nothing else than the pleasure of a good conscience. For what else is the joy of self-perfect-ing in altruistic thought and performance? The inward pleasure derivable by a philosopher from the possession of what he deems a good conscience will naturally assume nobler forms than the same pleasure in beings of less large discourse; to his reflective mind the consequences of a good action extend themselves in ever-widening circles till they touch the very limits of humanity, and, in fact, he attains to the conception of that subjective immortality which is to replace the heaven of old creeds.

Here, it can scarcely be doubted, we face the last stronghold of philosophical optimism. Demolish this, prove it a mere phantasm without solid foundation in the depths of human nature, and pessimism alone remains to us, conscious and consistent pessimism, with or without that degree of solace which will suffice to persuade men into still submitting to the burden of breath. Indulgence in prophetic forecast of the ultimate phases of man's life on earth may be resigned for an amusement to those who have no better occupation for their time; for those who acquiesce in the broad conclusions of our men of science regarding the material world, the cyclical future of the human race must remain the most insoluble of problems. But in discussing the probable issues of a struggle between optimism and pessimism for the possession of man's soul, we are but giving attention to a matter of immediate and pressing concern. To what extent of time our conclusions may be held to apply rests an unresolved doubt; that the struggle has commenced in earnest and will assume even greater importance in the minds of generations which shall succeed us, is the general consent of thinking men. Further than this assertion we may not go. Whether, the present period of questioning transition over, the guiding spirit of civilization will once more be found in the conclusions of philosophy (or a religion, call it as you will,) which can claim the allegiance of the foremost races, even for a space; or whether, the leading-bonds of supernaturalism cast aside, the world is henceforth given up to the license of individual opinion, sceptic being the only common denomination under which the majority can write; this we have again no means whatever of determining. In the meantime, the lists are thrown open. Let him who is so happy as to have convinced himself come forward to the contest with others' reason. The problems before us are old as human thought, yet as free to the mind's investigation as though they were now for the first time proposed. And if perchance some seeker after light discern what seems to him a hope-inspiring ray, far-off, dim-shining in the black void which is our intellectual firmament, shall he not direct thitherwards the eyes of other men, if haply they too may find solace in the vision?

To say that agnostic optimism is nothing more than what we call mankind's intuitive common-sense, seized upon and expanded to a coherent system by philosophic consciousness[,] would seem like anticipatory justification of its claim to acceptance, at all events would seem so to those who are practically earnest in their search for a new religion, who are more deeply impressed with the vulgar needs of vulgar humanity than solicitous for the logical completeness of abstract speculations. The very obviousness of its applications makes it especially attractive to practical, energetic minds, as also,—for a season,—to less easily satisfied intelligences, enticed by the prospect of rest from the never-ending search of unattainable truth. It is the philosophy of cheerful resignation; more, it applies to the totality of life that principle of making a virtue of necessity which is the wise man's best resource in daily details. Granting that we cannot rise to a perception of the absolute, that we are hopelessly imprisoned in our universe of phenomena, then let us not only accept these limitations, but make it a characteristic of moral excellence to resolutely shut the mind against yearnings for transcendental flights, and dedicate every thought to this so solid-seeming earth on which we tread, grapple with its material difficulties, study its conditions, enter into its transient joys and sorrows as though they were the be-all and end-all of human consciousness. The mass of mankind do not even possess the power of rising to abstract considerations. Such a thing as philosophical idealism is altogether beyond their intelligence. In a word, they are unquestioning *realists*; for them the world has an absolute, objective existence; they cannot so much as comprehend the existence of a doubt in the matter. And the majority are right. We will accept this common-sense attitude of theirs, base our ethical problem thereon, and thus assure for our creed their ready comprehension. But it would not do to stop here. We recognize in man the religious instinct, for all our realism, but we hold that hitherto it has been wasted upon imaginary divinities. We will no longer look up to the heavens when we worship. This spirit of man, the highest that we can know, we will dignify it with divine titles, will in fact worship. Is it not a law of nature that the individual is of no account in comparison with the race,—"so careful of the type she seems, So careless of the single life"? This, too, we will accept and convert to a means of moral good; we will extract from it our doctrine of altruism, by virtue of which I lose sight of my individual desires in a longing to make others happy, thus consciously co-operating with the blind natural law, which makes me of no account save in so far as I minister to the preservation and exaltation of humanity. Herein also is utilized the renunciative instinct; all men will own, theoretically, that it is more blessed to give than to receive. Perfection in self-sacrifice has made saints under the old dispensation, no less will it do so under the new; the only difference being that this sanctity will have its roots no longer in the love of God, but in the love of Man. Thus, equipped with these intellectual and moral safeguards, we will face life with cheerful courage. Do not the vast majority of mankind go about their every-day occupations in a spirit of, at least, contentment, often of absolute light-heartedness, when they could give you no satisfactory reason for their hopeful mood? This fact we will lay hold on as evidence that life is essentially a good and not an evil; on the strength of it we will be optimists. "Though nature, red in tooth and claw with ravine, shriek against our creed," we will maintain that the soul of the world is goodness, that all things work to noble ends, that life is the supreme blessing, and death, which puts an end to our joyful labours, the one dread foe.

We see, then, that Agnostic Optimism bases its hope of universal acceptance as a new religion on two assumptions. The first of these is, that it is possible to eradicate from the human mind that instinct which Schopenhauer calls *das metaphysische Bedürfnig*,—that standing revolt of the intellect against its circumscribed conditions, which has given birth to every form of supernatural religion, and has been hitherto the prime motive of philosophical enquiry. Man, it is taken for granted, will discover that the last attainment of philosophy consists in frank acceptance of his limitations, and will find rest in a realistic interpretation of the universe; the metaphysical stage will have been passed through, and, in the positive stage which shall succeed, the light-hearted study of phenomena will find no interruption from the troublesome consciousness of insoluble problems ever lurking in the rear.

The second assumption is, that such universal realism, and the optimism supposed to go hand in hand therewith, are compatible with that altruistic morality (practical, and not merely in theory,) which is relied upon as the future hope of the race. When we have ceased, —it is urged—to peer into the clouds after impossible explanations of our being; when we have convinced ourselves of the purely natural sanctions of morality; when we have learned to regard the earth as our true and only home, and one capable of being made delightful to all creatures; then, and not till then, will our hearts overflow with the single love of Humanity, and "to live for others" be recognized as at once the noblest moral theory and the highest practical blessedness.

In opposition to these postulates, I should like to endeavour to show that, so long as human nature remains as now we know it, the metaphysical instinct can never acquiesce in subordination to a realistic philosophy; secondly, that so far from deriving such subordination, we should do our utmost to cherish and strengthen the metaphysical tendencies of the human mind, seeing that in such tendencies alone, inevitably leading to the universal acceptance of a pessimistic philosophy, is at present discernible a hope of the better order of the common life of men.

One thing we may perhaps begin by conceding, namely, that a point has been gained in the recognition of the fact that religion and philosophy are henceforth one and inseparable, the two names merely indicating different phases of the same thing, the intellectual and the moral. It is a gain to openly confess this; that the truth is not for the first time felt is evident when we reflect how, in eras of prevailing supernaturalism, the wise man has generally ended with making a religion of his philosophy, whilst the mass of men have at all times made a philosophy of their religion. Perhaps the best thing, under such circumstances, would be to discontinue altogether the use of the word religion, and allow philosophy, which has absorbed the function of religion, henceforth to possess a supreme jurisdiction without even a rival in name. But we are met at once with the question: what is philosophy? Aristotle notes that philosophy has its origin in wonder, and herein provides us with a sufficient definition. The average man sees nothing to wonder at in the universe; its existence is for him its explanation. The philosopher wonders at every thing he sees; and it becomes the task of his life to seek an explanation of this being of his and all which it supposes; he has no rest from the questions: Whence, whither, wherefore? Filtered through the intelligence of successive ages, the questions reduce themselves to one simple interrogation; the modern philosopher asks with Kant: What *can* I know? Upon the answer which his reason supplies depends his view of the universe. But for our agnostic optimist all such speculation falls under the somewhat contemptuous title of metaphysics; and the study of metaphysics characterizes for him an earlier stage in the history of human development than that which it is his happiness to have attained. He has ceased to trouble himself with the question: What *can* I know? and holds that it is the philosopher's duty to confine himself to the enquiry: What *do* I actually know of the laws of this *Realwissenschaften,* and a completed system of such sciences, and co-ordinated view of all human knowledge, crowned by a self-consistent theory of the operation of the penalties whereby such knowledge is obtained,—for him constitutes Philosophy, the philosophy which in contradistinction to all those hitherto held, he calls the Positive. But, strangely, considering the rigidly scientific attitude assumed, he takes it for granted that this Philosophy of his is the final stage of speculation; makes such a conclusion tributary to his hopes. The spirit of our modern science is vehemently and dogmatically agnostic. Accordingly, we will not be content with demonstrating how all previous stages of thought have led up to this, which we may safely and scientifically do, but we will take it for granted that evolution henceforth means the strengthening and confirming of this actual condition. Because the human mind is passing through an agnostic and realistic stage, therefore agnosticism and realism will one day become its essential qualities, final conditions of its operation. The easy application of evolutionary symbols and analogies involves these theorists in an error of proportion. One might as well confidently assume with Sir Thomas Browne that one face of Janus holds no proportion to the other; 'tis too late to be ambitious, the great mutations of the world are acted, and our generations are ordained in the setting part of time. Because intellectual activity is for a season turned away from the ultimate problems of existence and given up to the study of the laws of phenomena, to what it pleases to call the study of actually existing things, this is surely no argument to prove that metaphysical speculation has therefore had its day and ceased to be. Nay, for that matter, if one is disposed to prophesy, does it not seem far more probable that the mind, after long and strenuous exertion in the pursuit of natural science, will, by dint of the very vastness of its attainments, in consequence whereof it strikes, so to speak, every moment against the barriers of the unknowable, become, Faust-like, weary of the vanity of its course, and turn to seek for truth by an altogether different way, so that mysticism, or something of the kind, may prove the true evolutionary outcome of agnostic realism?

Or, to put the same error in another way. Apparently it is taken for granted that, in virtue of the scientific principle of heredity, the prevalence of dogmatic agnosticism in one generation guarantees the prevalence of the same characteristic in the generation which succeeds. But philosophical views are not hereditary: were it so the mind would be fixed for ever in one construction of the universe. What a man does inherit from the generation which gives him birth is a certain accumulation of positive knowledge with intellectual capacity to avail himself thereof, and, in his turn, to add to the possession before transmitting it again. The mode in which a man shall make use of this heritage is, of course, in the earlier stages of his mental growth, greatly decided by the instruction he receives, but were there no possibility of ultimately outgrowing these influences, then, with all our present knowledge, we should still be adherents of fetichism or some such primitive philosophy. Every man must work out his own salvation. The mere renewal of generations is a constant danger to the persistence of a given form of faith; for the individual, no less than the race, has his systematic development, one stage of which is necessarily that of metaphysical enquiry. Nor is it difficult to give reasons for the belief that this stage will, as time goes on, come to be of more and more importance, rather than of less and less, as agnostic optimists hope and believe.

Suppose we try, in the first place, to realize what is meant by an agnostic world. That is to say, a world educated out of the bondage of supernaturalism, and so completely trained in the methods of philosophical enquiry, as to have finally recognized the limits of the human intelligence, to have definitely acquiesced in a system of *relative* realism. To put it concretely, a world in which the average man has quite mastered the "Kritik den Reinen Vernunft," and fully appreciates all its moral and intellectual consequences. For, short of this we may not stop. To assert that agnosticism of a kind sufficient for all practical purposes will ensue upon a conscientious rejection of supernatural faiths is simply to ignore that property of human nature, by virtue of which the mind not sufficiently self-conscious to grasp the reasonings of philosophy will, in spite of itself, entertain views of existence identical with those whereon are based the old religions. Gather your audience of intelligent, but only half-educated, working men, and convince them that modern science has overthrown belief in revealed religion. Well, so far you may prevail; so far you *have* prevailed through large masses of the population. But do you flatter yourself that these minds have become in the true sense of the word agnostic? Far from it. In all probability, the best of them have reached the stage of pantheism; but be sure that not one but, consciously or unconsciously, holds still a theological theory of the world, in all likelihood has still his anthropomorphic ideas of the deity. In very deed, if one thinks of it, you have only succeeded in bringing them to the threshold of metaphysical consciousness, to that phase of thought in which names stand for things. Cast one of your disciples into the midst of severe mental trouble, or even afflict him with bodily anguish not easy to be borne and threatening death,—and see whether his agnosticism be more than skin deep.

But we will pass over this initial difficulty, the difficulty which must lie in the pathway of every reformer who would have the masses of the people leap at a bound to a height of intellectual refinement which, in himself, represents ages of slow development. We will also say nothing, at present, of the circumstance that the direction of modern civilization seems becoming more and more unfavourable to the hope of anything like universal culture, inasmuch as the struggle for mere existence becomes daily more and more all-absorbing and leaves to the vast majority less and less leisure and inclination for abstract study. Let us repeat the supposition, that we have progressed so far as to see before us a truly agnostic world. This means, undoubtedly, a world advanced in the study of the "real" sciences to a point which we can hardly conceive, and, as already said, a world which has criticized the conditions of pure reason and recognized its limits. Is it not evident that, to such a reflective world, the circumstance of life, the totality of phenomena, will constitute a source of wonder as inexhaustible as to the most philosophic minds of our own day? Is it not in accordance with that fundamental human nature which seems unalterable by such lapses of time as we are at all justified in speaking of, that, the more clearly we recognize the limits of our knowledge, the more able we become to view life objectively, in the philosophical spirit, all the more wonder-inspiring will our position appear to us? Is it not, then, self-contradictory to take it for granted that a problem which must perforce grow to our consciousness ever more present, ever more tantalizing, will possess ever slighter influence on the minds of men, so that they will be able to put [it] aside calmly, as an importunate suitor whom they have once for all decided not to listen to? In earlier ages, when men were as yet children in knowledge, the searching mind was able to find rest in a very simple explanation of the world's origin, though the metaphysical instinct was already operative, consciousness of the mind's processes was still undeveloped, and it seemed quite satisfactory to explain the creation of the universe on the analogy of a design conceived by the human brain and executed by human hands. Such an explanation no longer suffices. Your very Philistine makes a mock of the first chapters of the Genesis, holding that a belief in such stories is incompatible with the dignity of his intellect, and untroubled by the circumstance of his having no more credible theory to substitute for that which he discards. Your average scientifically-cultured man trains himself in evolutionary modes of thought, and delights to pursue the course of development into the dark backward abysm of time, till some dimly-imaged act of spontaneous generation links for him the space between nothingness and being. Is he nearer to an understanding of the principle of life, to a sufficient comprehension of the sum of things? Lay your Philistine and your man of science on a bed of sickness, and let their conscious eye read the expression of relinquished hope in the faces of those about them; which of the two sees the further into the dark ahead of him, or derives the more strength from his philosophy which guided his active hours? The Philistine, in all probability, sinks into the anguish of despair, and at the last quiets his wretched soul in frantic acceptance of the faith he had contemned. The man of science acts his part better, preserves his self-respect in the face of a ruining world, but none the less confesses to himself the futility of his investigations, and even in the pangs of dissolution must smile at his own life-long credulity. Both have recognized the vanity of the mood in which man says to himself that the present life shall be his all-in-all; the dogmatic realism of both has yielded to the convincing metaphysics of death.

No; natural progress does not consist in diminution of self-consciousness; we have but to reflect for a moment on the history of the human intellect to acknowledge that the very opposite is the truth, that the metaphysical instinct strengthens with the advance of civilization, [in] spite of the superficial tendencies of a passing era. Far from content with once for all recognizing that all they know is that they can know nothing, men will find the consciousness of their strange, dread environment of shadows ever more present with them, till at length the intellectual phase of their nescience subordinates itself to the moral phase, and they will assert that they know nothing save that they are miserable. And herein, from the earthly point of view, lies the hope for our race,—a paradox which will establish itself now that we come to consider the second assumption of the agnostic optimist.

That universal realism, and the optimism supposed to go hand in hand therewith, are compatible with an altruistic morality.—This is putting it negatively; it is only necessary to assert that optimistic realism is the sole permanent foundation of such morality in order to make evident the grievous instability of a religion which should base itself on such an association. Surely, if there is one general principle of human nature justified by the observation of all times, it is, that to make this present life of ours an end in itself is equivalent to the discouragement of just those virtues which altruism presupposes. I know it may be urged that I am here misrepresenting the position I assail; that I am confusing the individual life with that larger life of the race which the altruist is supposed to always have

in view. Not in his poor day-to-day existence is he to find the nutri-
ment of his soul; but in the contemplation of that noble entity, the
human race, which, as an object of devotion, is held to be capable of
awakening and satisfying every religious instinct. Alas, and can we
really persuade ourselves that man will ever worship man in spirit
and in truth? Granting that Humanity is the highest we can ever
know, that it is vain to seek after another God, are we not too fatally
conscious of the distance between the utmost human goodness, and
that ideal which we are capable of conceiving? In very deed, it is
not Humanity which the new religion makes the object of its worship,
but an ideal embodiment of man's noblest faculties and attainments,
a terrene divinity such as will never find its avatar in human flesh.
Better to abandon the figure, and acknowledge that our only guide
is in our own good instincts. And how ineffectual such guidance
proves is sufficiently attested by the union of the highest degree of
civilization yet attained with the most flagrant social misery the
world has ever seen. Far be from me the cynical temperament which
delights in disparaging the grander possibilities of man's nature.
"How noble in reason! How infinite in faculty! In form and moving
how express and admirable! In action how like an angel, in apprehension how like a God!" Yes, and for all that but "the paragon of
animals." Can we, pray you, with our rationalistically established
scheme of altruism get beyond the moral force of that religion which
summed itself in the injunction that we should do unto others as we
would have them do unto us, for that such was the will of our Father
which is in Heaven? And, if even that religion has failed, then by
dint of what marvellous conceit, in consequence of what amazing
hallucination, do we dare to hope that our painfully excogitated
philosophy will approve itself the very water of life, a spring of final
regeneration for all mankind!

Lay to our souls what flattering unction we may, we shall not
escape from the eternal truth that the world is synonymous with evil.
If indeed it is true that the metaphysical instinct was but an element in an evolutionary stage which humanity is leaving behind,
and if indeed the state of things which we see around us is the fore-
shadowing of an age of universal realism, which shall have no spiritual guidance save in the contemplation of the virtues of ideal Man,

then let us rejoice that we have been born thus early and that our lives will have closed before the final establishment of the era of Agnostic Optimism. Imagine the intensifying through another generation or two of the social strife which every day grows more bitter; imagine wealth accumulated in the hands of yet fewer capitalists, and the immense majority toiling desperately for mere subsistence; then conceive the utter annihilation of all hopes of a future world, of all belief in a rewarding and avenging God, with the prevailing religion one which makes Man its supreme being, the earth its scene of final blessedness, and appeals to the unselfish instincts as the sole guarantee of morality. Do we not already recognize on every hand the one great and obvious result of such tendencies, in the strengthening of the natural forces of egotism? Let a man say to himself: This is my first and last existence; here on this earth must I find the development of my faculties, reap the delights of my senses, if ever I am to do so; it is now or never with me, miss this my one chance in all eternity and far better than I had never been;—suppose this impressed upon his mind as a vehement conviction, does it not perforce follow that he will set himself with desperate determination to win what he deems his just share in the enjoyments of life? Will he not brood himself into frenzy over the social wrong which holds him, as it were spell-bound, a mere famishing onlooker at the world's banquet? Will not envy, hatred, malice and all uncharitableness keep riot in his heart and brain? Of what use to point such a man to beautiful ideals, to preach to him the holy joys of self-forgetfulness, to bid him worship Humanity? Verily, if, as all men must, he arrive at his conception of humanity at large from a study of his own inner life, he will feel little inducement to fall in adoration before the altar of the race.

Did the supporters of the new religion make its universal acceptance dependent upon the prior success of a social revolution, the outcome of which was to be the establishment of a just order, we could then very well concede the logical strength of their position, think what we might of the calculations on which they based their hopes. But it is distinctly asserted that the only reasonable prospect of such new social order depends upon the operative influence of the Religion of Humanity. So it is to be feared that we shall wait long for our

Utopian constitution. For, if agnostic realism is obviously fraught with every greatest danger to the common weal, religion of earthly optimism is the very last instrument wherewith one would seek to counteract the threatening ill. For optimism of this kind is but egotism under another name. To the agnostic optimist life is something good in itself and for its own sake; the mere circumstance of birth into the world endows with a right to a share in the world's happiness. Let this constitute a man's creed, and, consciously or unconsciously, he will inevitably make it his first object to secure possession of his birthright. The social results which directly issue from such a conviction in the individual are only too plain before our eyes. Hence this scheme of commercial competition tempered by the police-code, to which we are pleased to give the name of a social order. The motto of our time is: Every man for himself, and the Devil take the hindmost. We will not listen to any of our socialistic nonsense, not we; let every man fight his way through life as best he can, one up, another down. The competitive system, depend on it, is the grandest outcome of civilization. It makes us robust and self-reliant: we expect no mercy in the battle, and accordingly give no quarter; the strong man will make his way; for the weak are there not workhouses and prisons? We are a growing population; our great problem is, how to make the food of two keep three alive; it is patent that we cannot stand upon ceremony, must e'en push our best to get a place at the board. Does not science—the very newest—assure us that only the fittest shall survive? If we tread upon a feeble competitor and have the misfortune to crush the life out of him, we are merely illustrating the law of natural selection. A man must live, we suppose?—This is the spirit of the time, the outcome of realism and devotion to the life of the world. How, in the face of such a state of things, are you to begin converting people to the doctrine of altruism, your medium nothing better than a philosophy of Agnostic Optimism? Whence the moral force which is to inspire men with the enthusiasm of Humanity? The man who can pin his faith on the conviction that life on earth is the highest attainable good, and, doing so, can yet sacrifice his share in this good for the sake of a fellow-being, is cast in heroic mould; and are we justified in taking it for granted that the spread of the new religion would make such heroism the common attitude of men?

We owe to Schopenhauer the metaphysical explanation of egotism. It is the outcome of what he calls *die Bejahung des Willens zum Leben,* the affirmation of the will to live, as opposed to that *Verneinung des Willens* with which alone genuine self-forgetfulness is compatible. Now optimism directly encourages the affirmation of the will to live, consequently cannot but encourage egotism, let sophists argue as they please. For Agnostic Optimism, as already said, is the restatement in terms of philosophical consciousness of the spirit which unconsciously possesses and actuates the mass of men. That this spirit is prevailingly egotistic no one will be found to deny. It is so, simply because it represents the instinct by virtue of which every living thing clings to life with the utmost energy of its nature, and finds the goal of being in the propagation of its kind. The very cattle led to slaughter are optimists, in precisely the same way that man is an optimist when he gives himself unreflectingly up to the current of active life. Are we to suppose that human progress consists in the strengthening of this tendency, and not rather in its final counteraction by the supreme powers of intelligence? We know that instinct can be overcome by reason; a man may, in a solitary instance, be capable of sacrificing his life at the prompting of reason, even though life seem to him an absolute good; or he may go further than this, and, by the practice of the severest asceticism, prove that the conquest of instinct has become the habit of his life, that he has attained to *die Verneinung des Willens.* Life is no longer a good to him; he is a Pessimist. And this is the final triumph of mind, the highest reach of human morality, the only hope of the destruction of egotism.

Can it really be necessary to argue against an optimistic view of human life? Has not the general voice of the wisest of all ages borne witness to the weariness of being, the sighing of unnumbered generations made mute protest against the burden of breath? We enter the gates of life with wailing, and anguish to the womb which brings us forth; we pass again into the outer darkness through the valley of ghastly terrors, and leave cold misery upon the lips of those that mourn us. The interval is but a feverish combat, the commonplace of moralists. Those brief intervals of rest which nature grants we embitter for each other by the inexhaustible envy of our hearts. Our passions rack us with the unspeakable torment of desire, and fruition is but another name for disillusion. Every epoch of existence feeds on the vision of some unattainable joy; from the rising to the going down of the sun we lament for that which we have not, and our nightly dreams mock us with a visioned happiness. We make unto ourselves idols of our vain beliefs, and rend each other for the supremacy of a name. From the ancient battle-field of earth goes up the reek of the blood of peoples, spilt that one man might lie in purple, or for the glory of gods that are not. Our bodily frame is a house of torment, and the seat of lusts which obscure the soul. The aching of a limb frustrates the keenest intellectual delight; disorder in a fragment of the brain sinks the philosopher below the beast. We lay our selfish plans as though for an eternity of life, and fate mocks the bitterness of our disappointment. We inherit but by the offices of death, and every possession to which we succeed puts us in mind of our own mortality. Each generation builds upon the grave of that which went before; the whole earth is but the cenotaph of vanished hopes; and, in the words of the golden-tongued preacher, "You can go no whither but you tread upon a dead man's bones."

In losing that larger hope which is the foundation of religious optimism, we are deprived of the only solace which could prevail against the misery of being. Well did Christianity insist upon the saving efficacy of faith, in the light whereof evil could show as a means of final good, and the daily martyrdoms of earth gleam under the fore-vision of the promised crown. This faith lost, sin and suffering and the last agony of death are to our reason inexplicable. Science comes with its doctrine of determinism to realize the image of a relentless Fate, which brings into existence but to torture and then destroy. Man becomes conscious that to represent himself as tempted by evil is a reversal of the truth; evil is the essence of his being; of good he is cognizant, but can only approach it in proportion as he denies himself, un-wills the instinct of life. The foremost religions of the world, Buddhism and Christianity, alike recognize this, vouched for as a truth by that inner persuasion, that subjective proof, which is our only revelation.

Physical anguish and the misery of sin all men inherit; he who has experienced the second birth of philosophical consciousness endows himself with a yet deeper woe; for him "but to think is to be full of sorrow and leaden-eyed despair." He is the spiritual alchemist, seeking to extract from the inadequate elements of the mind the gold of absolute knowledge, and for ever overcome by a perception of the vanity of endeavour. His eye, piercing the veil of things which seem, would penetrate to that which is; his despair is in the discovery that subject and object presuppose each other, and that if he would view this mutual relationship from without he must first transcend the conditions of his intelligence. The insoluble problem meets him on every hand and in a multitude of forms: the chain of causation without beginning or end, the meaning of force, the origin of matter and its infinite divisibility, the boundlessness of space, the eternity of time. Look up to the sky above you, and try to reconcile that logical necessity of belief in infinitude with that finite practical understanding which stubbornly revolts against the conception; in the effort the brain reels and the heart is sick, an immense self-pity takes possession of the imprisoned soul. Let us nourish this self-compassionate mood, hold desperately to it, strive to make it the familiar companion of our thoughts,—for herein lies what we may call the tangible issue of metaphysical speculation, the root of future good in the intercourse of man with man. Consider the lot of humanity from the first conscious thought, who knows how far back in time, to that moment, beyond the interval of unimagined ages, when the earth shall circle in its contracting orb, the grave of thought. No words can give utterance to the sadness of such contemplation, a sadness which must increase as mankind becomes more reflective, though the mind may gird itself against the onset of insidious fears, and the heart seek to find a joyous music in its own strong throbbing. From the earliest times men have sought to get at the significance of their strange, dread fate; one generation has solved it thus, another in another way; all have found a momentary solace and strength in the visions which their faith conjured up for them, and all, as we now believe, rested their hopes on foundations insubstantial as a ray of sunlight. In the grave was the goal of their striving, and Death laughed as he stilled with cold hand the fever of their foreheads. For us, the offspring of a later day, not even thus much happiness is allowed; we may not deceive ourselves with the visionary heritage of a life to come, still less with the hope of solving in this world the enigma of our destiny. The sphinx stands before us with ever more inexorable face, propounding a riddle which we listen to with ever deeper despair. We, too, shall find peace in the dissolution of being, and our minds shall rest from their anxious toil; but the last moment of consciousness is saddened by the thought that we depart with our task unaccomplished, hopeless of success forever. We cry for light, and, even as we speak, the eternal darkness envelops us. Generation shall succeed to generation, and race step in the footprints of race, and the incident of a human death-bed will still symbolize the triumph of woe. Then, in the lapse of cycles, will come the day when the last human soul has ceased to dash itself against the barriers of the unknowable, and the last prayer from human lips has wasted itself upon the unpitying void, and the great tragedy will have found its close.

In the pity of it we must find our salvation. The compassion which each man first feels for himself, let him extend to his fellow-sufferers. But this compassion, as it is the divinest feeling of which our nature is capable, so can it only be the offspring of that metaphysical consciousness which Agnostic Optimism would fain repress as vain and obstructive of the future hope. Suppose all men so far intellectually trained as to be capable of fully and intensely realizing the pathos of the human lot, the deeper pathos which goes so much beyond our every-day griefs, and indeed gives to such their significance,—were it not inevitable that their souls should be forthwith possessed by an overpowering mutual pity? Let us have done (they would say,) with making our poor little day so full of bitterness for each other. Let us see into the dark places of our brother's soul, and strive to solace him with sweetest sympathy. Not as a hardy, self-sufficient being, ripe to cope with circumstance, as a strong warrior competent against the odds which face him, as a conqueror marching on with front to the stars,—not thus let us regard man, for thence comes the hardening of the heart against him, the insistence on one's own miserable claims, the prevalence of the spirit of combat; so have we come to use that phrase, "the battle of life." No; rather cultivate our perception of man's weakness, learn thoroughly the pathos inherent in a struggle between the finite and the infinite. We are shipmates, tossed on the ocean of eternity, and one fate awaits us all.

94

Let this excite our tenderness. Let us move on to the real gulfs hand clasped in hand, not each one's raised in enmity against his fellow. So will the agony of the last drowning moment be lightened by the thought that we have not lived in vain. Save our brother we could not, knowing not, alas, how to save ourselves; but our last word to him was one of kindness, and on his anguished face we still recognize the gleam of gratitude.

"Sorrow is better than laughter, for by the sadness of the countenance the heart is made better." Sadness is the twin-sister of wisdom, and comes to us hand in hand with her. Upon the face of him that looks into the heart of things there rests the shadow of a great mystery, and the revelation which to the wise comes thus directly makes itself at certain seasons a presence in the being of the most unreflective. The world-old ballads chanted by "the spinsters and the knitters in the sun," the legends sacred to the cottage hearth, those melodies which linger through centuries in the homely corners of the earth, all bear a character of melancholy; they embody the philosophy of the unconscious. All music, indeed,—music, which is the most perfect utterance of the deepest truth,—lives by the spirit of sadness, and is a summoner at the gate of tears. This universal sense of pathos in the most secret places of our nature is the unconscious expression of the truth whereon Pessimism founds its creed. Our existence is something which should not be; the vehement desire of its continuance is sin. There is, in truth, only one kind of worldly optimism which justifies itself in the light of reason, and that is the optimism of the artist. The artistic mind, as Schopenhauer demonstrates, is *das reine Subject des Erkennens,* the subject contemplating the object without disturbing consciousness of self. In the mood of artistic contemplation the will is destroyed, self is eliminated, the world of phenomena resolves itself into pictures of absolute significance, and the heart rejoices itself before images of pure beauty. Here, indeed, good does prevail over evil, and there is excellence in the sum of things. Herein is one explanation of the optimism of the Hellenic religion: it was the faith of a people of artists. The thought did not go behind phenomena, and instinct embraced the world in the artistic sense. The earth was the abode of loveliness and delight; life was a hymn to the spirit of beauty; the state ensuing upon death was a

95

negation, a horrid absence of the active joy which possesses all things under the sun; better to be a live beggar than a king among the shades. Optimism in the religion of the Jews represented a moral error, was the outcome of a spirit of aggressive egotism; and one might say the same of Islam. Christianity, basing itself upon the recognition of original sin, was consistently pessimistic, and embodied in a noble symbolism those truths in the return to which lies the only hope of man's ultimate salvation.

Christianity in its modern form of optimistic protestantism is a delusion and a snare. In accommodating itself, step by step, to the growth of material civilization, this so-called religion of Christ has directly encouraged the spirit of egotism which inevitably accompanies an optimistic faith; its latest outcome is the predominance of commercial competition, with its doctrine of "Every man for himself, and the Devil take the hindmost." What has the Christianity of to-day in common with the "Imitatio Christi," what in common with the teachings of a prophet whose birth from a virgin mother, and whose own virginity, symbolized that renunciation of the world of flesh which was the strait and narrow way to the kingdom of heaven? It is in the pessimistic philosophy as developed by Schopenhauer that we find the true successor of pure Christianity. In former times the world had to be taught the lesson of salvation through the medium of a myth; hereafter, the developed understanding of mankind will grasp it in the abstract form. The establishment of the kingdom of righteousness can only ensue upon the destruction of egotism, and egotism only perishes together with optimism, together with "the will to live." Only with the absolute extinction of every lust of the flesh can sin cease to be; only with the final cessation of conscious life can evil disappear from the earth.

That kingdom will be long to come; but we may well, without offence to the most practical, anticipate that time when, in consequence of a prevailing consciousness of the pathos of human fate, compassion will so far weigh against egotism as to abolish the system of competitive greed, and make no longer socially applicable that terrible phrase: the battle of life. In the divine strength of Sorrow will this victory be achieved, even as of old was achieved the victory of the Cross. The prospect of happiness on earth is a chimera, but peace and good-will may prevail to an extent not easy as yet to realize, and thereby suffering man be strengthened under the burden of life. Death, too, persistently regarded as a consummation devoutly to be wished, will lose a portion of its terrors;—

"Nec mihi mors gravis est posituro morte dolores."

The grave will become a symbol of joy; those who have departed will be spoken of as the happy ones, and the tears of the mourner will be checked by his bitter reason. Pity is alone for the living.— Unless by the eyes of faith we may look onward to that day when compassion will extend itself to generations yet unborn. To create a being predestined to misery will come to be deemed a crime, even as the passion concerned is recognized as a sin. And so, perchance, where the condemnation of reason could not overcome, the dictates of emotion will be strong to chasten; a childless race will dedicate its breath to the eternal silence, and Mercy will have redeemed the world.

Along Shore

RARELY DID GISSING try his hand at the descriptive essay. In the whole of his career, only three were published: "On Battersea Bridge," which he wrote feverishly one evening after watching the sun set on the Thames, appeared in the *Pall Mall Gazette,* on November 30, 1883,* "Christmas on the Capitol," written to order for Tillotson's Newspaper Syndicate, was printed in the *Bolton Evening News* on December 28, 1889; a contribution to the *Daily Chronicle* entitled "At the Grave of Alaric," composed at the invitation of his friend Henry Norman, who was the editor of the great London newspaper, appeared on May 31, 1898.

The present essay, like "On Battersea Bridge," belongs to his Chelsea days (September, 1882–April, 1884). As the first words indicate, it was written in winter, and almost certainly after November, 1883, for it is natural to assume that, delighted by the unexpected acceptance of "On Battersea Bridge," he was tempted to try his luck again, in the hope of earning a couple of sorely needed guineas. The manuscript, which bears Gissing's full name and address, is almost six pages long. Whether or not it was rejected by a newspaper cannot be determined.

* See *The Private Papers of Henry Ryecroft*, Autumn XXI. The text of the essay is more readily accessible in *Selections, Autobiographical and Imaginative from the Works of George Gissing*, pp. 54–58. The two other essays are also reprinted in this volume, pp. 130–48 and 238–44.

HESE SHREWD WINTER NIGHTS, when the wind is sweeping clear the path of the moon, there is good rambling in the waterside country from Wapping to the Isle of Dogs. The tumult of the day has vanished; miles of narrow, devious roadway are unpeopled; your footstep echoes far between high warehouses and blank walls of wharf and dock as you walk in their dense shadow, looking forward into masses of vaguely-featured gloom. At times the front of a public-house beacons ahead, and voices, or perhaps music, break the stillness; or you reach the open gateway of some vast vaulted place of storage, where forms are moving among dimly-lighted piles of barrels and bales, a damp odour of indistinguishable merchandise burdening the air; or, again, the intermittent thud of hammers guides you to a bridge, from which you look down into a dry dock, where men with lanterns are working late at the repairing of a vessel. But the best is when you suddenly pass out of the shadow, and, without warning, stand on the swing-bridge, spanning an entrance to one of the great basins. The water sobs and gurgles in darkness between the restraining locks, and tethered boats grate against each other; before you is the free breadth of stream, silver-grey in the moon, dotted with red lights of barges, bounded by the dim shapes of the farther shore. Turn, and your eye rests upon the still dock, beautiful with the witch-grace of sleeping ships, masts and yards etched with delicate firmness upon the sky, the nearer hulls darkly distinct from stem to stern, majestic in repose. The wind which blows through the rigging seems to catch a note of sadness, the sigh of the strong, swift creatures, as they dream of glad conflict with Atlantic billows, or of the glory of southern seas. You pity them, moored here in the recesses of the narrow Thames, in the shadow of a great city to which they seem nothing akin. It is as though we had robbed them of liberty, perforce constrained them to do our spiriting over the waters, to be our messengers and carriers from land to land.

The by-ways up from the river lead to inhabited districts; but here again there is silence and darkness; all life would seem to have been attracted to the thoroughfares above, the high streets of Shadwell, Ratcliffe and Limehouse. Cramped streets,—a blear-eyed little shop here and there,—are intersected by alleys, courts and passages.

There are low archways, through which it is vain to peer, no gleam on the blackness beyond; other entrances where a lamp, fixed against the house-wall, half discloses with its yellow ray a vista of dirty white-washed dwellings, one storey high, the space between them measurable by the extended arms, the doors requiring a lowered head. To explore these inlets one must be, to say the least, adventurously minded. The doors on each hand generally stand open, but not an object within is discernible. Darkness here is more than deprivation of light; it is a presence whispering villainous suggestions, closing about you till you shudder as from a clammy touch. To look up to the narrow streak of silver sky is to feel more consciously the frowning of the low, black roofs; the glimmer in a window, coming often from behind a red curtain, sets the mind on weird imaginings. Perhaps there are ragged children sitting upon a door-sill, unchildlike, goblin, talking together of unintelligible things. Moving quickly on, you think to issue into a broader way, but, as often as not, become lost in some unpaved yard, amid confusion of lumber, or wheels, or in the door-ways of sheds, startling a stealthy cat, or scattering fowls into flapping flight. And amid all this fearsome squalor you feel the characteristic of the neighbourhood; the atmosphere at its closest has an ancient and fish-like smell, and where the wind has space to blow, you distinguish flavours of rope and tar, canvas and cargo.

At this hour of quiet, there is a peculiar attractiveness about the "stairs." At the end of a long passage between dark walls you catch a blue glimpse of the river, and, drawn towards it, reach the flight of stone steps leading down to the water-level. At the foot is the waterman's wherry; and barges, three or four deep, lying off the adjacent wharf. Occasionally there is life here which you had not suspected; descending to where the tide laps on the lowest step, you see lights in the front of the wharf, and cranes at work, hoisting and lowering. But oftener all is still and deserted; there lurks about the shadowed margin a spirit of melancholy solitude, and from the black depths rise fearful whisperings.

The Stairs at the foot of Old Gravel Lane in Wapping—maybe the identical Wapping Old Stairs,—have been made interesting in a curious way. An old waterman, with a praiseworthy desire to utilize his leisure for the public service, has tarred over some ten square feet of wall, and painted hereon, in neat rows of print, a record of all manner of noteworthy events, principally connected with the river. Here you can peruse the "pedigree" of the Thames Tunnel, and learn, if you care to, the exact number of bricks which went to the building of that structure; or note remarkable high and low tides, as far back as the eleventh century; or read a full account of the "Princess Alice" disaster, or be informed who were the last men hung at Execution Dock, for mutiny at sea. There are also matters of more general character, such as instances of extreme old age, particulars of the Plague and Fire of London, and distressing calamities of other kinds. The inscription completed, its author was at the pains to calculate the number of words his hand had traced, and found them to be 3465, as is duly set down. Among these must be reckoned a verse of poetry, the chosen motto of our industrious friend:—"Were I so tall to reach the pole, Or mete the Heavens with a span, I would be measured by my soul, The mind's the standard of the man." But the old waterman's activity has not ended here. On the opposite wall is another table, a list of the winners of Doggett's Coat and Badge, in the annual rowing match from London Bridge to Chelsea, for the last hundred years or so.

A less ancient waterman, who was standing alone late one night at the head of the Stairs, disappointed at first on finding that I had no need of his boat, grew more cheerful when I was able to serve him in the matter of a light for his pipe, and willingly chatted of the inscriptions, which he admired greatly: "So useful, you see," he said, "to settle a hargueyment." He went on to inform me that, some five and twenty years ago, the tables had already been completed on another part of the wall, though on a smaller scale; but then came the time of cholera in those regions, and, alas, sanitary coats of whitewash had obliterated the work. Dim traces yet remain, however, as he showed me with his finger. My informant, in reply to a question, turned the talk to his own personal affairs. Business is not flourishing, nor, for the matter of that, ever had been since the running of the railway through the old Thames Tunnel; and he pointed to Wapping Station with a half mournful, half contemptuous, gesture. Prior to that, he had known as many as sixty boats lying here at the Stairs, ferrying workmen and others to the south bank; he himself had been wont to earn his three shillings before breakfast. But at present there was little to be done, save carrying occasional seamen and travellers to the vessels off in the river. As he spoke he shook his head frequently, and, when I left him, went back to the head of the Stairs and stood looking at his idle boat below.

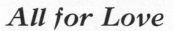

All for Love

LATE IN OCTOBER, 1879, Gissing completed his first published novel, *Workers in the Dawn,* which Remington and Company brought out the following June. Feeling that this fat three-decker had somewhat taxed his inventiveness and artistry, he turned within the next few weeks to shorter fiction. He had uppermost in his mind his various successes with American editors and wished to explore the potential English market for such pieces as had appeared in the *Chicago Tribune* and *Appleton's Journal* in 1877. He must have settled to work shortly after moving from 38 Edward Street to 5 Hanover Street on November 26, while the manuscript of *Workers* was in the hands of Chatto and Windus, as the fifty-eight-page manuscript of "All for Love," signed G. R. Gissing, bears the latter address.

A note on the back of p. 17 is dated February, 1880. Though no express mention of the story occurs in Gissing's correspondence, the date of composition is confirmed by an allusion he made to it in a letter of January 2 to his brother Algernon. He had "gone desperately to work on a few stories and novelettes," he wrote, "which I mean to sow broadcast among magazines and papers hoping that *some* at least may take root."*
Of his surviving fiction of the period, "All for Love" is the only text to which the word "novelette" can be applied.

When it was finished, probably in January, 1880, Gissing sent it, with the editor's permission, to a publication called *Novelist,* which was the property of one John Dicks, 313 Strand. Each weekly number of *Novelist* consisted of one complete original story. After three weeks Gissing inquired of the editor about the story. His manuscript was thereupon returned to him, three-quarters of it missing, without comment. The missing portions were sent him by two later posts. With characteristic bitterness, Gissing concluded his brief account of the episode: "The reward of dealing with blackguards."†

Novelist was one of many such pamphlets issued at regular intervals and intended for the mass of readers produced by Forster's Education Act of 1870—the millions which Gissing later called "the quarter-educated" in his *New Grub Street.* In presentation it was not unlike the series published by Methuen with the same title in the early 1900s, which included sixpenny reprints of *The Town Traveller* and *The Crown of Life.*

* *Letters of George Gissing to Members of His Family,* p. 53.
† Written on the reverse of manuscript page 17.

Chapter I: The End of the Honeymoon

HE SCENE OF OUR STORY is the quiet little town of Market Leyton, a prosperous but drowsy place, generally redolent of hay and clover, and regularly given up once a week to a stampede through the streets of bullocks, sheep and pigs, which is known as the cattle fair. As regards natural advantages one could not choose a more delightful place of residence, for it is situated in the heart of a charming agricultural district, in one of the midland counties. Though brought by a great steam-highway into connection with large and busy centres of industry, Market Leyton cares little, if anything, for towns whose prosperity does not depend upon cattle fairs. It is thoroughly impressed, moreover, with a sense of its own importance, firmly believing that, but for the strenuous patriotism of its inhabitants, England would not be the country she is. Doubtless the reader can, from this description, obtain a tolerably clear notion of Market Leyton.

At the time of which I write—no very remote epoch,—no name was better known in the neighbourhood than that of Bloomfield. Edward Bloomfield, Esquire, of Bloomfield House, who was thrice mayor of the town, had died rather more than two years since, but the House was still held by his widow and his only son, the former an amiable old lady of some sixty years, the latter, who was just turned twenty-six, a prosperous physician, with a reputation which extended considerably beyond the limits of his native town. The Bloomfields were at all times interesting people to the gossips of Market Leyton, but just at present the five-o'clock tea-tables were especially busy with their name, for the very sufficient reason that Laurence Bloomfield had lately seen fit to take unto himself a wife. Mothers of families, especially those with marriageable daughters, had of course been very angry with him for not deciding upon the step sooner; now they were still angrier on account of the choice he had made. "Who is she?" had been the universal question upon the wedding-day; a state of affairs, it need not be said, highly improper when the bridegroom was a young man of such extremely eligible qualities. Perhaps not half a dozen of the intimate friends of the Bloomfields had ever seen the bride before. That was no concern of theirs, Laurence had said. His mother had quite approved the choice, the wedding had taken place, and at the present moment everyone was expecting the return home of Dr.

Bloomfield and his wife from their two-months' tour on the Continent.

But, during the night preceding the appointed day occurred a very disagreeable incident indeed, nothing less than an attempt upon Bloomfield House by burglars. Very early in the morning the news of this event was spread about the town, and was received by all as a most exciting and delightful topic of conversation; novel, withal, for it was a long time since burglary had disturbed the repose of the good people of Market Leyton. Many were the kind inquiries made at the house with regard to Mrs. Bloomfield's health, in reply to all which the servant was instructed to say that her mistress was much obliged but happily she felt no ill result worth speaking of from the alarm of the night. Towards noon the house was full of friends and acquaintances, all of whom threw up their hands and expressed much astonishment at the calmness with which the old lady related the circumstances; for Mrs. Bloomfield, be it noted, was a woman remarkable above everything for common-sense, and but little given to the more distinctly female forms of excitement. The fuss which she now found herself the centre of was extremely distasteful to her, and it was with a sigh of relief that she at length saw the last visitor turn her back. But she was not to be allowed the peace she coveted. No sooner had she sat down in her drawing-room to the quiet perusal of a book than the door-bell once more rang, and, a moment after, there bounded into the room a lady whom the servant had scarcely time to announce as Miss Chad. She was apparently middle-aged, short and slim, not to say angular, in person, and, as regards her features, plain yet pleasing. Handsome she had never been, but there was on her countenance a marked expression of good humour, a lively geniality in eyes and lips, which made one from the first favourably disposed towards Miss Chad.

"Dear me! Dear me!" she exclaimed, in short, quick tones, as she burst through the doorway and hurried panting to the old lady's side. "How very shocking, Mrs. Bloomfield! How unspeakably dreadful! Why, *why* was I not telegraphed for? To think that such a thing should happen, and in my absence,—I, who certainly am not absent from Market Leyton more than half a dozen days in the whole year! I'm sure you must need support, Mrs. Bloomfield. So very shocking! Dear, dear!—Why *was* I not telegraphed for?"

"To do so would have been to alarm you most unnecessarily, my dear Miss Chad," replied the old lady, overcoming her first sentiment of annoyance, and smiling with a mixture of quiet irony and friendly feeling which was well adapted to her cast of countenance. "Doubtless the affair has been reported to you in a very exaggerated form; it seems to have excited the imagination of many of our friends, and they distort the truth without meaning to do so."

Mrs. Bloomfield's tone was very quiet and self-contained, the tone of one who was in the habit of forming her own opinion on matters and was not easily disturbed in it.

"Yes, yes; of course," pursued Miss Chad, eagerly. "Dreadful chatterboxes! Dreadful!—But do let me hear the story from your own lips, my dear Mrs. Bloomfield; I positively must hear it, if only to correct the false accounts which are flying about as thick—as thick as apples in your orchard, Mrs. Bloomfield." The simile was suggested by a glance through the window at the heavily-laden fruit-trees. "Now is it really true that you faced the whole gang with a pistol, and in your—in your night-dress, my dear Mrs. Bloomfield?"

The old lady laughed quietly, perhaps a trifle contemptuously.

"Pooh!" she replied. "What silly tales people invent! In the first place, the gang certainly did not consist of more than two men, and, secondly, I do not believe there is a pistol in the house, if I had the courage to think of one. The facts are these. I happened to wake in the middle of the night, as I very frequently do, and I was busy in my thoughts about Laurence's return, when all at once it seemed to me as if I heard a bed-room door open, one of those on the opposite side of the landing to my own. I was a little alarmed, and sat up to listen intently. Suddenly something fell, some light weight, also in the same direction, and at the same time I felt sure I heard the creak of a footstep. Walton and the two girls were of course sleeping in the house as usual, but I had no means of communicating with them, without leaving my room, which you may suppose I did not care to do. The only plan that occurred to me was to ring the bell in the servants'-hall, and this I at once did, vigorously. The noise echoed through the house immediately, and at once I heard a scamper of feet on the staircase. Then I slightly opened the door and called Walton loudly. In a few minutes he came, followed by the frightened girls, and together we all went over the house. We discovered that it was Laurence's bed-room the thieves had entered for the door stood open, and one of Bertha's trunks had been forced. Some of the clothing it contained had been scattered on the floor, but I cannot say whether anything was actually stolen. I scarcely think, however, that the box contained anything of sufficient value."

"Dear me! Dear me!" broke in Miss Chad, who, with her twin-kling eyes fixed upon the speaker's face, had eagerly devoured every word. "A mere collection of old clothes, I presume. The idea!—But however did those terrible ruffians get into the house, Mrs. Bloom-field?"

"They can scarcely have been very terrible," returned the old lady, smiling, "remembering how they scampered upon the first fright. It was very evident that they had entered by the scullery-window. Strangely enough, the dog in the yard had got loose and must have been roaming about the country at the time when he should have de-fended his master's house. It is lucky the affair has not been more serious. One of the trunks in the room contained quite a number of valuable wedding-presents. I'm very glad for poor Bertha's sake that the thieves did not get at them."

"Indeed, I am enraptured that the bloodthirsty villains were balked!" exclaimed Miss Chad. "I wonder, now, how many there were? 1 am sure at least half a dozen?"

"Certainly not more than two, as I think I said. Walton feels sure of it, from observation of the footmarks in the scullery. It was a wet and muddy night, you know; and the burglars left distinct traces."

"Ha!" exclaimed Miss Chad, with a gasp expressive of satisfied curiosity; then, after a pause which was long for her, but which did not last more than half a minute, the stream of chatter once more bubbled from her lips. "But how very shocking, my dear Mrs. Bloom-field, to think of such a—a tragedy I may say, happening the very night before the arrival of the happy pair! Extremely shocking, I'm sure!—And you must be expecting them every moment, Mrs. Bloom-field! And to think of them returning to find your nerves so dreadfully shattered"—

"Not in the least, my dear Miss Chad," broke in the old lady, a little sharply. "Not in the least. Do I look as if I were nervous or terrified?"

"Well, when I come to look at you," replied the other, "I declare you look wonderfully well, considering! Indeed, I envy you, Mrs. Bloomfield. Your nerves must be wonderfully strong, as—as strong as cobbler's wax!"

Ordinarily, Mrs. Bloomfield had no objection to sacrifice an hour or so to Miss Chad's somewhat entertaining gossip, but at present there were arrangements to be made in the house in preparation for the evening, and perhaps, if the truth must be told, Mrs. Bloomfield's nerves were *not* quite in their usual condition. Consequently the old lady had no scruple in giving quiet hints, that, having satisfied her visitor's curiosity, she should rather like to be left alone. Miss Chad had of course an infinitude of questions to ask, more or less in relation to the expected arrival; and, as soon as all these had been very briefly responded to, she rose to leave.

"Once more I must heartily congratulate you," she cried, on her way out, "that matters are no worse. Indeed I felt at first quite cross with you for not having telegraphed for me. Oh, how I envy you your treat this evening, Mrs. Bloomfield,—to be the very first to greet the —the happy pair! But depend upon it I shall not wait long before I give myself the pleasure. Perhaps to-morrow morning,—the afternoon at latest. Good-bye, Mrs. Bloomfield; good-bye."

Though not looking forward to the meeting with quite such excessive rapture as Miss Chad imagined, Mrs. Bloomfield was yet sufficiently disturbed as the time drew near for the arrival of her son and his wife. They had telegraphed from London that they hoped to be at home shortly after seven o'clock, and by that hour the old lady was pacing somewhat restlessly up and down the drawing-room, one moment consulting her watch, the next inspecting the clock which ticked upon the mantel-piece. She had arrayed herself for the occasion in a heavy and somewhat old-fashioned black-silk dress, one which was seldom taken from its repository; around her neck hung a triply folded watch-chain, ending in the pocket at her girdle; at her throat was a rather large cameo-brooch, representing a chariot and horses careering towards the goal. The widow's cap upon her head became her well, giving relief to the well-defined lines of her countenance. Mrs. Bloomfield was in many respects a proud woman, and there was something in her face and mien, particularly upon occasions of some solemnity, such as the present, which made one involuntarily think of a Roman matron.

She had not to wait beyond the appointed time. Exactly at five minutes past seven Dr. Bloomfield's well-known carriage drove through the gate. The front of the house looked towards the west, and just at this moment all the windows were reflecting the intensely red glow of the setting sun; it was as though the illumination were in honour of the returning pair.

Mrs. Bloomfield could not wait to consider ceremony, but hastened out into the hall, and with an exclamation of "My dear children!" cordially embraced the pair. Then she led the way into the drawing-room with delighted utterance of welcome.

"And how are you both?" she cried, her face aglow with joy, as she took their hands in her own. "Come and turn your faces to the window that I may see how you look. Oh, no need to look at *you*, Laurence; you are always as red-cheeked as a schoolboy. But how is Bertha?"

"In admirable health, my dear mother," replied Bertha, blushing slightly before the old lady's gaze. "Indeed I never felt so well."

"Still too pale; still too pale," said Mrs. Bloomfield, caressing her daughter's hand. "I shall begin to think the defect is natural, for really you look happy."

"But mother," broke in Laurence, "whatever is all this talk about burglars with which we are overwhelmed as soon as we reach home? Bertha and I feared that we should find the whole house stolen away and you in it."

"Psha!" exclaimed his mother, with a look of annoyance on her face. "You know about it already? Whoever has found an opportunity of telling you? Not Miss —"

"Yes," interrupted Laurence, with a hearty laugh. "Miss Chad, and no other; wasn't it, Bertha? She set upon us the very moment we stepped out of the train,—must have been waiting on purpose. But, seriously, mother, has anything been lost?"

"No, nothing at all, my dear; the whole affair is not worth mentioning again. I am heartily sick of it."

"But the burglars escaped I am told?"

"Yes, they escaped, and seem to have left no clue. Of course the affair is in the hands of the police. In short, I forbid either of you to plague me about it during the rest of the evening.—Bertha, I will take you upstairs.—I suppose you are hungry, Laurence. The bell will ring in a quarter of an hour, not a minute sooner or later; so dispose of yourself as you please, sir."

Chapter II: Loss and Gain

Before Mrs. Bloomfield leads her daughter-in-law from the room let us look at husband and wife as they stand side by side, facing the glow of the sunset. To begin with, their external appearance is far from that of an ideally suited couple; for whereas Laurence Bloomfield is tall and admirably developed, with perhaps some slight indications of robustness threatening to become corpulence, unless kept down by an active habit of life, Bertha, his wife, scarcely reaches above his shoulder, and, though of symmetrical figure, shows a tendency to anything rather than robustness. Indeed she has all the appearance of a frail and not very healthy woman. Again, Laurence is dark, darker than ever just at present, when his handsome, intellectual face is deeply tanned by the sun of the Mediterranean; Bertha, on the other hand, is very fair, her skin of marvellously delicate texture, and her hair, slightly drooping about her forehead from the fatigue of the journey, is of a very light gold, like that of a child. Upon the features of the husband are strongly impressed the signs of a vigorous will, of a nature which can determine quickly and boldly, and act upon its determinations unfalteringly. But the countenance of the wife has a far other tale to tell to one who knows as much as the alphabet of physiognomy; weakness and doubt are to be read unmistakably in the tremulous outlines of the mouth and the moulding of the delicate chin. Yet her face is very loveable, perhaps all the more so for its weakness; there is a sweet, pleading expression in the eyes, a hesitating smile on the lips, both of which are inexpressibly attractive. One does not wonder, after all, that Laurence Bloomfield passed unscathed from amid the luxuriant, rose-like beauties abounding in the principal families of the town, to lay his heart at length before the feet of this pale, trembling lily.

Bertha Williamson had been her name before she was married, and as already hinted, she was regarded by the gossips of Market Leyton as somewhat of a mystery. How and when she had first come to the town no one but her husband and her mother-in-law certainly knew. It was settled upon all sides that she must always have been very poor and have come of a poor family, for she had earned a scanty living by keeping an infants' school, and had never been known to refer in any way to friends or relatives of her own. When once he had discovered her in her retreat, it was only with the utmost difficulty that Laurence had won her confidence, and with still more that he had at length induced her to accept an invitation from his mother to visit Bloomfield House. When at length he heard her story from her own lips it seemed so simple that there was nothing at all left to wonder at. She told him that she believed herself to be absolutely without a relation in the world, and was certainly without a friend, with the exception of the very few she had made in Market Leyton. Her father she had never known; her mother had died when she was about sixteen. Up to that age she had lived in London, but, upon her mother's death, she obtained a situation as governess in a family residing in the south of England. To the step she had been compelled by absolute need; her mother had possessed a small annuity, but only for her own lifetime, and Bertha was left almost penniless. Since that time (at present she was not quite twenty-five,) she had lived by her own exertions as a teacher. In her last situation as governess she had been able to save a little money, part of which she had laid out in the purchase of her school. This she had discovered by means of an advertisement in a country paper; and it was thus by pure chance alone that she had come to live in Market Leyton. Such was her story; and, on Laurence expressing some wonder that she should ever have cared to make a mystery of it, she declared that the mystery was none of her making, that she was by nature reticent and retiring, and on this account alone she had seemed to have something to conceal.

Having done our duty in so far enlightening the reader, we proceed with our narrative in order due. Laurence had inwardly lauded his mother's appreciativeness when she said he must be hungry, and accordingly it was with some impatience that he paced up and down the room when the dinner-bell had actually rung without either his wife or his mother putting in an appearance. At length the old lady rustled in.

"What!" she exclaimed. "Hasn't Bertha come down yet?"

"It seems not," replied Laurence. "I must go and hasten her on, for I assure you I feel in no mood to delay."

His mother laughed as he strode past her and went upstairs three steps at once. "Bertha!" he called, on reaching her door; but, receiving no answer, he turned the handle and entered. He was astonished to see his wife, still in her travelling garments, on her knees before an open trunk. All the contents lay scattered on the floor, Bertha, apparently unconscious of his presence, was staring into the empty box with a blank look of despair which amazed and horrified him. She had been weeping too; and the tears still clung to her pale cheeks.

"Bertha!" exclaimed the young man, touching her on the shoulder. "Whatever are you doing! For Heaven's sake, what is the matter? Speak, dearest!"

She had started quickly to her feet at the sound of his voice, and her face, the moment before so deadly pale, now burned with a deep blush. Laurence redoubled his inquiries.

"It is nothing, dear," she replied, speaking with obvious effort, and with eyes cast down. "I was foolish to distress myself so much about such a little matter. Look, this—this box was broken open by the thieves last night, mamma tells me; and now that I come to examine it, I find that—that something has been stolen."

"What is it? Anything of value?"

"Oh, no, no! It is really nothing. Only—an old writing-case that I have had for many years, and that I very much regretted to lose."

"An old writing-case!" exclaimed Laurence, with a laugh. "Pooh! A memento of the days when you made bricks in Egypt. Is that all you miss?"

"I—I think so."

"Why then, I think we shall survive the loss. You foolish girl, you frightened me out of my wits, to see you kneeling there like a domestic Niobe, in mute despair. Come, do you know the dinner-bell has rung, and that I am hungry enough to turn cannibal and eat both you and mother if I am not soon appeased? Come; three minutes I allow you and no more."

At the dinner-table, ten minutes afterwards, Laurence amused his mother by a humorous description of Bertha's grief for the loss she had sustained.

"You do wrong to ridicule her distress," replied the old lady. "I'm sure I had lots of old knick-knacks which it would almost drive me crazy to lose. No doubt, Bertha, the thieves thought it was your jewel-case, and kept hold of it at any price.—Never mind him, Bertha," she added. "I sympathize with you sincerely. Suppose you advertized, Laurence? I have heard of stolen things being restored on the offer of a reward."

"It looks too much like compounding a felony," replied Laurence smiling. "But still, if Bertha is really grieved at the loss, I will certainly see what can be done."

"Oh, no!" broke in Bertha, earnestly. "I beg you will not think of it, Laurence. It is not of the least importance, mamma, I assure you. I beg you will not think any more of it."

"And yet you look horribly upset," put in the doctor. "Confoundedly unfortunate that this should be your first experience in your new home."

Bertha protested that she was not at all distressed, and, as she did so, flushed scarlet over her face and neck. She could not raise her eyes to meet those of her companions at table, and from beginning to end of the meal she scarcely made a pretence to eat. Mrs. Bloomfield, with natural delicacy, abstained from making any further reference to the distressing subject, and Laurence sat in mute surprise at his wife's disturbed appearance. He could only attribute it to nervous excitement consequent upon fatigue, but it robbed him of his mirth and made the meal rather a sombre one.

Mrs. Bloomfield had dreaded lest their evening should be disturbed by a visit from the irrepressible Miss Chad, but fortunately this did not happen, and the three passed a very agreeable hour in chatting over all that had happened during the past two months. Bertha was very silent, but it was her nature to be so, and she seemed by degrees to have recovered from her agitation. Her mother-in-law now and then observed her carefully, though cautiously, and it gladdened her heart to see the pale face occasionally glow with pleasure, and the sweet eyes once or twice twinkle merrily, as Laurence related some of their pleasant adventures in Italy. Mrs. Bloomfield was a warm-hearted woman, and one who, perhaps on account of her own strength of character and constitution, always felt an especial tenderness for those who were weak and needed sympathy. From her first acquaintance with Bertha she had loved her, and it was with a calm but deep joy that she looked forward to their future united life.

That any cloud could ever settle upon their future and envelop it in hopeless gloom was very far from her thoughts that evening.

Chapter III: The Writing-Case

At a distance of some five miles north of Market Leyton is the village of Brent, and hither we must beg our readers to follow us, to a small public-house known as the "Coach and Horses." It was not a house of any particular reputation, and in entering it we must not expect to find ourselves in genteel company. At nine o'clock on the night of the burglary at Bloomfield House the "Coach and Horses" was empty, and the landlord had begun to relinquish the hope of any guests for that night when the latch of the front-door was suddenly raised, and a man stepped forward into the bar-parlour, taking off his hat as he did so and shaking the rain off it. He was evidently a labouring man, one of the class that usually sought the shelter of the "Coach and Horses," and, judging from the state of his boots, appeared to have tramped the muddy roads the whole day. Such indeed was the account he gave of himself to the landlord, adding that he had a couple of companions who had been detained late by a job at a little distance, but whom he expected to follow him and arrive some time during the night. He then asked for some supper, and, when it was brought, invited the landlord to join him.

"Quiet house this," remarked the stranger as they sat down together.

"Yes, yes," returned the landlord, in the dialect of the district. "A quiet house is a good thing now and then."

The man looked curiously at the other's face on hearing these words, and the landlord, seeming to understand the gaze, waited with a peculiar significance. After this their conversation was carried on in a lower tone, and with less mutual restraint. A change, too, was soon evident in the stranger's manner of speaking; at first he had spoken in a broad country dialect, but this was now dropped, and his pronunciation became very much that of an educated man. Indeed the difference between his speech and his attire was somewhat singular.

At twelve o'clock the landlord locked all the doors, and made ready to go to bed.

"Then you'd rather stay where you are?" he said to his guest, as he took up a candle and lit it.

"Yes, yes," replied the other. "They'll be here before very long, I expect. It's a nasty night for tramping, too, and I daresay they'd like a bit of fire to dry themselves."

The landlord laughed, said good-night, and left his guest alone. There were several very dirty newspapers on the table, and with these the stranger at once began to occupy himself. Occasionally he threw them aside and walked for a few minutes impatiently up and down the room, and at times he consulted a watch which he drew from underneath his labourer's blouse. At length, when the tall clock in the corner pointed to half past two, there came a light tap at the front door. At once the man started up, and, taking the poker from the fire-place, knocked the ceiling with it. The knock was responded to, and in a very few minutes the landlord came downstairs, candle in hand. After a word or two on both sides, he opened the front door, and admitted a man and a boy. They all went together into the parlour. Here the light showed that the newcomers were also attired as labourers. The boy carried a coarse sack, which, on entering, he threw down in a corner. Already the landlord had retired and left the three alone.

"What!" exclaimed the man who had been waiting. "Empty?"

"Aye, empty enough," replied the other man, who spoke in a tone unmistakably cockney. "I feared as how it 'ud be so from the fust. I told yer, you wasn't careful enough, Phil."

"Why, what's that the lad's got under his arm?" asked Phil.

"Why, we was surprised, yer see," returned the fellow, who rejoiced in the name of Dick Dodman. "We got one o' the boxes open, and was a goin' to work to bag what we could, when all at once all the bells in the 'ouse begins a ringin', an' then the old woman opens her door an' begins a screamin' out, an' what could we do but run?"

117

The conversation of these worthies was, from the beginning, thickly seasoned with oaths and curses, which we have seen fit to spare the reader. Acting on the same principle, we shall not report the various exclamations to which the man called Phil gave utterance on hearing this account of the night's work.

"So that's all we have got?" he cried, at last; "that scrubby writing-case."

"Why yes," returned Dodman. "We stuck to it yer see, thinkin' as how there might be val'bles in it; but when we looked into it on the road, we found nothing but papers. Young Charlie here wanted to chuck 'em away, but I thought as it 'ud be better to give 'em a look through and then, if they was worth nothing, burn 'em. Was I right, Phil?"

The landlord now knocked at the door, and brought in some bread and cheese, with beer. This plain fare seemed highly acceptable to Dodman and the boy, for without saying another word, they sat down and fell to with a will. The landlord and Phil exchanged a few words in a whisper, after which the former again withdrew.

Whilst his companions were satisfying their hunger, Phil took up the writing-case from the table and proceeded to examine its contents. One or two papers he glanced at and threw into the fire, but the next which he took out, a letter, seemed to rivet his attention strangely. He read it through carefully, his features, as he did so, becoming fixed in an expression of the utmost astonishment. Then he kept turning it over in his hands, looking first at the corner where the address and date were written, then at the final signature. At length, with a muttered exclamation of wonder, he folded the letter carefully, replaced it, and proceeded to examine the rest. A few of these he burnt, but most of them appeared to possess an extraordinary interest for him. When he had gone through them all, he carefully shut up the case, and, taking a piece of string from his pocket, tied it round to prevent the papers escaping, for the writing-case was a very old and worn one, and there was no means of fastening it. Then he walked once or twice up and down the room, passing his hand over his forehead, and showing signs of deep thought.

"Don't take on about it, Phil," said Dodman at length, with his mouth full of bread and cheese. "Better luck next time."

"Where do you say you found the case?" asked Phil, paying no heed to the proffered consolation.

"Why, in a big box, along with a whole lot o' woman's togs."

Dodman and the boy having at length finished eating, a conference was held, to which at length the landlord was summoned. The end of it was that Dodman and the boy left the house just as dawn was beginning to break, whilst Phil repaired to a room above and flung himself on a bed for a few hours' sleep. At about nine o'clock he rose, and shortly after, came down for breakfast. But his appearance now was entirely different from what it had been on the previous evening. Instead of wearing the rough garb of a labourer, he was dressed in the ordinary morning attire of a gentleman. Even his face appeared to have changed. Whereas he had previously been clean shaven about his lips and chin, he now wore a handsome dark moustache. In fact his appearance was rather prepossessing than otherwise; his features were those of a handsome man, and his age appeared to be about thirty. The disappearance of a rather large bundle which he had last night carried over his shoulder on the end of a rough stick might possibly afford some explanation of this metamorphosis.

Thus equipped, Mr. Philip Vanstone, as he was known by those who were not sufficiently intimate with him to use the abbreviation Phil, started about ten o'clock to walk to Market Leyton. It was a fine sunny morning, and he had all the appearance of a gentleman taking a morning stroll for his pleasure. On arriving in the town, he made his way to a small hotel called "The Bull," entered it like an ordinary guest and ordered a light lunch. Whilst he was engaged upon this, he kept his eye very attentive to everyone who happened to enter the coffee-room. At length a man came in who seemed to be a gentleman's servant out of livery. The two interchanged glances of recognition, and the new-comer, after calling for a glass of beer, took up a newspaper and sat down at the same table with Phil. The beer was brought and the two were left alone in the room.

"You're sure they don't know you here?" asked Phil, in a low voice, leaning over the table.

"Not they," replied the other. "They're new people, and you see I haven't my livery on."

"Well," pursued Phil, in a rather angry tone, "what have you got to say for yourself? The fellows got nothing at all."

"That was their fault," returned the other, sullenly.

"No, it wasn't. Why didn't you let them in, and take them to the right room, as you promised?"

"I set the dog loose, and left the window open. What more could they expect? I told them clear enough where to go."

"Did they get to the right room then?"

"Yes, right enough. But they began with the wrong trunk, and then they made such an infernal row. I was standing at my bed-room door listening, and I felt sure the old woman would hear them."

"Curse the old woman! Why didn't you go and persuade her it was all a mistake, and that there was no one in the house? The fellows waited in the garden I don't know how long for you to come to them."

"It was impossible. You don't know old Mrs. Bloomfield, or you wouldn't talk in that way."

Phil went on with his lunch, and the other (whom the reader has already guessed to be Walton, the man-servant at Bloomfield House,) took up the newspaper. As he read, Phil looked at him curiously from under his eyebrows.

"Then the people come back to-day?" he asked, at length, pushing his plate away from him.

"To-night," replied Walton, nodding.

"And so the chance is lost?"

Walton shrugged his shoulders.

"By the bye," resumed Phil, after a brief pause, speaking in a tone of affected indifference; "who is this Mrs. Bloomfield, the woman the doctor has married?"

"How should I know?" returned the man with a look of surprise. "What does that matter?"

"Never mind what it matters. Who is she? I mean, what was her name?"

"Miss Williamson."

"Ah!" returned Phil, with a careless nod. "Has she lived here long?"

"Don't know. A year or so, I think."

"Hum!—I should like to see her."

"To see her?"

"I don't mean to speak to her; but just to see her. Never you mind why; you owe me a good deal of work yet, you know."

Walton turned away his head with an anxious look at the door, but no one entered, and Phil continued to speak.

"Come, how is it to be managed?"

"Does not matter for her seeing you, I suppose?"

"She mustn't on any account see me. Stop though; it doesn't much matter whether she sees me or not. I suppose I can buy a wig or false beard here."

"Well," said Walton, with hesitation, "I don't know nothing of her habits, you see. I must wait till she's been at home a day or two."

"Well, I leave here to-day, but I shall be back on Monday. Meet me here again on Monday at twelve, can you?"

"I'll try, but I can't be certain. I may be wanted."

"Do your best. If not on Monday, then on Tuesday. But stop; if you can't come on Monday at twelve, address a note to me here and appoint your own time."

Very shortly the man-servant left the hotel, whereupon Phil paid for his lunch, and was on the point of leaving the coffee-room when the waiter called out, "You're leaving something, sir."

Phil turned quickly, with a muttered oath, and took from the waiter's hand a small brown-paper parcel.

"I must be careful," he said to himself as he went out. "It won't do to lose that."

Of course he spoke of the writing-case.

Chapter IV: A Slighted Beauty

Of all Dr. Bloomfield's patients perhaps the most regular and the most persistent in her ailments was Mrs. Golland, the wife of the principal draper in Market Leyton. Mr. Golland himself was a very small and a very inoffensive man, one who made the very least possible demands upon those with whom he came into connection; his wife, on the other hand, was very stout, very impatient, and mortally offended if she were not treated on all sides with the greatest possible deference and attention. One of Mrs. Golland's many devices for securing this attention was that of perpetually suffering from some ailment or other. All day long she would sit in her drawing-room, which was situated over the shop, with the blinds drawn down, and extra mats spread all over the floor for persons to tread upon, lest her shattered nerves should receive another shock from some thoughtless intruder. Especially violent were these attacks of her extremely vague disorder whenever anything had occurred to annoy her, and, on the morning after Dr. Bloomfield's return, both the cause and the effect were present in an unusual degree.

The cause was a simple one. Mrs. Golland had an only daughter, a young lady of nineteen years, whom everyone acknowledged to be one of the very finest girls in Market Leyton. For the last two years it had been the good lady's constant endeavour to find a suitable mate for Miss Harriet Golland, urged not only by the ordinary maternal solicitude for her daughter's welfare, but also in a great degree by the fact that an unpleasant discrepancy existed between her own and Harriet's temper. In short seldom a day passed without mother and daughter quarrelling violently, Harriet losing patience with her mother's absurdities, and the latter recriminating with charges of undutifulness and want of feeling. Among the many eligible bachelors upon whom Mrs. Golland had cast her eye, Laurence Bloomfield had been for a long time the most approved, and it is possible that the desire of frequently bringing her daughter in contact with the young doctor had greatly tended to increase her susceptibility to nervous ailments. When at length Dr. Bloomfield's engagement with the unknown Miss Williamson was announced, the news had excited Mrs. Golland to the utmost, her anger knew no bounds; she declared that the doctor had deceived her and that he should never again enter her house. But if Mrs. Golland was passionate, she was also easily appeased, and she very soon began seriously to miss her wonted medical attendant; she had not liked to openly declare the breach by calling in another doctor, and to be without advice entirely was impossible for her. On the present morning she had, then, proposed to Harriet to forget her grievance and send for Dr. Bloomfield. But the young lady, though less demonstrative than her mother, was more steadfast in her likes and dislikes. Whether she had really loved Laurence it would be difficult to say. However that may have been, she now strenuously opposed her mother's proposition, and hence the state of distress into which the latter had fallen.

"Harriet!" she called, petulantly, as she lay back in her great easy-chair, with a pocket-handkerchief tied round her forehead. "Harriet! Do you hear me?"

"Of course I do, mamma," returned the young lady, who was sitting at a very little distance, engaged in some crochet-work.

"Of course you do!" repeated Mrs. Golland, angrily. "Is that the way to answer your suffering mother?—I tell you that I must positively see Dr. Bloomfield."

"And I say, mamma, that I shall not remain in the house if he comes. Dr. Bloomfield is not a gentleman! I thought you had done with him for good?"

Certainly those were not wrong who spoke of Harriet Golland as the belle of Market Leyton. As she raised her face with an expression of indignant surprise upon it, her features were wonderfully beautiful. Here was one of those faces better fitted for the expression of scorn, contempt or passionate anger than for receiving the impress of the amiable emotions. Her lip seemed to adapt itself naturally to a sarcastic curl, her eyes were never seen at their best save when flashing with defiance.

"Harriet," returned her mother, "you are of a nasty, spiteful disposition! I could not bear malice as you do, indeed I couldn't!"

The girl was on the point of making passionate retort, when a servant knocked at the door and announced a visitor—Miss Chad.

"Oh, let her come up at once!" exclaimed Mrs. Golland. "How glad I am! *She* at least will sympathize with me."

"I should think," said her daughter, when the servant had left the room, "that your headache would make you dread her above all persons. I'm sure I shall not stay to listen to her interminable chatter."

But Harriet had not time to escape before Miss Chad came bouncing in, in her usual impulsive manner.

"My dear Harriet! How are you this morning?" she exclaimed, of course quite out of breath. "And your poor mamma?—Oh, there she is!—Dear me! How you *do* suffer, to be sure, Mrs. Golland! You are quite a martyr, I declare.—And oh, what do you think? I have seen her!"

"Seen who?" asked Mrs. Golland, groaning slightly. The good lady was not always unimpeachable in the matter of grammar.

"Who? Why young Mrs. Bloomfield, to be sure. I happened to be in the railway-station, last night, by the *merest* chance, just as they arrived!"

At the mention of Mrs. Bloomfield's name, Harriet Golland, instead of leaving the room, as she had intended, sat down in a corner, and, whilst pretending to be very intent upon her crochet-work, did not lose a word.

"Indeed!" said Mrs. Golland, slightly raising herself, speaking in a less moribund tone. "Then they have returned?"

"Oh yes," pursued Miss Chad, her face glowing with the delight she always experienced in being the first to impart news. "The doctor is looking wonderfully well, but poor Mrs. Bloomfield is still extremely pale.—Do you know, Mrs. Golland, the poor young woman always gives me the impression that she has something on her mind.— But of course it is only her look; no doubt her conscience is as pure as that of any of us."

Harriet slightly raised her dark eyes with a singular gleam in them. As for Miss Chad, she had spoken without the slightest touch of malice; it was merely her inveterate talkativeness which led her to utter such thoughts.

"But how distressed I am," she pursued, "to find you so ill, my dear Mrs. Golland. I have not as yet paid my formal visit to the young people, and I came in the intention of asking you to go with me. But of course I see it is impossible."

Mrs. Golland would gladly have gone, but, for very shame, could not be so inconsistent as to declare herself able. She merely replied with a groan.

"Really," continued Miss Chad, "you should see a physician. It is extremely distressing that you cannot call on Dr. Bloomfield. He always did you so much good, now."

"Indeed," began Mrs. Golland, with another groan, "I think I shall be compelled to see him, though of course I would rather not.—

Yes, Harriet, you may look as much as you like!—Would you believe it, Miss Chad, that Harriet would rather see me die than have Dr. Bloomfield in the house?"

"There are many other good doctors in the town," put in Harriet, sharply.

"Ah!" sighed Miss Chad, shaking her head, and turning round with a sympathetic look at the girl. "Poor Harriet must be excused for feeling rather sore.—But, indeed, if—if I might suggest such a thing, it—it might not be a bad thing, Harriet dear, to accustom yourself to see Dr. Bloomfield again. The habit of regarding him as—as a married man, you know—"

"Surely, Miss Chad," broke in Harriet, in offended accents, "you don't suppose that I care anything for Dr. Bloomfield, or ever did? It is not that at all, but simply that he has behaved in a very ungentlemanly manner. No one can deny that he made distinct advances, and, after that, for him suddenly to go off, and, without a word, propose to this Miss—Miss What's-her-name,—it wasn't the conduct of a gentleman!"

Miss Chad, who never quarrelled with anyone, or even contested anyone's opinion, yielded a hasty assent, and the conversation continued for some half hour. The vivacious lady then took her leave, and trotted off to pay her visit at Bloomfield House. It may be observed that Miss Chad had once pursued young Mrs. Bloomfield's former calling, and had been a schoolmistress in Market Leyton; but a wealthy relative dying and leaving her a little property, she had henceforth relinquished her school and assumed the function of head-gossip in the town. Her personal activity was wonderful, and only exceeded by her genius for collecting news of all kinds and spreading it abroad. On an occasion like the present, the return home of a newly-married lady, Miss Chad felt as if the duty were imposed upon her of at once qualifying herself to respond to all and every question which could possibly be put to her. She had, as we have seen, actually gone to the railway-station on the preceding evening, and she was now hastening to be among the first to pay a morning-call at Bloomfield House.

She was fortunate enough to find Mrs. Bloomfield and her daughter-in-law alone.

"Ah! my dear Mrs. Laurence," she panted out, as soon as she was seated, addressing the younger lady thus by way of distinction. "Would you believe it that your happiness is creating jealousy already?"

"Indeed!" returned Bertha, who was always extremely quiet, and did not know how to reply to such a remark.

"Oh yes. Mrs. Bloomfield will tell you all about it, no doubt. I just dropped in to speak to the Gollands, my dear Mrs. Bloomfield, on my way here. Poor Harriet seems in dreadful distress."

"Really, Miss Chad," replied the old lady, in her direct way, "I am somewhat tired of hearing about Miss Golland. I am sure Laurence never gave her the least encouragement."

"Who is the lady spoken of, mamma?" asked Bertha.

"Don't you know the Gollands, dear? Drapers, in High Street. I myself scarcely know them, but Laurence has frequently attended Mrs. Golland. It appears that Miss Golland did your husband the honour to fall in love with him, and is terribly aggrieved at being so slighted. Is not that the true state of affairs, Miss Chad?"

"Exactly, my dear Mrs. Bloomfield, exactly."

"You must catechize Laurence on the subject, dear," said the old lady. "Perhaps you may bring him to confess that he was not always indifferent to the love-lorn damsel. I should certainly investigate the subject."

Mrs. Bloomfield spoke with the slightly contemptuous tone she usually displayed in mentioning a matter of foolish gossip; Bertha merely smiled and was silent. Very shortly after, two or three new visitors were announced, and Miss Golland's woes were forgotten.

Chapter V: In His Power

It was now mid-autumn, and the country around Market Leyton had put on its most charming attire. To Bertha and her husband, fresh from the glories of Italy and Switzerland, there could be nothing very striking in the quiet English landscapes amidst which they now dwelt, yet, for the former at all events, there was more true happiness to be found in gazing upon these rich tracts of undulating corn-land, now ripe for harvest, these quiet country homes, so unassuming in their simple beauty, the deep, green lanes, skirted here and there by an overshadowing copse, than she had experienced in the face of the grandest Alpine scenery or beneath the bluest heaven which lends its colour to the Mediterranean. Bertha's was a nature which, above all things, shunned excitement. Her longing for quietness went so far as to make her shy and restless in the presence of the smallest gathering of friends, though when alone with one, one whom she really loved, she could be even talkative and lively. Since her marriage it had become evident that her modesty and love for retirement were genuine, owing nothing to affectation; for with every opportunity of making an important figure in the aristocratic circles of Market Leyton, with every temptation to display her happiness and make others envious of her conquest, she associated with strangers no more than she felt absolutely necessary on the grounds of politeness, and was so seldom seen in the town that many inquisitive people had to wait weeks before their desire to see her was gratified.

Among these inquisitive people not the least anxious was Miss Harriet Golland. This young lady could at once, if she had seen fit, have established herself on the footing of an intimate visitor at Bloomfield House, for Miss Chad was ready to lead her thither with the utmost state any moment. But this was impossible; Harriet felt sure she could not exchange a friendly word with Mrs. Bloomfield if her life depended upon it. But for all that she was extremely anxious to see the doctor's wife: she had only seen her once previous to the marriage, and was desirous to observe what difference social elevation had produced in the quondam schoolmistress's appearance. She was therefore inwardly gratified when her mother, sitting at the drawing-room window one rainy morning, called out to her that Dr. Bloomfield's carriage had driven up to the shop and that Mrs. Bloomfield was getting out.

Harriet would have very much liked to run down into the shop, and, out of some corner or other, have had a good gaze at her fortunate rival; but to do so would have been to attract the attention of the young-lady assistants, who very probably had heard something of the state of affairs. Accordingly, she sat at the window, waiting till Bertha should return; and when at last Mrs. Bloomfield reappeared, escorted by Mr. Golland who was all bows and smiles, the girl's dark eyes flashed with an expression of hatred, and her teeth clenched firmly on her lower lip.

"At all events she has a ladylike appearance," said Mrs. Golland, who took some little pleasure in tormenting her daughter on this subject, in return for the scorn with which she was so frequently treated by the self-willed young lady.

"Very likely," returned Harriet, with a sneer. "No doubt she has been lady's maid to some one or other, and so caught a few tricks, like a monkey does."

"Upon my word!" exclaimed stout Mrs. Golland, leaning back to laugh. "You are spite itself, Harriet."

Bertha returned home in happy unconsciousness of the remarks that had been made about her. She had now been in Market Leyton a little more than a fortnight, and was regulating her life in accordance with the quiet routine which suited her. As she entered the drawing-room she found her mother-in-law in conversation with a man whom she did not remember to have seen before.

"This gentleman," said the old lady, turning to Bertha, "has kindly called to let us know that nothing has yet been heard of the burglars."

Bertha bowed slightly and uttered a few confused words, then turned away and seemed to be busy with her work-basket.

"We feel pretty sure," she heard the man say, "that they were London hands. There have been several such affairs in this part of the country lately."

In a minute or two he left, and the ladies were alone.

"Have you matched the wools, dear?" asked Mrs. Bloomfield.

"All but one, mamma; and that they will procure for me."

"Since you have been away," pursued the old lady, "the new Magazines have arrived. I promise myself much delight in hearing you read aloud from them. Do you care much for novels, dear?"

"I like good ones," replied Bertha, "but I have read very few."

"You are like myself. I sometimes commence one of the serials, but I find they nearly always turn on the subject of husbands deceiving their wives, or wives deceiving their husbands, or at all events some of the miseries of domestic life, and I prefer not to make myself uncomfortable by reading them."

Bertha endeavoured to smile, but immediately after was obliged to turn away her face to hide the paleness which had come over it. Mrs. Bloomfield did not observe anything and Bertha very shortly left the room.

In the afternoon the weather cleared up and the sun shone gloriously. Mrs. Bloomfield had a few visits to pay in town, but did not trouble Bertha to accompany her, knowing her dislike of such occasions. Dr. Bloomfield happened to be absent on a visit to a patient some ten miles off. Left quite alone, Bertha was sitting in the drawing-room, one moment turning over the leaves of a book which lay on her lap, the next forgetting all about the book and losing herself in reverie, when suddenly she was startled by some dark shadow coming between her and the sunshine. Looking up, she saw that the glass doors which opened onto the lawn had been pushed wide open, and that someone, to all appearances a gentleman, was in the act of stepping into the room. At once she rose from her seat, and stood, gazing surprisedly into the face of her unceremonious visitor. At first her countenance showed no more than astonishment, but in a moment a change was visible. She turned deadly pale, shrank a step backwards, and caught at the back of the chair to support herself. For a second it seemed as though she would fall to the ground; but, by an immense exertion of will, she shook off the all but overmastering faintness, and faced the stranger resolutely.

"I am afraid," she began at length, seeing that her visitor showed no disposition to speak, "that I have not the pleasure of knowing you. Probably you wish to see Dr. Bloomfield?"

"Certainly not," replied the other, with a malicious smile. "It is you that I wish to see, Mrs. Bloomfield. Are you quite sure that you have not the pleasure of knowing me?"

He spoke the last words in sarcastic imitation of her tone. Her face was the hue of death, and she grasped the chair, by which she still supported herself, with convulsive violence. But still she forced herself to look him in the face.

"Quite sure," she said, though her voice scarcely rose above a whisper. "I cannot understand what right you have to intrude upon me in this way."

"Cannot you? Allow me to submit something to your notice, Mrs. Bloomfield."

He put his hand into an underpocket, and drew out two or three letters which he opened and held before her eyes. Her strength now failed her and she sank into the chair. With the same malicious smile, the stranger (if such he was), put back the letters and assumed a seat at a little distance.

"Good God!" groaned Bertha, hiding her face with both her hands. "Good God! Then it was *you* who robbed the house!"

"Oh, by no means," he replied. "These have merely come into my possession,—hem! indirectly. Are they a sufficient introduction, Mrs. Bloomfield?"

Once more Bertha rose to her feet, and now she had need of no support.

"Leave this house at once!" she exclaimed, in a hollow whisper. "Leave the house, or I will ring and have you secured. The police are already on your track."

The other laughed slightly, and stepping up to the bell-rope, said, "Shall I relieve you of the trouble, Mrs. Bloomfield?"

She shrank back before his glance, and, after a moment's internal strife, once more sank upon her chair, weeping violently.

"What is it you want?" she exclaimed, between her choking sobs. "Why do you come here to drive me mad. I thought, I *hoped* you were dead!"

"Very possibly," replied the man, coolly; "but you see I am not. And, being alive, I must have the means of continuing to live. In short, I am none too amply supplied with money. That is why I have come to you."

"Money? I cannot give you money!"

"Indeed! I scarcely thought the worthy Dr. Bloomfield behaved so shabbily to his handsome wife as that."

"I tell you I cannot get you money!" she repeated, hysterically. "I dare not! I will not!"

"Very well," said the other, calmly, rising from his chair. "In that case I must see Dr. Bloomfield himself. Perhaps he will not be so niggardly."

He made as though he would step out again onto the lawn, but the same instant she had grasped him by the arm.

"Do you mean what you say?" she asked, looking into his face like one distracted. "Do you mean that you are heartless enough to ruin me a second time, to bring innocent people to despair, just because I refuse to rob my husband for your sake? Do you mean it?"

"Oh, your *husband*," he said emphasizing the words, and grinning as he spoke, "is not so poor that he could not afford a few pounds to keep unpleasant company out of his house. Perhaps it was a mistake not to apply to him at first. Good-morning, Mrs. Bloomfield."

He was going, but again she detained him with all her strength.

"In God's name," she cried, "wait! I will—I will give you what I can! I will indeed.—Have mercy on me, and be satisfied with what I can give you!"

"Oh, I should never be hard on a lady," he replied, once more sitting himself. "But you won't be long?"

She hastened from the room and quickly returned with two or three bank-notes in her hand.

"Take them," she said. "It is all I have."

The man looked at the money, smiled, and put it in his purse.

"It is not unlikely," he said, "that I may wish to have a little further conversation with you some day. But I don't care to see you here; we might be disturbed. Do you know a place about a mile away called Red Lane Cross?"

She nodded.

"It is a nice quiet place," he pursued, "and we might talk there at our ease. If ever you receive a note requesting an interview at a certain time, the place of meeting will be Red Lane Cross. You understand?"

She would have uttered an entreaty, but her voice failed her.

"Stop," he said, as he was on the point of going. "You may like to put my card among those of your other visitors. I will lay it on the table. Good-morning."

He laid down a card which bore the name of "Philip Vanstone," then stepped quickly onto the lawn, heedless that Bertha had sunk senseless upon the floor.

Chapter VI: A Husband's Love

Dr. Bloomfield and his mother returned almost at the same time, just before the ordinary dinner-hour. The doctor and his wife had already taken their seats at table, when the old lady entered the dining-room, evidently in a flurry.

"What a very strange thing!" she exclaimed. "You remember,

Bertha, that I took off my watch this morning because it would not go, and put it on the drawing-room mantel-piece that I might be reminded to have it seen to?"

"Certainly, mamma," replied Bertha.

"Well, it has entirely disappeared. I can't find it anywhere. I didn't take it out with me because I was not going in the direction of the watchmaker's. Surely I must have put it down somewhere in an absent fit. And yet I certainly have no recollection of removing it from the mantel-piece."

Poor Bertha looked dreadfully ill as she sat throughout the meal, scarcely touching a mouthful of food, and with the greatest difficulty replying to an occasional question. At the first mention of the missing watch a horrible suspicion flashed across her mind, a suspicion which was all but a certainty. She felt as guilty as though she had herself been the thief. It was impossible that her companions should not remark her suffering.

"How terribly out of sorts you look, dear," Laurence said to her, in his kind, manly tone. "Have you been out to-day?"

"I went to Golland's in the morning, but in the afternoon I did not feel well enough to walk."

"She must certainly get more exercise, mother," said Laurence. "I thought, Bertha, you promised to make me some sketches of the neighbourhood. I thought of it this afternoon. As it was so wonderfully fine I got out at Brent station and walked the rest of the way, and as I came along Red Lane I thought I had never seen such delightful spots for a sketcher. You know Red Lane, Bertha?"

"Yes."

"We must go there together some fine morning. The trees just now are in wonderful colour; I am sure you could get some very fine effects."

After dinner Laurence was called away to see a patient. On returning he looked in vain for Bertha in the drawing-room; then he opened the door of the parlour she sometimes used, but, seeing that it was dark within, was on the point of searching elsewhere, when he thought he heard the sound of a sob in the darkness.

"Bertha!" he called, gently.

There came a low sobbing reply. Taking a box of matches from his pocket, he quickly lit the gas. His wife was lying upon the couch, her eyes red with weeping, her forehead feverish. With an expression of the utmost concern on his face, Laurence drew a chair to the side of the couch, sat down, and, taking one of Bertha's hands in his own, spoke in a low, soothing voice.

"What are you distressing yourself about, darling? You quite frighten me by your constant depression. How hot your hands are! Do you feel ill? Tell me why you seem to be constantly suffering, Bertha."

"I do not know, myself, Laurence," she replied, throwing her arms about his neck and leaning her head against his bosom, whilst the tears continued to stream from her eyes. "I think I must be ill, for if ever I had cause for deep happiness it is now, and yet I never felt so miserable. Oh, my life is fated to be a wretched one!"

She uttered the last words with almost hysterical violence, and Laurence began to fear that she was really ill. Yet his medical skill could discern no real indication of bodily ailment; rather everything pointed to mental agitation as the cause of her suffering.

"Bertha!" he exclaimed. "You pain me beyond measure. How can you say that your life is fated to be wretched. Have you ceased to love me? Has all my devotion no power to render you happy?"

"Ceased to love you, Laurence? Oh, I love you but too well, too well."

"Too well, dearest?" he repeated with surprise. "How is that possible? My love for you, darling, is beyond my power to utter, but if it were ten times as strong I could not think that I loved you too well!"

"Forgive me!" she whispered, hiding her face from his look. "I was thinking that I had not been just to you in becoming your wife. I am so spiritless, so shy, so unable to fill the place in society which, as your wife, I should. All my life I have been a poor, lonely girl. It was presumption in me to think I could so change my nature at will as to be fit for the position to which you desired to raise me."

"Whatever is all this nonsense, Bertha?" asked her husband, laughing. " 'Not just to me!'—'Spiritless!'—'Unable to fill your place in society!'—My dear child, what ever are you talking about? Do you think I had not studied your character in its every detail long before I even asked you to be my wife? Do you think I expected you to transform yourself from the wedding-day henceforth into something entirely different from what you ever were or could be? If I had wanted a wife for no other reason than to see her fill a place in society, as you put it, was there not the charming Miss Golland ready to fall into my arms, like a ripe apple as soon as ever I presented myself before her! Ha, ha! Think of me with such a wife as that!— Or, better still, I might have married Miss Chad; there's a social woman for you!—Who on earth has been putting such ideas as these into your head, Bertha?"

She could not reply a word, but still held her arms tightly round him, and her head pressed against his bosom. Passing his hand with fond tenderness over her light-gold hair, Laurence continued to encourage her.

"Let us recall the days when we first knew each other, Bertha. You remember how I was called in one night to see a poor old woman who had met with a severe accident in some household work, and how I found someone nursing her who was not in the least connected with her, but, happening to live next door, had come in out of pure charity, and was doing everything that good sense and a good heart could suggest? Well, this someone who was acting the nurse so cleverly made a strange impression upon me at the time, and I did not rest till I had discovered who she was. Then I learned that she was the mistress of a small infant-school, a poor and lonely girl (to use your own words,) who had only one object in life, and that to do her duty to those who trusted her. She did not seem unhappy, I thought, even though she always looked a little pale. That I put down to overwork. Well, what was the result of my acquaintance with her? Acting, I am afraid, with some little rudeness, I forced upon her my friendship, I compelled her to come and see my mother, I did my best to drag her out of her loneliness,—and all this for the very simple reason that I had fallen in love with her! And now, when I have succeeded, against a thousand unheard-of difficulties, in persuading her to become my wife, when we have passed together the most delightful honeymoon that ever mortals were blessed with, when I have brought her back and made her the mistress of my house,—after all this, this strange, wilful girl gets paler and more miserable every day, and at length tells plainly that she is sorry she ever married me—"

"No, no, no!" broke in Bertha, pressing her lips upon those of her husband in one long, passionate kiss. "No, darling. I did not mean it! I can never be sorry for that, come what may! Who could ever have understood me as you have done? Who could have treated me with such respect, such delicacy of feeling, so as never, from the first day of our acquaintance, to have wounded feelings which were sensitive to exaggeration? There was but one man in the whole world, Laurence, who could so completely have won my confidence, my reverence, and at the same time awakened in my heart so infinitely strong and pure an affection; there was but one ideal husband for me, and that was you, my dearest! Forgive my weakness, Laurence! I scarcely remember what I said; it was a moment of delirium. —No, nothing shall ever part me from you; I will live and die at your side, your true, true wife!"

"What *could* part us, darling," asked Laurence, "save death?" He had never seen her so vehement before. The strength of her passion almost frightened him.

"No, no! Nothing can part us! What *could?*" she exclaimed, clinging closely to him, and laughing hysterically. "I am yours forever, yours, yours!"

He pressed her passionately in his arms, whispering all manner of tender words, words which seem childish if written down and read in calm moments, but which on his lips were instinct with life and love. Her tears had begun to flow once more, and between her sobs she kept replying to all his tenderness with words of equal devotion. He knew not how long he held her thus, clasped to his heart, but at length he perceived that her sobbing was stilled, and that her breath came regularly. Softly raising her so as to look at her face, he saw that she had fallen asleep. Carefully he let her head sink upon the cushion, fearful lest he should awake her. But agitation had brought with it such fatigue that her sleep could not so easily be broken. Pressing a kiss upon the pure forehead, Laurence rose and gently left the room.

Chapter VII: Red Lane Cross

The lost watch remained a complete mystery; no one could offer the least suggestion in the matter. Of course a disagreeable suspicion fell for a time upon the servants in the house, but at length Dr. Bloomfield gave it as his decided opinion that, whilst the drawing-room was empty, some thief must have stepped in through the glass doors, seen the watch, and run away with it. And there was an end of the affair.

But in the meantime poor Bertha's condition excited much anxiety. Laurence concluded that his wife was suffering from a nervous disorder, and henceforth made it his constant effort to ward off everything that could in the least offend her delicate sensibility, as well as to provide her every opportunity of congenial amusement and occupation. Perhaps it was the sudden change from a lonely and hopeless life, he thought, which was working thus upon her. Day by day his tender solicitude increased and Bertha often said that she possessed the most affectionate and considerate husband in the world. All the time which he could spare from his professional engagements was devoted to conversing with and entertaining her, and certainly not without effect. Bertha became as the weeks passed on, unmistakably improved in health and spirits; at times she would even display something of the bright and joyous temperament which had delighted her husband during their honeymoon, in the sunny lands of the south. She applied herself, too, more continuously and with greater zest to her books, her music, her drawing. The reader, who has more insight into the real causes of her suffering, will understand that this improvement was due to her having had no second visit from the man who held such a dreadful power over her. True, she ever had his parting threat in her mind; but there was always hope to counterbalance its gloomy weight, hope which grew as time went on and left her undisturbed, hope which found unceasing food in the endless devotion of her husband and in his apparent power to save her from all dangers.

The autumn passed away, and cold, dark nights, followed by mornings which displayed the leafless trees and hedges hung with hoar-frost, told that winter had set his foot upon the earth and was preparing to reign long and rigorously. By the good folks of Market Leyton times of holiday and feasting were naturally looked forward to with long and earnest expectations, and, above all festivals, Christmas was kept in real old English fashion. As early as the beginning of December there was earnest talk in Bloomfield House with regard to the preparations it behoved the family to make, as to who should be invited for Christmas Eve and Christmas Day, for New Year's Eve, and for New Year's Day, for upon people of such importance as the Bloomfields lay heavy responsibilities at this time of the year, and closely would their behaviour be watched and criticized. Bertha naturally looked forward with much timidity to the ordeal, but she felt that to face it bravely was a duty she owed her husband, and to all appearances she was very interested in all the arrangements discussed.

It wanted rather more than a week to Christmas Day. One morning, as Bertha was sitting alone, busied on the illumination of a Christmas text, a servant brought her a small note which had just been delivered at the door by a little boy. Was any answer required? she asked. No; the messenger had gone away at once on delivering it. Bertha was just tearing open the envelope, wondering quietly what the contents could be, when, like a flash of lightning, a sudden terror shot through her mind. She had been standing, but now, holding the note half-opened, she sank again upon her chair. For a moment her suffering was terrible, and it required the strongest effort to open the sheet of paper and peruse what was written there. At last she succeeded, and the following words swam before her eyes:

"Be at the appointed place at 12 to-morrow, and bring with you as much as you can. I am hard up and must have it. Disappoint me at your peril.—Phil."

Five minutes before she had been perfectly happy in the forgetfulness of everything save the pleasant task before her; now she was once more subject to the old terror in its fullest force. The anguish of mind which overcame her was unspeakable. She could not collect her force and form plans upon which to act; her whole nature seemed paralysed by the one sense of sickening dread. It was as though, in the midst of the calm, bright winter's day, sudden darkness had enveloped her, darkness which teemed with horrors unutterable. For some minutes she could not move. When at length she began to recover her powers of thought, her first action was to press her hands against her throbbing forehead, muttering to herself—"I shall go mad! I shall go mad!"

She rose from her chair and paced the room. No thought now of completing her illumination. An hour passed, and still she was pacing up and down, almost in despair. Once or twice she had half resolved that she would see her husband as soon as possible, give into his hands the note she had received, and disburden her heart of the dreadful secret which formed the key to its interpretation. But Bertha was in character very weak and irresolute; she *could* not force herself to such a step as this, a step which she felt could be nothing less than the renunciation of all future hope in life. Without the courage to face such a prospect, yet without the power to force down, or even dissemble, her agitation, she could only exclaim repeatedly in her heart—"God help me! God *forgive* me!"

Fortunately old Mrs. Bloomfield was engaged in shopping till late that morning, and as for Dr. Bloomfield, he was not expected to return before dinner-time. By when the old lady returned, Bertha had succeeded in suppressing at least the more violent signs of distress, and what remained she was able to account for by the excuse of a severe headache. That evening she retired very early; but throughout the long, dreary night, she scarcely slept. On the morrow it required some little artifice to enable her to start alone and privately for the rendezvous, but she succeeded in doing so, and, exactly at twelve o'clock had reached the spot known as Red Lane Cross.

This was distant not more than a quarter of an hour's walk from Bloomfield House, which of course lay on the outskirts of the town. Just at this point, Red Lane, which ran between high banks, surmounted by thick quickset hedges, was traversed by a lane still narrower, only very occasionally used by carts going to and coming from a neighbouring farm. At this point of meeting was a fragment of a curious old cross, such as is met with here and there on English country-roads, the origin of which was a moot point with Market Leyton antiquaries. In addition to the cart-road, the Lane was also crossed here by a footpath, transversely, leading from the village of Brent into the town. So thick were the hedges and so deep the roadway, that for anyone coming over the fields even the cross was invisible till the stile was surmounted. Thus Bertha had no opportunity of viewing the man who waited for her till she was actually in his presence. She had drawn her veil closely over her face, and did not raise it throughout the interview.

Philip Vanstone stepped forward to meet her, but, at the sight of his face, Bertha stepped back in surprise.

"Who—who are you?" she stammered.

"Your very obedient," returned the other, laughing. "I'm glad you didn't know me. The beard makes a difference, don't it? And then the hair isn't the same colour it used to be,—but never mind that. What have you brought me?"

Without speaking she handed to him a five-pound note.

"What do you mean?" he exclaimed, scornfully thrusting her hand away. "What's the good of that?"

"It's all I can give you," she replied, in a choking voice. "Indeed it is! I cannot obtain more without attracting attention."

He was silent for a moment. When at length he spoke, it was with knitted brows and a low, decided voice.

"I must have twenty pounds,—you hear? Twenty. I want it for a special purpose."

"But how can I get it you?" she asked, appealingly. "I will do my best to get ten; but more is impossible. All would be discovered."

He swore a violent oath.

"All *shall* be discovered, and that soon, if you don't get me what I want.—So you don't think it worth while to pay me for keeping quiet?—Very well, Mrs. Bloomfield. Either you bring me twenty pounds to-morrow at this time or,—you know what will happen."

As he ceased speaking he nodded significantly, and walked quickly away, whilst Bertha, unable even to call him back, stood supporting herself by the ruined cross. The sky had been growing dark ever since she started from home, and now, as she remained in mute and motionless despair, flakes of snow began to fall. Suddenly she started, as a familiar voice, close by her, broke the silence. It was no other than Miss Chad.

"Really, Mrs. Bloomfield! How very imprudent of you! To come out such a day as this without your umbrella!—How very fortunate that I met you!—You seem tired, too.—Taking a walk, I suppose?—They tell me you are very fond of solitary walks.— Really, I am delighted to have your company back. I have just been across the fields to Lowther's Farm;—you don't know the Lowthers, I think? Very good, plain people."

With the most extreme effort, Bertha forced herself to reply a word or two, and they walked together homewards. Bertha could only now and then utter a "yes" or a "no," but Miss Chad's talkativeness made up for her companion's silence. Bertha kept asking herself whether Miss Chad had seen the stranger with her, but, so perfectly unconstrained was the little woman's tone and manner, that she could not think it possible. Surely there would have been some question, some hint. Nevertheless she was heartily glad when their paths at last separated; she was not even capable of the politeness of asking her companion to enter the house.

Nor, strange to say, would Miss Chad have accepted the invitation, had it been uttered. No sooner alone than she hurried away as fast as she could walk into the town. Arrived at the house of the Gollands she flew upstairs without waiting to be asked, feeling quite sure that she should find Mrs. Golland, as usual, in the drawing-room above the shop. But she was disappointed. Miss Harriet Golland was there, sitting alone.

"Your mother out?" she exclaimed. "Dear me!—How very imprudent; a day like this!—I had something rather important to tell her.—When will she return?"

But it was impossible for Miss Chad, having commenced to talk, to hold her tongue before it had uttered all the weighty intelligence beneath which it trembled. In the course of a long and round-about narration, she imparted to Miss Golland a piece of the most secret intelligence, that, as she was returning from a short walk outside the town, she had suddenly come upon no less a person than Mrs. Bloomfield *tête-à-tête* with—a *man*, a perfect stranger to Miss Chad, whose acquaintance in Market Leyton was extensive, nevertheless. She described how, on being discovered, Mrs. Bloomfield had shown the greatest agitation, being scarcely able to speak. Last of all, she impressed on Miss Golland the absolute necessity of keeping all this a profound secret.

Harriet was wonderfully interested, much more than she usually showed herself in Miss Chad's eager narratives. She put on an air of solemnity before replying.

"My dear Miss Chad, depend upon it there is something wrong! From the first I have been suspicious of Mrs. Bloomfield. I shouldn't be the least surprised at any scandal.—But of course we must consider poor Dr. Bloomfield. Really, I pity him. I hope you won't let this story become public?"

As she spoke, the girl's eyes flashed with a peculiar light, half humorous, half fierce. The prospect of gratified jealousy was unutterably sweet; and she knew very well that by recommending silence to her informant she was adopting the very means of spreading the news far and wide. From this moment she was a firm ally of Miss Chad's, resolving to use for malicious purposes whatever the latter's inquisitiveness might discover.

The same night Harriet penned a short note, in a feigned hand, and without signature; then, having carefully addressed it to Dr. Bloomfield, sent it to the post.

Chapter VIII: The Fatal Secret

"Take care of your wife. She meets a stranger at Red Lane Cross."

Such were the words which met Dr. Bloomfield's eyes on his opening the first of a little pile of letters at breakfast next morning. The envelope showed him that the letter had been posted in Market Leyton, but beyond this there was not a clue to the identity or the whereabouts of the writer. The writing was reversed and to all appearances might have been from the hand of either a man or a woman. It was a blow from a hidden enemy.

It would be scarcely possible to find a man naturally more free from the vices of suspicion and jealousy than Laurence Bloomfield was. Himself perfectly honest and straightforward in every word and deed, it was natural to him to regard all other people as equally upright, all, that is to say, against whom there stood no indisputable proof of dishonesty. It had been a singular instance of this wide-reaching charity that, despite the somewhat strange circumstances under which he had first of all discovered Bertha, it had never for a moment occurred to him to seek for them any other than the simplest of explanations. When she had subsequently related to him the brief story of her life with which the reader has been made acquainted, Laurence heard it with the most absolute good faith, not a shadow of doubt crossing his mind either then or subsequently. To be sure it might be said that in this case love blinded him, but, in the first place, this was merely an example of his usual habits of mind, and, secondly, it would be in no sense correct to say that he was rendered oblivious by his love to circumstances which would otherwise have excited his curiosity. Laurence was the very opposite of an easily-impressionable or excitable man. At first he had merely been actuated by a feeling of friendly interest in Bertha; it was only by degrees that increased acquaintance with her many virtues heightened his interest to a sentiment of respect, thence to one of admiration, and finally to strong love. That he was capable of love no one who observed his behaviour to his wife could deny. He was, in fact, a man who could love but once in his life, and then with a concentration of his nature which would set at defiance every obstacle to perfect happiness.

Confront such a nature as this with a piece of anonymous malice such as that Laurence now held in his hands, and, under ordinary circumstances he would have dashed it aside with a contemptuous laugh. But, though supremely trustful, the man was yet clear-sighted enough when he met with an object worthy of his scrupulous examination, and with such he felt that he was now face to face. The note alone was nothing, or something capable, no doubt, of the easiest explanation; but the note combined with Bertha's abnormal state of mind and body formed a serious consideration. Throughout the night Bertha had not once closed her eyes; at times she had wept hysterically, at others she had seemed crushed by a mute sense of despair. Laurence's medical knowledge told him that this was a state of affairs wholly unaccountable on mere physical grounds, and, during the long, painful hours of watching, it had been for the first time forced upon his mind that there must be some mystery in it all at which he could make no conjecture. His suffering under these rising doubts, doubts respecting one whose absolute purity and truth he would have vindicated with his life, was unutterably severe. How should he act? It was impossible to decide at once upon any course to pursue. His was a mind which worked slowly, though in the end it almost invariably hit upon the kernel of the affair in question.

Fortunately he was breakfasting alone, his mother being detained in Bertha's room, or his agitation would certainly have been observed. He had commenced to eat and to read his letters simultaneously, but after the opening of the first envelope not a morsel passed his lips. For half an hour he sat, plunged in deep thought; at length, with a deep and troubled sigh, he hurriedly began to examine the rest of his correspondence. Engagements compelled him to start from home about ten o'clock, but he consoled himself with the thought that the fresh air would bring order and perspicuity into his thoughts. He had a rather long journey before him, and had at first intended to go by train; but now he altered his mind, and ordered the trap to be got ready. As he was leaving the house, his mother descended the stairs.

"Poor Bertha is in a strange state," said the old lady, gazing into Laurence's face with a look of anxious inquiry. She spoke in a low voice, too, and her tone seemed to convey more than was contained in the mere words.

"She is," replied Laurence, returning her look steadily. "Is she still so feverish?"

"Very; I fear she is going to have a bad illness."

"Let her continue to take the draught at intervals. I shall be back before three o'clock. Good-bye, dear mother."

He stooped down to receive her kiss.

"You are sadly troubled, dear," she whispered, "I can see it in your face. Perhaps this will cease in time."

He smiled sadly, and left the house.

Throughout the morning Bertha lay in absolute silence, save for a sob which now and then broke from her. During the night she had determined how to act. Looking forward to a life of torture such as this, ever repeated at longer or shorter intervals, she found the prospect quite intolerable. Sooner or later the end of it must come, and why not at once? Had she possessed the courage, she would have killed herself; but for that she was too feeble, morally considered. There remained then, but one course. She would fail in her engagement at the Cross, and would await the result, be it what it might. Anything better than this fearful suffering. She had scarcely contemplated the thought of revealing all to her husband, and so cutting the knot of her difficulties. She felt that this would have required more courage than even suicide.

About three o'clock Laurence returned. He entered Bertha's

room, felt her pulse, laid his hand upon her forehead; but did not speak a word, for his mother was in the room. The feverish symptoms were rapidly heightening. Going to the window he wrote out a prescription. His mother followed him out onto the landing.

"Brain fever, I fear," he whispered, in reply to her inquiring look. "Had you not better write and put off all the Christmas invitations?"

"I was thinking of it, and I will see to it to-night."

She continued to look curiously into his face, till at length he half turned away. Then she took his hand.

"Don't you think, dear," she whispered, "that you had better ask her if there is anything she—she wishes to say to you?"

"You are right, mother," he replied, pressing her hand. "It is the best way."

He re-entered the room, alone, and sat down by the bed. Bertha turned away her face, with a slight shudder.

"Bertha," he began, in a low, endearing tone, "why do you hide from me this trouble which is on your mind? Cannot you confide in me, your husband? Why do you suffer so needlessly? I am sure you are hiding some cause of trouble from me. It is cruel to do so, Bertha!"

She made no reply, and still held her face averted.

"Bertha!"

No reply. He rose and leaned over her, looking into her face.

"There is nothing, nothing!" she exclaimed, hurriedly. "Only I am so hot,—my forehead burns so.—There is nothing else!"

Again he left the room, and, in reply to his mother's look, shook his head.

"Nurse her carefully," he said. "I shall see her often, but I am afraid the fever will have its way."

He went down-stairs. As he was crossing the hall to his study, the servant had just taken a note from someone at the door.

"For me?" he asked.

"No sir; for Mrs. Bloomfield."

"I will take it."

The servant gave him the letter, and he entered his study, with it in his hand. His brow had darkened as he looked at the direction,

144

and it grew still darker as he opened the envelope, and read what it contained.

"Have you kept away on purpose, or because something prevented your coming? Either you meet me at eight to-night and bring me the money, or *your husband* learns everything. If it is impossible for you to come secretly, send a messenger, and appoint your own time. But remember that I am in earnest; the money, or the secret out."

For Laurence the secret was already out. The line drawn under "your husband," and the whole tone of the note pointed unmistakably to one explanation as regards the writer's identity. Though prepared for the discovery, sooner or later, of some strange secret, he had never anticipated such a one as this; the shock was terrible. Still holding the paper crushed in his fingers, he covered his face and wept like a child.

As soon as some degree of calmness had returned, he at once prepared to face manfully the difficulties of his position. First of all, should he acquaint his mother with the circumstance of the note? Between himself and her there had always been the most complete confidence, and, what was more, it was evident that the old lady's clear sight had already discerned the existence of some mystery in Bertha's illness. Yet, spite of all this, Laurence did not feel that he possessed courage enough to tell his mother all that he feared. Besides, there still lingered in his heart a few ineradicable traces of hope that this affair might not really be as dark as it seemed. Bertha was constitutionally very weak, and who could tell whether she had not become in some strange way the victim of a mere plot,—seeing that the object of her correspondent was confessedly nothing more than to obtain money. Laurence *hoped,* for his nature was hopeful, yet his hope did not afford strong enough support to his own mind to permit of his imparting it for the encouragement of another. No; he could not as yet say anything to his mother. As to Bertha, to her it was still less possible to speak. Otherwise, he had no doubts as to how he should act. Of course this man must be met and compelled to give an account of himself. A strong arm and a firm will were the best weapons against such an underhand rascal, and Laurence doubted not that both would be at his command. It only remained, then, to pass the time before half-past seven, when he intended to start.

Chapter IX: Strange Rivals

The night was pitch-dark, for throughout the afternoon snow had been falling in slight quantities from time to time, and the sky was still overhung with thick snow-clouds. Laurence dined with his mother at six o'clock, but during the meal neither spoke much. At its conclusion both went up together to Bertha's room. Bertha had just fallen into a troubled slumber when Mrs. Bloomfield left her, and in this condition she still continued. She was muttering slightly in her sleep, but not words which could be understood. Laurence examined her condition, gave his mother a few directions with regard to her, then, saying that he was obliged to be away for a couple of hours, he descended to his study and prepared for the walk.

As it was intensely cold, he muffled himself up well, and, before buttoning his great-coat, strapped to his waist a small bull's-eye lantern which he had occasional need of. Then he went to a drawer in his desk, unlocked it, and took out a loaded revolver, which he deposited carefully in his pocket. This done, he was prepared to start.

As we have already said, it was not much more than a quarter of an hour's walk from Bloomfield House to Red Lane Cross. It yet wanted, however, a few minutes to half past seven. Nevertheless, Laurence would not wait longer, so great was his impatience, and at once started forth on the road. The road had soon to be abandoned for the fields, and here so great was the darkness that it required considerable care to avoid the deep ditch which ran along one side of the path. But Laurence was well acquainted with the ground, and, so quickly did he walk in his excitement, that he could hear one of the church clocks in the town chiming the three quarters just as he arrived at the stile which led down into the lane.

Here he paused, and, bringing his lantern from underneath his coat, allowed a stream of light to fall upon the road and the ruined cross. Apparently no one had as yet arrived. He crossed the stile, and took up his position close by the Cross. It was so dark here that he could scarcely see his hand.

An interminable time now seemed to elapse, as he stood in the bitter cold. At length he made sure that he must have been waiting fully half an hour, and was just on the point of uncovering his lantern to look at his watch, when all at once he distinctly heard footsteps upon the hard road. They drew nearer, nearer, and, just as the person, whoever it was, had approached close to the Cross, Laurence cast the light from his lantern full upon him. At once the bright beam was answered by a corresponding one from a lantern carried by the new-comer, who was a tallish man closely wrapped in a great coat, and with a hat which quite concealed his face. For a moment neither spoke, but the stranger was the first to break silence.

"Good-evening, friend," he said. "You are waiting for someone?"

"And you also, are you not?" replied Laurence.

"Oh no," replied the other, shrugging his shoulders. "But you startled me with your lamp."

"Then you did not expect to find a lady here?" asked Laurence, after a moment's pause, doubtful whether this were the right man or not. "I had a message for someone who was to meet a lady here at eight o'clock."

"You had?" asked the other, turning his light full on Laurence's face, and speaking in a lower voice. "Then you may give me the message, for I am the man you expect."

"Then the message is this," began Laurence, calmly. "The lady will have nothing more to do with you, but has sent her husband that you may do your business directly with him."

The man made a quick movement, but Laurence was quicker still. In a second his pistol was pointing full at the other's face, and the light of the lamp gleamed on its barrels.

"Now mind what you are about," said the young man, seriously, "for you are in my power. If I whistle, a couple of policemen will secure you in a moment."

This was of course a fiction, but necessity suggested it, and it had its instantaneous effect. "You have been guilty of trying to extort money by threats. If a certain sum were not paid, you threatened to reveal some secret to me. I am here, but I have got no money for you, nor has my wife either; so now for your secret."

There was silence for a moment, when the stranger laughed slightly.

"There is no secret," he said. "It was a joke, and there's the end of it."

"Indeed, then I shall at once summon the policemen and give you into their hands."

Laurence made as though he were about to whistle, but the other stopped him with a sudden gesture.

"You'd be sorry if you did," he said in a low voice, drawing nearer.

"Why? If you satisfy me on that point, you are free to go."

"I will tell you. Any moment I chose I could bring disgrace upon you by proving that you had married another man's wife."

The words were spoken in a low, emphatic tone, and after a slight pause. Evidently the speaker had been discussing with himself the best thing to do and had decided that to declare the secret was his only course. Had he not had the fear of the policemen before his eyes he might have acted differently.

"And who is that other man?" asked Laurence, his voice trembling very slightly.

"Myself."

"Can you prove it?"

"Any moment."

Again there was silence, during which Laurence reflected. Despite the fearful agony which the confirmation of his fears created in his mind, he felt that the present was the opportunity for decided action, and an opportunity which must not be let slip. He spoke, slowly and emphatically.

"Tell me if I understand you. The woman I have married is in reality your wife. For some reason or other you have deserted her—or she you—and now that you have discovered her again you wish to make profit out of my misfortune. You have no wish to reclaim her as your wife?"

"None whatever, I assure you," replied the other, in the cynical tone natural to him. "Don't think, however," he added quickly, "that on that account you have done with me. If you refuse to pay me for keeping this a secret, I will disclose it for spite."

"And how if I do not care, if I purpose myself getting rid of my wife to-morrow?"

"You don't purpose any such thing, Dr. Bloomfield," said the other, confidently. "I know you too well."

"You know me?"

"Perfectly well; though that is a very different thing from saying that you know *me*."

"Well, you are right," said Laurence, after a pause. "I should prefer to still call this woman my wife. And now, scoundrel, what are your terms?"

He spoke the last words in passion, half maddened by the thought of his position, yet seeing no escape.

"No hard words, doctor," said the other, who grew more cool as he saw that, after all, he could command the situation. "At all events I am prepared to deal honestly with you.—If you pay me five hundred pounds I will leave you alone henceforth forever."

"You are modest in your demand," returned Laurence. "So that is your figure?—Well, before I say either yes or no, I must have absolute proofs of your identity. Will you accompany me to my house and conclude our business there?"

"I will," replied the other, after a brief pause. "If you betray me, you know the penalty. I shall at once let out everything."

"I know the penalty, as you say," returned Laurence. "First let me whistle away my policemen to a respectful distance. I daresay they are gentlemen with whom you do not care to come into too close connection.—Now, will you go?"

They walked off, side by side, each still holding his lantern to show the way and to guard himself against any possible treachery. They reached Bloomfield House thus, and Laurence led the way through a side-door into his own study. No one had perceived their entrance.

"Now for the proofs," said Laurence, as he locked the door and turned to face his companion. The latter drew from his pocket a number of letters, tied together, and began to take them from their envelopes.

"You know Bertha's writing pretty well, I suppose?" he asked.

149

Laurence nodded, pained excessively to hear his wife's name on the lips of such a man. At once the other put into his hands a letter, dated some seven years previous, which began "My Dear Husband," and was signed "Bertha Vanstone." Though time had slightly altered it, he yet recognised distinctly Bertha's handwriting. Several others he looked at, which began and ended in the same way, all written in an affectionate strain, and mostly occupied with accounts of the wife's simple home-life during the husband's temporary absence. Laurence did not read them all, but in a few moments handed them back, sick at heart.

"But how am I to know," he asked after a slight pause, "that these are not forgeries?"

"Does Bertha deny me?" asked the other, in return. "If so, I can refer you to the registry of the church where we were married."

"But, supposing I am convinced of the marriage, how shall I know that the husband is not dead, and you an impostor?"

"Confront me with her," said the other, laughing. "But do you think she would have been fool enough to let me screw money out of her unless I had her in my power?—But you had better confront me with her."

"She has already given you money?"

"Oh yes. I am surprised she preferred to run the risk of refusing me this time."

"That is easily explained," said Laurence. "She is ill with a bad fever, and could not have come to meet you, even if she had wished. Your note fell into my hands on that account."

"And how did you know where to meet me?"

"I had received information of her former meeting with you, so concluded it must be the same place."

Laurence would much have liked to ask questions with regard to Bertha's first marriage, but a sense of pride, a feeling of disgust at the thought of speaking on these subjects with such a man, kept him silent. One question, however, he felt bound to put.

"What was the cause of your separation?"

"That I shall say nothing about."

Laurence turned and walked up and down the room several times, reflecting. After all, he could entertain no reasonable doubt that the man's story was true, though he could not forget that there might be imposture. Yet poor Bertha's own behaviour was a strong confirmation of the account he had just heard, and, seen from this point of view, a multitude of slight circumstances, hitherto thought nothing of, came back to his mind with a strong significance. Then again came the question—Is this woman worthy of the sacrifices I am about to make for her? Would it not be better to let things take their natural course and be severed from one whose life had been one long falsehood ever since he had known her? But his love, his love was still strong in the depths of his heart and spoke loudly against such a course. He *could not* resign Bertha; nay, he *could not* believe her so guilty! If he knew all, there must be some extenuation of her conduct; perhaps, from the standpoint of a higher than conventional morality, he might be able entirely to justify her. No, love would still have its own. He must retain Bertha at all hazards.

"Listen," he said to the man; "you must give me time. If you are in good faith, you can well afford to wait a week or two. You know it is not in my power to escape from you. You must wait till my—till *she* is well enough to speak on the subject; then she will tell me everything, and I shall know whether to believe you."

Vanstone did not at first reply, but looked suspiciously at Laurence from under his eyebrows.

"In any case, you will *have* to wait," pursued the latter. "I refuse to take any step [until] I have heard my wife's confession."

"And when will your wife—as you call her—be able to confess?" asked Vanstone, with a sneering laugh.

"That I cannot tell you," said Laurence, suppressing his inclination to strike the rascal to the ground. "Let me have some means of communicating with you, and you shall hear as soon as possible. That is the last word I have to say."

"Well, I agree," returned the other, somewhat reluctantly. "Write to this address when you are ready;—but mind, it must not be too long."

He scribbled a few words on a piece of paper, and Laurence took it. He saw that the address was in London, but at present paid no closer attention to it. Then he led the way out of the house by the same side-door, and Vanstone at once vanished in the darkness.

Chapter X: All for Love

As soon as Laurence was left alone, he rang the bell, and bade the servant request Mrs. Edward Bloomfield (so the old lady was called, in contradistinction to Bertha,) to step down to the study. The servant returned with a message that the patient had become highly delirious, and it was impossible for her to be left. Laurence at once ran upstairs, and entered the room where his wife lay. He found his mother in a state of great distress, scarcely able to restrain Bertha from springing out of bed in her delirium. As soon as the sufferer saw Laurence, she cowered back, as if in terror.

"Keep away! Keep away!" she exclaimed, whilst her eyes glared with the terrible expression of madness. "You are not my husband; I have another now.—What right have you to torture me after all these years?—You shall not ill-use me now; I have someone to protect me.—Laurence! Laurence!—Cannot you save me from that man?"

Hereupon she broke into terrible shrieks and Laurence had to exert all his strength to hold her down. The scene was inexpressibly painful, and Mrs. Bloomfield was unable to refrain from weeping.

"Mother," said Laurence, as soon as Bertha had become less violent, and had for a moment sunk back in exhaustion, "you had better go and rest a little. I will attend to Bertha myself. Never mind my engagements, they must be put off."

"Perhaps it would be better," replied the old lady, "for me to get a little rest now, then I can relieve you later. Fortunately I am strong and can sit up all night without much difficulty."

"You shall not be taxed too much, mother, but your presence here now is indeed a godsend. You see how impossible it would be to have a strange nurse."

Mrs. Bloomfield sighed, and exchanged a look of sad meaning with her son; then she pressed his hand and left the room.

For nearly a week Bertha continued delirious, scarcely ceasing day or night to talk aloud of her past life, disclosing all the secrets which had weighed so dreadfully upon her mind. Once or twice Laurence all but despaired of her life; yet, by dint of the most unceasing care, by exertions where tender affection and consummate medical skill mutually helped each other, the patient was at length brought safely out of her delirium, and once more hope might be entertained of her complete recovery.

In the meantime, Laurence had decided in his own mind how he should behave upon his wife's discovery. Clearly the only means of securing peace for the future was to bring his wife to confess freely to him all her secrets, and, in return, to disclose to her the means he had adopted to provide against further molestation. In his compromise with Vanstone he could see nothing to be ashamed of, nothing immoral; but naturally he was anxious to hear the story of Bertha's marriage, to be sure that his love had not been spent upon an unworthy object, that he had done right in submitting to any sacrifice rather than lose her.

In the early days of her convalescence, Bertha was very quiet, scarcely speaking either to Laurence or to his mother, and, though slowly improving in bodily health, still evidently afflicted in her mind. Laurence endeavoured to prove to her by constant kindness in word and deed that his affection for her had not in the least diminished, but his tenderness appeared rather to distress than to console her. He felt that there was but one means of putting an end to this mental trouble, and he chose as early a day as possible to entreat her to unburden her heart of all its sorrows.

One morning just after the commencement of the New Year, he entered her room alone, and, after an affectionate greeting, sat down on her bed-side with her hand in his own.

"You begin to feel much stronger, darling, do you not?" he asked, gazing tenderly into her pale, yet beautiful, face.

"A little," she replied, faintly. "But I fear I shall never be quite well again, Laurence."

"Oh, you must not have such thoughts as that," he exclaimed, merrily. "Why, we shall have you getting about again in no time. See what a thing it is to have a husband who is a doctor."

The last sentence was not spoken with any special intention, but Laurence could feel her hand tremble as he uttered it. He was on the point of broaching the subject uppermost in his mind, just considering what words he should begin with, when Bertha anticipated him.

"I was delirious for a long time, was I not, Laurence?" she asked.

"A long time, darling," he replied, looking earnestly into her face.

She endeavoured to raise herself, and drew nearer to him.

"Did I—did I talk much in my delirium?" she asked, her voice failing her as she spoke, so that the last word was scarcely audible.

"Yes, Bertha, a great deal," he said, firmly, keeping his eyes fixed on hers. "You said much that I understood, but many things that were unintelligible to me."

"And—did your mother hear me?" she asked, in a tone scarcely above a whisper.

"She did, dearest."

Bertha broke out into bitter weeping.

"Calm yourself, Bertha," he said, caressing her long hair as it lay loose upon the pillow. "There is no doubt that in your delirium you unburdened yourself of a secret which had weighed long upon your mind; but was it not better that you should do so? What though my mother and I heard you? No one else did, and our love for you is strong enough to overlook everything. Not a single harsh word has my mother spoken of you; and I, darling, would die rather than condemn you for being the victim of terrible misfortune.—Listen, Bertha. I have even seen this man, and talked with him."

"You have?" she exclaimed, in terror.

"Yes, dearest. On the first day of your illness a note from him which was meant for you came into my hands. I met him, and he left me so well satisfied that he promised never to trouble us again."

Laurence spoke as if his transactions with Vanstone were concluded, for the sake of putting Bertha's mind at ease. She had hidden her face from him, and was still weeping.

"But now, dearest," he went on, "I want there to be no more secrets between us. Will you trust me perfectly and let me hear once for all the whole of the wretched story? As yet I understand it only vaguely. Make me your confidant, and the matter shall never be once again referred to by either of us."

"Oh, you are very good, Laurence!" she sobbed. "How can you be so kind, so forbearing to one who has brought trouble and sin into your house. Then you will not send me away from you? I must not go back once more to my lonely life, covered with shame?"

"Leave me? Never, darling!" he exclaimed, fervently. "You are my wife; let the world and its prejudices say what they will. I now know what you meant when you said that nothing should part us, and I am determined that nothing *shall!*"

Bertha lay back on the pillow for a few moments with her eyes closed; then she began to speak in a low tone, and so related the story of her life before she knew Laurence. As she continued, sobs and tears frequently interrupted her words, but Laurence encouraged her with expressions of love and trust, and at length the narrative was concluded. It was a simple one, and I shall merely give its principal outlines. At about the age of seventeen she had been left, an orphan, in the care of an aunt who was her only relative, and who was sufficiently well-to-do to permit her niece to complete her education at a superior school. The aunt resided in London, but the school was at a Sussex watering-place, and consequently Bertha was a boarder. Whilst here, she was so imprudent as to commence a secret correspondence with a young man whom she had become acquainted with at the house of a friend who was a day-pupil, where she occasionally visited. Bertha was in those days young and romantic, and it required but little persuasion to induce her to escape from the school and be secretly married at another watering-place on the south-coast. As soon as the ceremony was over, she wrote to her aunt, and told her all that she had done, begging her forgiveness. But her relative replied with the utmost harshness, refusing ever to see her again or have anything to do with her. The name of Bertha's husband was Philip Vanstone. He was about twenty-two, and, it soon appeared, was living upon a little money which had come into his hands at his majority. Previous to that he had been a clerk in London, but, on obtaining his money, he had thrown up all occupation, and was now wasting his means as fast as he could. At first he was kind to his wife, appearing to truly love her, but as soon as poverty began to show itself, his behaviour altered entirely, and he treated the poor girl brutally. At length he deserted her, and the next thing she heard of him was that he had been sentenced to eighteen months imprisonment for a robbery in which he was detected. Hereupon, Bertha had sold what little property she possessed and made her way to London, where she revealed everything to her aunt, and begged for a little assistance, at least till she could earn some kind of living for herself. Her relative was at first inexorable, but at length gave her a very small sum of money and dismissed her with a command never to return. With the utmost difficulty she obtained a place as teacher in a little school, and, from this time onwards, her life had really been such as she had always said. Her husband had never discovered her till just after her return from the Continent with Laurence.

"And how did the discovery then come about?" asked Laurence, who had listened with the utmost attention, and felt a great load taken from his breast.

"I am almost ashamed to tell you," she returned, still much distressed. "You remember the burglary which took place here the night before our return? He was either one of the men, or was connected with them; for it was by means of the papers in the writing-case which I then lost that he discovered me."

"Poor child! Poor child!" murmured Laurence, as she drew near to him and hid her face against his breast. "It is no sin that you have committed; I swear it is not! If ever this man could call you his wife he has long since forfeited the claim by his brutality and villainy. Now you are mine, darling, and shall be mine for ever!"

"And your mother, Laurence?" she sobbed. "How shall I face her?"

"My mother must know all, I will myself tell her," he answered, firmly. "Do not fear her ill opinion, dearest. I shall justify you to her, I am sure; for she has more strength of mind and more liberality of judgment than most women.—Now rest, Bertha. It is all over; forget it, as if it were a dream which had tortured you in your illness."

Chapter XI: Intrigue

Bertha's illness had of course been the subject of much talk among the gossips of Market Leyton, and for the circles in which Miss Chad and the Gollands were familiar it acquired a significance only to be explained by female spite and love of exaggeration. To do Miss Chad justice she was by no means a malicious woman; but it was so natural to her to talk about everything and everybody on every possible occasion that she could scarcely have kept silent if the life of her dearest friend had depended upon it. So it was with no special malice against Bertha that she had told the story of having seen her talking to a stranger at Red Lane Cross; but this story when repeated by Harriet Golland held up poor Bertha in very dark colours indeed to the reprobation of the virtuous ladies of Market Leyton. Nor was the illness which followed almost immediately left unused for malicious purposes. Miss Golland industriously spread the report that it was anything rather than brain-fever from which Mrs. Bloomfield was suffering; and she whispered that the truth of the matter was this: Bertha had been discovered in correspondence with the much-talked-of-stranger by her husband, who, in his anger, had severely beaten her, thus compelling her to take to her bed. Absurd as this story was, there were plenty of people found ready to believe it.

In the meantime Miss Golland was herself becoming a centre of attention, for no less a reason than that she was about to be married. Yes, Harriet had at length resolved to give up her hopes of an aristocratic match—such as she felt the Bloomfield one would have been—and had been graciously pleased to accept the hand and heart of Mr. Thomas Stonehouse, a very substantial provision-dealer, who had promised her that she should have her carriage and hold her head as high as the best. For some time Miss Golland had hesitated before even such an advantageous offer as this, the counter-attraction being Dr. Simmonds, her mother's new medical attendant; for Harriet had gained her point, and Dr. Bloomfield had been dismissed from the house of the Gollands. Harriet had an idea that to be a doctor's wife would be a fine position indeed, but when, on making inquiries, she found that Dr. Simmonds was the very reverse of rich, she had begun to look with a more favourable eye on Mr. Stonehouse and the promised carriage, and very early in the new year, had accepted both.

Mr. Stonehouse kept his promises. Harriet had her carriage,—a very small phaeton, drawn by a diminutive pony which rumour said had once done duty in a cart belonging to the shop,—invited her friends to tea very frequently, and had even once or twice a ceremonious dinner-party. But, above all these social advantages, there was one she specially advertised; namely, the fact that she possessed a lady's maid.

This young lady, by name Selina, was a species of general servant in the house as well as lady's maid, but, considered in the latter capacity, Harriet did not scruple to treat her with a certain amount of familiarity and even to make use of her for the gratification of that quiet and long-enduring malice which was Mrs. Stonehouse's most notable characteristic. In the course of conversations between the mistress and maid it soon became known to the former that Selina was "keeping company" with a young man, and this young man no other than the manservant in Dr. Bloomfield's house, with whom the reader has already some acquaintance under the name of Walton. Harriet experienced considerable inward pleasure on first hearing of this, for she felt instinctively that it ought to afford some means of getting at sundry little secrets in the domestic life of the Bloomfields, though at first she did not see very clearly how. The opportunity came of its own accord. One day Selina had been talking with her mistress in a rather more confidential tone than usual, and, among other things, she said that Robert—that is, Walton—had been in a very bad temper on the preceding Sunday when they saw each other, that he had spoken of being ill-treated by his master, and that he had thought of leaving his place; but, what was strangest of all, he said that he knew of some secret which he could tell if he liked, and which some people, evidently meaning Dr. Bloomfield, would not care to have told.

At this Harriet pricked up her ears, if the expression may be used of a young lady, and did her best to get more definite information from the girl; at length plainly promising her that, for every secret she could discover through Walton, regarding the Bloomfields, she would reward her well. Selina was somewhat surprised at the interest taken by her mistress in such matters, but readily enough promised to find out all she could.

She could not at once discover anything of importance, for the simple reason that the source of her information was but little wiser than herself. Walton's discontent and vague threats had come about in this way. When Vanstone had consented to wait a few weeks before coming to an agreement with his victim, he had not been so careless of human interests as to quit Market Leyton without leaving someone behind him who might act as spy upon the Bloomfields' movements. This spy Vanstone had ready to his hands in Walton, with whom he had had constant relations ever since their first contact in the matter of the burglary. But though he thus made use of Walton, Vanstone had no intention of letting him into his secrets, so that the former could only suspect that there was some strange business going on between his two (very different) employers, without precisely knowing what is was. Now, very shortly after hearing Bertha's story from her own lips, Laurence faithfully fulfilled his agreement with Vanstone. A second meeting took place privately in the study, and Laurence paid down the sum of five hundred pounds, Vanstone promising in turn never to trouble him again, and never, on any account, to disclose the common secret. Fortunately, Laurence possessed a competency in addition to what he derived from his practice, so that he was able to afford this sum without serious embarrassment ensuing. He well knew that in this affair he was dealing with an arrant rogue, but he *hoped* that Vanstone would adhere to the agrement. Moreover, he was already contemplating a removal with Bertha and his mother to some remote part of England, perhaps even to the Continent, by means of which he certainly thought he could avoid any further importunity.

I have not thought it necessary to enlighten the reader with regard to the particulars of Philip Vanstone's mode of life; doubtless it has by this time been made pretty evident to all that, if not a rogue of the first water, it was owing to no lack of good will and experience on his part. Living at times by his wits, more often by his fingers, his first visit to Market Leyton had been pure chance, and it was only owing to hearing the gossip about the Bloomfields then prevalent that he had been induced to plan the burglary. Of course he was a character very well known to the police, but, owing to his skill in the matter of disguises, he had now for some time succeeded in keeping out of their hands. Since his discovery of Bertha, he had utilized the period of his necessary stay in Market Leyton for the purpose of carrying out one or two successful burglaries in the surrounding neighbourhood. With the results of these, and the large sum he had extorted from Laurence Bloomfield he was now preparing to get away to "fresh fields and pastures new." Before he went, he entertained his accomplice, Walton, in a lordly style one night at the "Bull" Hotel, and, during the carouse, in his excitement he let fall several hints regarding the sum he had obtained from Laurence. Walton, also swelled with drink, pressed to be told the secret, but Vanstone was not so imprudent as to gratify his curiosity. The fellow then became quarrelsome, and complained that Vanstone had treated him shabbily, had not given him a share of his profits, and so on. The end of it was that Vanstone got off the same night, and Walton had to return home, much intoxicated. Laurence heard of this, and, the following morning, summoned the man to his room and reproved him soundly, threatening, if ever the thing recurred, to dismiss him at once. And hence the complaints and the threats which Walton, who was a cowardly rascal in the main, gave vent to, on his Sunday walk with Miss Selina.

At present there seemed but little food here for Mrs. Stonehouse's malice. Yet Harriet was far-sighted, above all in matters of revenge, and would not permit herself to resign the hope of one day finding a key to these somewhat curious complications.

Chapter XII: Thunder-Clouds

Nearly a year passes, a year very quiet and uneventful for the inhabitants of Bloomfield House. Bertha, after passing through the various stages of convalescence, regained sufficient strength to be sent early in the spring to a pleasant watering-place in Devonshire, where she remained for nearly three months, together with Mrs. Bloomfield. For the latter, as well as Bertha, the change was very requisite; the old lady's strength, both of mind and body, had been sadly tried during the past winter. Yet she still entertained the old affection for her daughter-in-law; it was a plant which had taken up too deep a root in her heart to be readily torn up. Bertha's story she had heard in full from Laurence, all except that which related to Vanstone's presence in Market Leyton. Of this Laurence did not speak a word[,] allowing his mother to conclude that it was the poor girl's conscience only which had wrought such dire effect upon her health. The explanation once given, not a word more was ever spoken on the subject by one of the three. Their life henceforth was to be as though the wretched disclosure had never been made.

But, by the rules of human nature, such an ignoring of the past was impossible. Bertha regained, it is true, a moderate degree of health; but her happiness, her interest even in life, was forever vanished. Very shortly after her return to the town, too, her physical health began once more evidently to suffer. Laurence had to seriously consider the project of removing to a more favourable climate.

One morning early in December, Bertha and Mrs. Bloomfield were sitting together at the breakfast-table, waiting for Laurence, when suddenly the latter entered with a most disturbed countenance. He held in his hand two or three articles of female ornament, a brooch, a ring, a bracelet.

"It was as I suspected," he exclaimed. "The losses were becoming altogether too frequent to be owing to chance. Bertha, is not this brooch yours?—Mother, haven't I seen you wearing this bracelet?"

"Certainly," exclaimed both ladies at once.

"Then I have discovered the thief," went on Laurence, angrily. "I should not wonder if even the watch you once lost, mother, could not be traced into the same hand."

"Whoever was it, Laurence?" asked Mrs. Bloomfield.

"You will be surprised; no other than Walton. The number of losses lately has struck me as being very curious, and I have watched all the servants when we spoke of them in their presence. I thought I noticed something curious in Walton's face, so this morning I sent him out on an errand, and immediately visited his bedroom. These are the fruits of my search."

"Whatever shall you do, dear?" asked the old lady, whilst Bertha, afflicted with painful thoughts, sat pale and silent. Laurence looked at her, and thought he could read entreaty in her countenance.

"Well," he replied, "if I did my duty I should certainly bring the fellow to justice. In any case, I shall get rid of him at once."

"I do not see how you can do otherwise," said Mrs. Bloomfield.

That same morning, Walton, who had profited by the evil lessons of Philip Vanstone, was confronted with his thefts, at once confessed, and begged pitifully to be spared. Laurence told him that he should forgive him so far as not giving him up to the police went, but that he must at once leave the house. The fellow straightway went, vowing vengeance in his ungrateful heart.

"Well, my dear," exclaimed Miss Chad, the next morning, as she bounced into her friend Mrs. Stonehouse's drawing-room, "it is all arranged! The Bloomfields are going!"

"Going? When?"

"Oh, not immediately of course, my dear Harriet. Mrs. Bloomfield tells me they mean to leave in the early spring. They will go to some place or other in the south of France; I think they have not quite made their choice yet.—Poor Mrs. Laurence's health absolutely requires it. The poor child is, I declare, as weak as water and as pale as—as the vases on your mantel-piece."

"Yes, Miss Chad," returned Harriet, knowingly; "they will never persuade me that there is not something at the bottom of that illness.—Poor dear; I pity her indeed.—But, what do you think? Have you heard of poor Walton?"

"Walton, at the Bloomfields'?"

"Yes, he is dismissed. Selina told me of it last night. The poor thing is crying her eyes out about it."

"Dismissed! And why, I wonder? I'm sure I always thought Walton a very decent sort of man."

"Well, the affair seems to me shameful. It came about in this way. (I have it all from Selina, so it must be true, you know.) It seems that Dr. Bloomfield had asked Walton to light a fire in his study, and Walton did so. Half an hour after he meets Walton in the hall, and says 'I thought I told you to light my fire?'—'I did so, sir,' replies the man; and at once the doctor calls him a liar—the very word—and strikes him a savage blow on the face, bidding him leave the house at once. I declare it seems shameful. If I were Walton I would prosecute him for assault.—For, after all, the fire had only gone out again."

For once, Harriet was not spreading a fiction of her own making. As soon as he left Bloomfield House, the scamp Walton had set himself to make current the above story in explanation of his sudden dismissal. Harriet well knew that, in order to make the report known throughout Market Leyton, she had only to relate it to Miss Chad. And, indeed, before night the latter lady must have repeated it two hundred times, though, to do her justice, we must say that she always concluded with—"But, my dear, of course I don't believe a single word of it!"

It was true, however, that the Bloomfields had decided to leave the town, both on account of Bertha's health, and because Laurence began to feel that it had been a mistake to continue in their old home after its peace had once been so terribly marred. Perhaps in a new home, in a new land, the peace might return. Very bitter was it to Laurence, this experience of the fatality which, in some mysterious way, always follows in the track of wrong, involving, as often as not, innocent and guilty in the same dread punishment. Poor Bertha's deceit had had its origin in no less pure a feeling than passionate and devoted love, yet, for all that, it had still been deceit, and, to a certain extent, cruel deceit. During these long months of illness and suffering she saw but too clearly her own fault, and she could not free herself from a dreadful presentiment of truth impending over her and hers. Often she asked herself whether it was still too late to turn in her path; whether she might not still, even at the expense of her own unspeakable suffering, save those she loved so well. If she killed herself, doubtless it would be to inflict the keenest pain on Laurence for a while, but none the less certainly it would be freeing him from danger. But these were only thoughts; her innate weakness of character forbade their ever transforming themselves into acts.

Poor Bertha! Her presentiments of calamity were but too well founded. It was about a week after Walton's dismissal when, about ten o'clock at night, a stranger rang the door-bell and requested to see Dr. Bloomfield. Laurence happened to be at home, so the stranger was at once shown into the consulting-room and requested to take a seat.

Laurence entered. The stranger rose and bowed, with a peculiar smile upon his face. He was a man with thick black beard and moustache, and with a bandage over one of his eyes.

"You require my professional assistance?" asked Laurence, somewhat surprised that his visitor did not speak.

"If you please," returned the stranger.

How was it that Laurence's nerves seemed to thrill at the sound of the voice. He looked closely into the speaker's face, then uttered a slight sigh of relief.

"Have you hurt your eye?" he asked. "Or is it some natural affection?"

"I will take off the bandage, doctor, and let you see for yourself," was the reply; and again Laurence started at the voice, and looked closely into his visitor's face. As he did so, the bandage was removed; but the eye was, to all appearances, perfectly whole.

"What is the matter with the eye?" asked Laurence. "I can see nothing wrong."

"Can't you?" returned the other. "Then either you must have an uncommonly short memory, or my disguise must be uncommonly good. Do you see anything wrong now?" he asked, laughing, and, at the same time, removing a false beard and moustache.

Laurence started back, pale as death.

"Good God!" he exclaimed. "Vanstone!—Why do you come here? What do you want?"

"Well," returned the other, putting his hands in his pockets and speaking with cool impudence, "a little more of the same sort, doctor."

Laurence gazed at his face for some moments without speaking. He saw upon it evident traces of the dissolute life which the man had led during the past year, and, loathsome as the visage was to him, it seemed to exercise a certain hideous attraction, compelling him to gaze. As they stood thus, face to face, his blood grew hot, his pulses began to beat fiercely, he gasped for breath. At the same moment his brain seemed on fire, and in his ears was a dreadful hissing, as of snakes. It was a terrible instant.

"I don't understand you," he said at length, forcing himself to be calm. "I thought you agreed never to let me see your hateful face again?"

"Did I? Oh, that's a long time ago. Many things happen in a year, doctor!—By the bye, how's Bertha?"

"Tell me what you want at once!" exclaimed Laurence, "unless you wish to madden me to some rash act."

"I should have thought you were sharp enough to guess. I must have some more money."

Laurence turned away, and paced the room for a few seconds.

"How much do you want?" he asked, at length, in a hoarse voice.

"Oh, I'm not particular. Suppose we say the same as before?"

"Are you drunk?" asked Laurence, sharply. "You smell of liquor."

"I had a drop before I came; but nothing worth speaking of. Trust me. I'm quite up to business."

Again there was a silence, this time for nearly five minutes.

" I can give you no answer to-night," said Laurence, then. "You must see me again."

"When?"

"To-morrow night at the same time."

There was a dreadful kind of emphasis on the words as they fell from the speaker's lips; but Vanstone did not appear to observe this.

"Well, I am agreeable," he said.

"And you must come to me secretly," said Laurence, "as you did before. If anyone notices you are with me so long it might attract attention. Be at the side-door here at ten o'clock, and I will open it. You need not even knock; only be punctual."

"Right," returned Vanstone. "It'll suit me."

"And me," remarked Laurence, also with a strange emphasis.

Hereupon Vanstone resumed his disguises, together with the bandage over his eye, and Laurence accompanied him to the front door, where they parted with a mutual "good-night." Then Laurence repaired to his study. Presently Bertha knocked at his door, asking if he would not return and finish his supper, from which he had been called away. He replied in the negative, saying he had some important business to transact, and bidding Bertha an affectionate "good-night." For several hours he paced up and down his study floor, plunged in gloomy reverie.

Chapter XIII: Into the Lion's Den

All the following day Laurence did not leave the house, and, with the exception of the short time spent at table, remained shut up in his study. Both his mother and his wife observed that he was very different from his usual self, and both questioned him slightly. He merely replied, however, that he was not quite well, that he had a severe headache; and the ladies did not press him further. What was the character of his thoughts during the whole of that dreary winter's day, as he paced hour after hour the floor of the room, with pale, troubled countenance, occasionally passing his hand with an air of distraction over his knitted brows; what dire images, what terrible calculations occupied his mind, who shall say?

Shortly after lunch there came a knock at his door, and Bertha entered.

"Are you busy, dear?" she asked. Then, with a sudden shiver, she added, "But how dreadfully cold your room is! I declare you have let your fire out.—Let me ring and get the servant to relight it."

"Ah!—Is it out?" returned Laurence, absently. "I had not noticed."

"I am sure the atmosphere must be nearly at freezing-point," continued Bertha, who appeared in unusually good spirits. "But what is it that is troubling you so, dear? Is your head still bad?"

"Bad,—very bad!" muttered her husband, passing his hand over his brow.

"Is anything troubling you?" she went on, resting her hand upon his shoulder, and gazing affectionately into his face. "Have you any troublesome business on hand, dear?"

"No, no," he replied, hastily, averting his wife. "No, nothing to speak of. But my head is splitting. I had a bad night, you know; I scarcely slept at all."

"Yes, and when you did drop off for a moment you talked incessantly," said Bertha.

"Talked?" he asked, quickly, regarding her with a strange look. "What did I say?"

"Oh, nothing that I could understand. You spoke once or twice of somebody's eye, no doubt you were thinking of some patient."

"Yes, yes," he replied. "I had a man here last night with an injured eye. Yes; that must have been it."

She continued to look uneasily in his face, no doubt noticing some peculiarity in his tone and manner. At length he suddenly clasped his arms tight around her, and kissed her lips passionately.

"Do you love me, Bertha?" he asked. "Do you still love me as much as ever? Will you always love me?"

"Why do you ask me, Laurence?" she returned. "Love you! I shall love you till I give up my last breath; my last thought shall be of you, my last utterance shall be your name!"

She returned his burning kiss, and for a moment they stood thus, encircled by each other's arms.

"Leave me now, dearest," he said at length. "I have a great deal to do, despite my head-ache."

"Shall you be engaged long? At least you will spend the evening with us?"

"I will see," he returned, hurriedly. "Perhaps so; I will see."

She left him, and he once more began to pace the room, even more gloomy than before.

The long day of anguish at length faded into night, and night drew on to the hour of ten, the hour of his appointment with Vanstone. The side-door by which the latter was to be admitted was one which led into the surgery, which, in its turn, was connected with the consulting-room. At ten precisely Laurence went to this door, and opened it; he had only to wait a moment before a dark figure sauntered up the path, and drew near to the door.

"Good-evening," said Vanstone, with a nod of the head.

Laurence returned the greeting, though in a lower tone, and at once admitted his visitor, closing the door. A bright fire was burning in the consulting-room. The house was very still, for it was the practice of Bertha and the old lady to retire very early, and the servants always preceded them.

"Strange smell, here," remarked Vanstone, sniffing as he entered the room.

"Yes, perhaps there is," replied the other. "I have been conducting an operation here to-day and have used an anaesthetic."

Had the visitor noticed Laurence's face as he spoke, he would have seen that it was the hue of death, and that the forehead was covered with an oozing perspiration.

"Take a seat," said Laurence, and at the same time he sat down by the fire. The seat which Vanstone took had its back to the door which led into the surgery.

"Cold night," said the visitor, warming his hands. "Thawing though."

"Is it?" asked Laurence, quickly. "The ice on the canal was very firm this afternoon, I was told."

"Ah, I dare say. But it can't hold till morning."

There was a pause, during which Laurence's eye surveyed Vanstone's countenance stealthily, then wandered round the room with a restless glance.

"Well, let's get to business," said the visitor. "Have you thought the matter over, doctor?"

Instead of replying, Laurence began to sniff, as though conscious of an unpleasant odour.

"You're right," he said, rising from his chair. "There is a horrible smell here. Some stopper must have been left out in the surgery."

He rose and slipped into the little room behind whilst Vanstone, with a grin on his face, stooped forward to warm his hands again. He heard Laurence's step once more entering, and was on the point of turning his head, when suddenly he felt a damp cloth thrown over his face and pulled tight with an iron grasp. He had only time to be aware of this when, almost instantly, his senses left him and he fell back in the chair. Immediately Laurence took from a corner a piece of strong cord, and with this proceeded to bind together the arms of the helpless man; afterwards doing the same with his legs, and so firmly, that, even if Vanstone's senses had returned, it would have been impossible for him to stir. This done, Laurence hurriedly stepped to the outer door, opened it, and looked up at the sky. It was pitch dark. Underfoot the snow had all melted, and nothing but a constantly dissolving slush remained. He left the door open and returned to the consulting-room, where he rapidly put on his hat and great-coat. Then he bent on his knees by the side of his helpless victim, and, seizing with both hands the cord which bound Vanstone's arms, with an immense effort raised the body, like a sack, onto his shoulders. In this position he was able to carry it, though of course at no great speed. He went with it through the surgery as far as the outer door; then paused a moment to gather breath, and to look around. Nothing could be seen through the intense darkness, not even the low wall, which, at the distance of a few paces, separated the garden from a large ploughed field. Re-collecting all his strength, and bending almost double beneath the weight, Laurence groped his way to this wall, and with a great effort, flung the body over it into the field. Leaping after it, he attempted once more to raise it onto his shoulders, but his strength was too much exhausted for this. He was obliged to rest a few moments. But at length he once more raised his burden, and proceeded a hundred yards or so along the slushy furrows. Then he had to rest again; and so he went on, toiling and resting, till at length he had crossed the field and found himself once more before a low wall, over which, after a moment's careful listening, he heaved the body, again jumping after it. He now stood on the tow-path of a canal. Kneeling on the edge, he felt down in the darkness, and found that the canal, though still frozen over, was rapidly thawing. He endeavoured to break the ice with his fists, but it was still too strong for that. He then took off one of his boots, and hammered upon the ice with it, till at length he had succeeded in making an aperture; after which he soon tore out a large piece, rending the ice in every direction. The cold water clung to his hands, but he did not feel it. Drawing out his pocket-knife he now cut the bonds of the senseless or dead man, and carefully put the pieces of cord in his pocket; then, with a great effort, he dragged the body to the edge and pushed it over. There was a great splash, a few minutes' gurgling and rushing of the exposed water; then absolute silence.

Hitherto the murderer's nerves had resisted all the influences of horror, and he had acted with that strange calmness which men often show when once they have succeeded in working up their courage to the execution of a terrible purpose. But as soon as the effects of the splash had ceased to make themselves heard, and dead silence had ensued, terror seized upon his mind; he turned and fled, as though for his life. He had half crossed the field before he perceived that he had only one boot on; and, despite his dread of returning, the still greater dread of discovery forced him back to the side of the canal. It was some time before he found the boot, and, just as he was drawing it over his mud-clogged stocking, a fearful thought flashed across his mind, and, for a moment, rendered him incapable of stirring. In his excitement he had forgotten to rifle his victim's pockets! Who could tell what they might have contained? There might even be something in them which would declare immediately the motive and the perpetrator of the crime. Moments of unutterable horror passed as Laurence stood in the darkness, reflecting on these possibilities. He even once more leaned over the edge, and felt down into the ice-cold water, with some hope of recovering the body; but of course the stream had already floated it away, and he only cut his hands against the sharp edges of the ice. Resigning himself to the inevitable, he once more crossed the wall, and toiled back over the field, homewards. Arrived in the consulting-room, he looked at his watch, and was astounded to see that he had been absent more than two hours. Before leaving he had locked the door leading into the hall, so that no one could have entered during his absence. The house was in absolute silence. It was impossible that his absence should have been noticed.

For half an hour he was employed in removing all traces of mud from his boots and clothing, and in burning the cord and the cloth which he had used in the murder. Then he turned out the gas, and, taking a candle in his hand, went upstairs to bed.

Chapter XIV: Discoveries

Throughout that night the thaw continued, and in the morning the surface of the canal was only scattered over here and there with a few pieces of floating ice. From an early hour barges had commenced to force a way along, and this had aided the complete breaking up of the hard surface.

It was about eleven o'clock in the morning when some men passing along on one of these barges observed a human body floating in the water, and, with some little difficulty, succeeded in dragging it on board. The barge at once stopped, and one of the men walked into Market Leyton, communicating his news to the first policeman he met. Within half an hour the corpse was removed to the police-station. Here it was of course examined, and the clothing searched for means of identification. In the pockets were very few things: a purse full of silver, a pocket knife, and a few papers. By means of the papers it was at once conjectured that the deceased belonged to the criminal class, and, when aided by the comparison of his features with a photograph which had shortly before been sent to the police to aid them in discovering a celebrated burglar, speedily led to the conclusion that the body was that of the man whose real name was Philip Vanstone, but who was well known to the authorities by a dozen aliases. The circumstances of the death being inexplicable, preparations for an inquest were at once made. In the meantime a medical examination of the corpse was necessary, and this task devolved upon Dr. Laurence Bloomfield.

The inquest was held at the "Wheat Sheaf" inn, where the crowd usual on such occasions collected at an early hour. Already it had been made public by means of the "Market Leyton Express" that the body of a notorious criminal had been found drowned under strange circumstances in the canal hard by, and naturally the case excited much curiosity. After viewing the body the coroner and jurymen proceeded to the discharge of their functions. First of all the body was identified by a detective-officer as that of Philip Vanstone, alias James Stone, etc. etc; after which Dr. Bloomfield was called upon to give the results of his post-mortem examination. Laurence rose in his place, and, with a perfectly firm voice and a countenance only ever so little pallid, stated that the case was evidently one of death by drowning, with no concomitant circumstances that he had been able to discover. The body had certainly not been in the water more than ten hours. In his opinion the deceased must have been attempting on the previous evening to cross the frozen surface of the canal, unaware how far the thaw had proceeded, and, the ice giving way, had sunk and been drowned immediately. Further police evidence went to show that deceased's presence in the neighbourhood could easily be accounted for on the supposition of a contemplated burglary, of which several had of late been perpetrated in the district. After this there was little if anything to be said, and the result of the inquest was summed up in the customary form—"Death by drowning."

As soon as Laurence heard that the dead man's identity had been discovered, his thoughts turned at once to Bertha. Of course it would be impossible to prevent her from hearing of the case, and if she did not read the name of Philip Vanstone in the newspaper, it would be sure to be pronounced in her presence by some visitor at the house, for an affair like the present afforded a topic of conversation not to be neglected by the Market Leytoners. By a singular coincidence, one which produced an effect little less than ghastly upon the murderer's tortured mind, Bertha had not for a long time been in such good spirits as during the last few days. Laurence longed to be able to tell her the news, yet he could not utter it; he revolved in his thoughts a thousand turns of expression which appeared to him likely to convey the intelligence as it might have been conveyed by an innocent man; yet these one and all seemed to his guilty conscience stamped with a half-confession of his crime, he felt that if he uttered the name of his victim he would inevitably stand revealed as his murderer.

The inquest took place on the day after the finding of the body, and it was the same morning that the "Market Leyton Express" issued full particulars regarding the deceased. Laurence had the newspaper in his hand all through breakfast. He would not permit either his mother or Bertha to have a glimpse at it, pretending to be all the time busy in perusing it, though in reality his eyes remained fixed as by a hideous magic on that one paragraph. The heading in large type: A BODY FOUND IN THE CANAL, stamped itself upon his brain as though it stood in letters of fire. A thousand times he was on the point of making some reference to it, which might act as the introduction to a subsequent private conversation with Bertha; but each time his tongue failed him. At length he could endure the torture no longer; he rose hastily, still holding the paper, and went to his study.

He had scarcely left the room when a shrill, cheerful voice was heard in the hall, and, immediately after, Miss Chad, whose visits, even for a country town, were often curiously timed, put her head into the breakfast room, crying, "May I come in?"

"By all means," returned Mrs. Bloomfield. "You are just in time to have a cup of coffee with us. Laurence has suddenly left us, no doubt reminded of some piece of business which could not be neglected."

"Oh, I'm so sorry he's gone!" exclaimed Miss Chad. "I came on purpose to ask him for particulars about the body."

"What body?" asked Mrs. Bloomfield.

"Why, the body found in the Canal," returned the gossipy lady. "Do you mean to tell me you know nothing of it?—Nor you, Mrs. Laurence?—I declare if I—he, he!—had a husband, he shouldn't have so many secrets from me.—Haven't you seen this morning's "Express"? I have got it here. Let me read you the paragraph."

And she began to read aloud. After a long preliminary account, she came to the words, "The man, though known to the police under a multitude of aliases, was in reality called Philip Vanstone"; when suddenly she was startled by a faint scream from Bertha, and, on raising her eyes, saw that the latter had fallen back in a fainting-fit. Of course there was an immense bustle at once, and as Bertha did not immediately revive she was carried upstairs to her bed-room. Mrs. Bloomfield, who had never known the name of Bertha's first husband, was as much at a loss to account for the fit as Miss Chad herself. She at once ran to her son's study, and told him what had happened. Laurence, who did not seem readily to understand his mother, went up to Bertha's room and remained alone with her.

It was a long time before the poor girl regained consciousness, but when at length her eyes opened and at once fell upon her husband, she smiled sweetly.

"Kiss me, darling," she whispered, holding out her arms to him.

"Then you know, Bertha?" he asked; and his voice seemed strangely hollow in his own ears.

"I know," she replied. "Yours forever, darling; yours forever now!"

He sank into her embrace, and hot tears broke in torrents from his eyes.

In the excitement Miss Chad at once hurried away, her destination the house of Mrs. Stonehouse. Bounding into Harriet's presence she related, with many an interjection, the extraordinary scene of which she had just been a witness. Harriet's eyes gleamed with a strange look.

"And what do you think!" she exclaimed, in return. "I have heard something from Selina which seems to me to have some connection with what you have just seen. I sent her out on an errand this morning, and on the way she met Walton. They began to talk about the body, and what do you think Walton said? 'Ah!' said he, 'there are some people I know of that won't be sorry to hear about that man's death.' Selina pressed him hard to explain what he meant, and at last she found that it was Dr. Bloomfield who had some cause or other to be afraid of this man who had been found drowned. What the cause was, Walton either didn't know, or wouldn't tell.—But, my dear Miss Chad, doesn't it strike you as curious? Here's the husband has cause to be glad of a man's death, and the wife faints away when she hears of it for the first time. I'd give my head to know the meaning of it! There's something at the bottom of it, trust me!"

Vague as the hint was which Harriet had got hold of, she determined to avail herself of it. Once before she had dealt a keen blow with an anonymous letter; now she would try to do the same again. The same day she wrote the following words, put them in an envelope, and dispatched them to Dr. Bloomfield:

"It's an ill wind that blows nobody luck. A drowned body has put your mind at ease. What does your wife think about it?"

Chapter XV: The End

On the occasion of receiving the first anonymous letter, which apprised him of the meeting at Red Lane Cross, Laurence had felt more of annoyance than fear, that is as far as the letter itself was concerned. Anyone might have seen the meeting by chance, and there were very many people malicious enough to take this means of inflicting pain. But this second communication smote him as with a blow. Ever since, in a moment of madness, he had stained his soul with murder, his terrified conscience had been on the alert to find danger in every trivial incident of every-day life. But here he seemed to hold in his hand irrefragable evidence of his secret being known to someone. Could he for a moment suppose that this person, whoever it was, would be content with making such a use of his knowledge as this? Would he not rather make it the means of his victim's ruin? Laurence's excited fancy was incapable of nice reflection. He did not look closely at the words to see exactly how much they conveyed. Instead of seeing in them merely the shrewd and spiteful guess of one who was far from divining the dreadful secret, he fancied that they must come from one who had become, in some mysterious manner, cognisant of his crime.

Already all but mad with the torture of remorse, this letter deprived him of all show of equanimity. At once he locked himself up in his study and yielded without the least resistance to every torment which his conscience could inflict. Little did Mrs. Stonehouse suppose that her malicious jest would smite so deep into the soul of her victim as to drive him to despair; but so it very often is in this world, and an unmeaning utterance has ere now been the cause of the ruin of many an innocent life. Laurence was not innocent; his mind, already tenanted by legions of remorseless torturing demons, only awaited such an impulse as this in order to become the prey of one more terrible than all,—the demon of self-murder. By nature noble and ambitious of the respect of his fellow men, he saw himself dragged down by a train of fatal circumstances into hideous depths such as his imagination had never even contemplated. The secret agony would have been sufficient to render life bitter past endurance; but now that the prospect of discovery and all the infamy attendant upon an accusation of murder were added to his sufferings, they proved too great for the stability of his intellect. During the rest of the day he was a madman, though a madman dangerous to no one but himself.

Shortly after dark that night Bertha, in passing the door of the study, felt sure that she heard movement within. Throughout the day

Laurence had not been seen, and it had been concluded that business kept him away from home. The study door had been tried and knocked at, but as no response had been elicited, it was thought that Laurence had locked it before leaving and taken the key with him, as he occasionally did. On hearing what she thought to be the sound of someone moving within, Bertha paused and knocked once more. No reply came, however, and she concluded she must have been mistaken.

The evening passed away, and yet Laurence had not returned. The two companions began to feel uneasy. About eleven o'clock, Mrs. Bloomfield rose from her chair, evidently much disturbed.

"I never knew Laurence remain away such a long time without sending some message," she said.

They exchanged a glance.

"You—you don't think it possible," stammered Bertha, "that he has been taken ill in the study. I felt almost certain about five o'clock that I heard some noise from within."

The old lady turned deadly pale.

"Surely not, surely not!" she exclaimed hastily. "But have we no key that will fit the door?"

"I know of none but Laurence's own," replied Bertha.

"Could we get in by the surgery?" asked Mrs. Bloomfield.

"The outer door is always kept locked. But I will go and see."

Bertha started to leave the room, but was stopped by her mother-in-law.

"I will send a servant," said the latter. "If we cannot get in that way we must break open the study-door at all risks."

The outer door was found locked as always, but it was found that the surgery window could be opened from outside, and the man-servant effected an entrance that way. The result was that their worst fears were relieved. The study was found empty.

The two ladies sat up together till one o'clock when, with the utmost reluctance, they decided to retire, doing their best to comfort each other with the supposition that Laurence had been unavoidably detained somewhere, and would return in the morning. He was frequently away all night, but never before without previous notice or a message sent in the course of the evening. There was little rest for poor Bertha this night.

Once more the morning came. At breakfast there were several letters for Laurence, but not a word from him. At noon both ladies left the house to make enquiries of their nearest friends. They did not go together, but each sought a different house, in hopes of hearing some news. Shortly after two o'clock Mrs. Bloomfield returned, quite without intelligence. Bertha had not yet reached home, but a gentleman —so the servant said—had called to see Mrs. Bloomfield, and, on being told she was out, had appeared much disappointed. He had promised to call again in half an hour. A very few minutes after the visitor once more rang the bell, and was at once introduced into the old lady's presence.

Mrs. Bloomfield did not know him at all, and it was apparently with great effort that he began to speak. He introduced himself as an inspector of police, and, with many attempts to soften the effect of the ill news he brought, at length announced that, about an hour before, the body of Dr. Bloomfield had been found floating in the Canal, almost in the precise spot where the other body had been found but a day or two previously. Life was completely extinct, and it was evident from several circumstances that the doctor had commited suicide.

It was a terrible shock, but the poor woman bore it bravely. It was not of herself she thought, but of Bertha; how could *she* be told? And yet the task must be performed, and by her; for who else would undertake it? About half an hour after, Bertha entered the house, weary with walking, having heard nothing of her husband. Mrs. Bloomfield allowed her to rest a short while, and then induced her to take a little food; after which she commenced the terrible duty of disclosing Laurence's fate. In vain all her efforts to break the news gently; from the first word Bertha knew what was coming, and, with agony in her look and voice, demanded to be told the worst at once. She heard it, and immediately fell into violent convulsions. Medical aid was forthwith sought, but it proved useless. Within a couple of hours Bertha was dead.

As for the secret, it perished with Laurence and Bertha. Philip Vanstone had apparently confided it to no one, doubtless wishing to reap all the profit himself; all his wife's letters he had given up to Laurence when he received his payment; and they had been at once destroyed. On hearing of the fearful ends of Dr. Bloomfield and his wife, Mrs. Stonehouse and Miss Chad were more than ever convinced that there was some extraordinary mystery at the root of the matter, but even with the help of all Market Leyton they were never able to hit upon the exact truth. Poor Mrs. Bloomfield, though she knew Bertha's story, was herself completely ignorant of the relation between her and the dead man found in the canal, and, what was still more fortunate, she never had the faintest suspicion of the fact that her son had been a murderer before becoming a suicide.

The Last Half-Crown

LIKE "ALL FOR LOVE," the present short story, the text of which, written in the large handwriting typical of Gissing early in his career and thirteen manuscript pages in length, was composed at 5 Hanover Street, Islington. The signature at the bottom still includes his middle initial and can with certainty be attributed to the period December, 1879–February, 1880, for on February 26 he signed an agreement with Remington for the publication of *Workers in the Dawn,* and, though this apparent triumph involved the payment of £125 by the author, was sufficiently elated by the prospect of seeing his novel in print to decide to abandon short stories, which he looked upon as a poor substitute, for a time. Early in March he began another novel, *A Child of the Age,* retitled *Will-o'-the Wisps* and finally discarded before completion. "The Last Half-Crown" may well be one of the several short stories Gissing mentions in a letter of February 7 as being in the hands of magazine editors.* At all events, it went into a drawer and was rediscovered only after his death.

* Letter to Algernon Gissing, *LMF*, p. 57.

HERE!" EXCLAIMED THE LITTLE GIRL, with a start, and stood looking up into the young man's face in such a queer, old-fashioned way that the latter could not help laughing.

Yet Harold was in no laughing mood; his pale, emaciated face bore witness at once to bodily privations and that sickness of the heart which comes from ever-deferred hope. A few moments before, he had stepped out of the house with his last half-crown in his hand, and, instead of walking away, had stood at the door in a wretched reverie, turning the coin over and over mechanically, and endeavouring to think what he should do with it. Suddenly it slipped from between his fingers, clinked on the pavement, rolled away,—and disappeared through the grating, beneath which was the window of the miserable little cellar-kitchen. There it lay in the sunshine which streamed through the grate, only to be regained by making a descent into the kitchen and reaching out through the window. Harold repeated the little girl's exclamation of "There!" and laughed quietly.

"You'll have to wait till they come back," went on the little girl, whom Harold knew well by sight, for she lived next door, and in this bright summer weather sat all day long upon the pavement playing with her poor, make-believe doll. "Mrs. Wilson and Lizzie is both out; I see them go just now."

"Indeed? Then I must take a walk till they come back, I suppose. Good-bye!"

It was in Colville Place, a narrow out-of-the-way passage just behind Tottenham-Court-Road. No vehicles pass through Colville Place, for it is paved all across, and so makes a capital play-ground for the poor children who swarm in the neighbourhood. Harold Sansom would scarcely have chosen such modest lodgings of his own free will; once he had known the comforts of a very different home, but a miserable train of circumstances had changed all that, and for some months he had been glad to rent a little garret at half-a-crown a week, furnished with a bed, a broken-seated chair, and an apology for a table. The sloping roof scarcely permitted him to stand upright, but that mattered little, for, when not wandering about in hopeless search for employment, he either lay upon his bed, seeking forgetfulness in the pages of one or two dear old books which still remained to him, or else sat at the crazy table, making desperate efforts to write something which might bring him bread. He had always been unsuccessful, and for the last few weeks had written nothing; how could he scribble about fictitious joys and woes when his own heart was racked day and night with anguish and despair? He had no friend, and sadly little of that courageous energy which enables men to conquer single-handed in the battle of life. So his little capital had dwindled, dwindled. This morning he had two half-crowns; one of them had gone to pay the week's rent which the businesslike Mrs. Higgs always demanded in advance, whilst the other lay at this moment down beneath the grating, only to be got at through the cellar window.

In such quarters as Colville Place human beings are accustomed to pack themselves into the smallest practicable space, and this cellar-kitchen of which we speak was at once bed-room, sitting-room and work-room for a mother and daughter. By peering down through the grate on a bright day like this, one could see two little cards hanging in the window, one of which informed all whom it might concern that mangling was done below, the other that plain-sewing could be executed here well and cheaply. Mrs. Wilson and her daughter were, in a certain sense, friends of Harold's; since he had lodged here they had been his laundresses, and, finding they were painfully poor, the kind-hearted fellow had paid for the little jobs more, perhaps, than, considering his circumstances, he was justified in doing. Mrs. Wilson was a poor-spirited, broken-down woman, who often had scarcely strength to turn her mangle, and Lizzie, her daughter, was a pale, consumptive girl of sixteen or seventeen, whose unceasing toil over the needle was killing her day by day. Poor child, if only her cheeks had been fuller and her eyes less haggard, she would have possessed no little beauty; as it was, her suffering face had from the first deeply touched Harold, and, as often as he had occasion to speak to her, he lingered as long as possible, using every excuse to listen longer to her voice, and then pondering miserably for hours over her sad fate. Possibly to Lizzie also there was something strangely sweet in these moments of talk; but who shall say what are the sentiments of creatures whose home is a cellar-kitchen and who live on plain-sewing?

Harold paced the streets for more than an hour, in that dogged, aimless way which had become his habit of late. Walk about London, reader, any part of it, and at any time of the day, and you are sure to notice more than one such figure, the bent shoulders, the drooping head, the worn, careless attire, above all that fixed, hopeless look indicating too clearly a mind warped and spirit crushed in the brutalizing struggle with his fellow men, a struggle compared with which to have fought with beasts at Ephesus were nought. The coarser natures wear long, resist to the end; those of more delicate mould are soon driven to strange extremities, and become familiar with dread ideas from which a healthy mind shrinks in horror. For days past such ideas had haunted Harold. Why should he endure this unceasing torture when an end might so easily be put to it, at once and forever?

It was past noon, but to-day he had not broken his fast, and hunger was making him so faint that his weak frame staggered as he walked. The only means of satisfying it was to return home and ask Mrs. Wilson to reach the half-crown for him; if she had come back most likely the little girl had already told her the story. The coin was literally all he possessed, except the poor clothing which decency compelled him to retain; everything else had gone bit by bit to supply his wants. Indeed it would soon be impossible to leave the house till after nightfall; already one or two business-men to whom he had applied for a situation had openly sneered at his shabby appearance. A few months ago the sneer would have cut him like a knife; as it was, it seemed a mere matter of course. Society prescribes a brutal demeanour towards all who are so inconsiderate as to appear in rags.

On reaching the house, a glance told him that the half-crown had already been taken in. His little friend from next door was no longer playing about, but by dint of peering he could see someone moving in the kitchen. He entered with his latchkey, went down the dark stone steps, and knocked at the kitchen-door. It was opened at once by Mrs. Wilson, who, as well as Lizzie in the background, wore a look of joy which Harold could not but notice, so unwonted was it. He had not long to wait for an explanation, for the mother at once poured out a stream of talk.

"O, Mr. Sansom, sir, and what *do* you think? The queerest

thing I ever know'd, I do declare! Why, here was Lizzie an' me only a quarter of an hour ago cryin' our very heyes out—wasn't we, Lizzie? —'cos we hadn't got nothink like enough to pay the rent,—an' Mrs. Iggs is one as *will* have it, you know, come what may—and we was a wonderin' whatever we should do, seein' as we've hard a thing left we can pledge, an' goodness only knows how we're to find ourselves food through the week, an' Mrs. Iggs wouldn't let the rent run on for a week, no, not if it was ever so!—though I'm sure she's know'd us long enough;—well, as I said, I was just a-goin' to hopen the winder, it was so very 'ot in the room, when what should I see lyin' just out-side but a 'ole 'alf-crownd, upon my word! And I cries out with a little scream like to Lizzie to come an' look, for I really couldn't trust my own heyes, thinkin' it might only be a shinin' like, as I'd been cryin' so; 'Why, Lizzie,' I says, 'If 'ere isn't a 'alf crownd!' 'Why,' says Lizzie, 'someone must a' dropped it, mother!' 'Well,' says I, 'if they has, no doubt they've knocked at the door for it; let's arst Mrs. Iggs.' But no, Mrs. Iggs know'd no more on it than me an' Lizzie, an' if that ain't a cur'ous thing, I don't know! An' to think it should come just when we wanted it so bad as never was! I've bit it, an' knocked it, an' it seems a good 'un; what do *you* say, Mr. Sansom, sir?"

Harold stood throughout this long speech, struggling with him-self. So the little girl from next door had evidently not seen the two when they returned; they had no idea that the coin was his. He took it from the woman and made a pretence of examining it, then gave it back with a remark that it was doubtless good. He could not have held it for longer than a few seconds, yet so many thoughts battled through his mind the while that he seemed to have been standing there for quite a long time. He had surveyed the wretched room, with its little bed stowed away in one dark corner, the table strewn with a few odds and ends of needle-work, the mangle for which there was to-day no employment, the shelves whereon were ranged a few of the humblest articles of household use, and half a loaf of bread,— all the food that remained. He saw all this, and yet he never seemed to move his eyes from Lizzie's face. The draught caused by the open door had given her a fit of coughing; and the mixture of bodily suf-fering with mental relief which her countenance displayed affected him unspeakably. At his entrance she had drawn a little backwards, away from the light of the window, but for all that he had not missed the slight tinge which momentarily rose to her cheek; it was not the first time he had noticed it. Was it possible to claim the money and throw them once again into despair? This half-crown, good reader, which you throw away without a thought on the first whim that strikes you, represented an important sum to all the actors in this very vulgar scene. Harold Sansom knew that he could live on it for a whole week, and to Lizzie and her mother it made all the difference between solvency and the most hopeless distress.

"I am very pleased at your good fortune," Harold said, his mind already made up; then added, with the pleasant smile which looked so strange upon his haggard face, "I came to ask you if you would kindly tell the milkman not to leave my ha'p'orth when he comes this afternoon. I see Mrs. Iggs isn't in, or I wouldn't have given you the trouble."

"O dear, no trouble at all, sir," exclaimed Mrs. Wilson. "You're goin' out this fine day, sir?"

"Yes, I'm going out," returned Harold; then nodded, smiled to Lizzie, and ran up the steps.

About half an hour after the little girl next door returned from a long errand upon which she had been sent by her mother, and the first thing she did was to peep down the grating to see if the half-crown was still there. No, it was gone.

"Has he fetched it?" she called out to Lizzie, who was standing near the window.

"Fetched what, Annie?"

"Has the gen'l'm fetched his 'alf-crownd as he dropped?"

"Half-crownd? Gentleman? What do you mean?"

"Why, the gen'l'm as lives upstairs, to be sure. As he come out, he dropped a 'alf-crownd through your grating, and said as h'd ask you for it when you come back. I see him drop it myself, so you mustn't go to say as 'ow he didn't, 'cos I know better."

Harold Sansom did not return that night. After much discussion between Lizzie and her mother, the half-crown was paid to Mrs. Iggs for rent, it being decided that this was a piece of intentional benevolence on Harold's part, who had adopted this method lest he should offend them. It was agreed, moreover, that the money should only be regarded as a loan; the washing and starching must of course be done for nothing till the amount was made up. Mrs. Wilson was loud in the praise of their benefactor; Lizzie said much less, but went about with a glad light in her eyes which was seldom seen there.

Strange to say, the next day passed, and the next, and still Harold had not returned, nor was anything to be heard of him. But when Sunday came, and just as Lizzie and her mother were sitting down to their dinner,—bread and butter and a cup of tea,—Mrs. Iggs suddenly startled them by running into the kitchen with the weekly newspaper in her hand, uttering all manner of exclamations.

"Well, an' who *would* a' thought it, now! Lord bless *me*! As sure as I'm a livin' woman, if that 'ere poor young feller ain't been an' gone an' drownded hisself! An' there's been a inquest, see if there ain't, an' they couldn't find nothink to hidentify of him, only that he 'ad a old card in his pocket with *Mr. H. Sansom* a-printed on it. Think o' that, now! Eh, God 'elp us, an' he must a' been driven to it by want, they say,—poor-young-feller! An' that's the reason as he never come back, for 'ow could he come, yer know, when he was all the while drownded?"

Whilst the landlady chattered on in this fashion, Lizzie and her mother gazed at each other fixedly, the former pale as death. The poor girl had clasped her hands over her breast, and her eyes were full of tears.

"O, mother," she cried, "how good he was! How kind he was!" and fell upon her mother's neck, sobbing bitterly.

Cain and Abel

No MYSTERY HANGS over the composition of "Cain and Abel." The manuscript bears the inscription "G. R. Gissing / 5 Hanover St. / Islington" in the top right-hand corner of the first of its twelve pages, on which no compositor's marks are to be seen. Gissing signed the story with his middle initial on the last page. He completed it on January 2, 1880, as indicated by a letter of that date to his brother Algernon: "I have tonight finished a horrible story—'Cain and Abel,' the writing of which has made me shiver. It is rather in Poe's style, be it said. It is a tale of two brothers. The elder is christened Abel, after his father; and the younger through a curious circumstance receives the name of Cain. The name haunts him like a Fate, and he ends as the convicted murderer of his brother Abel. Rather horrible this, eh? But I assure you it is dreadfully effective."*

If anyone, apart from review editors, was privileged to read this gruesome tale in Gissing's lifetime, it must have been Eduard Bertz, with whom he was on intimate terms at the time. However modest, Bertz's lodgings offered better conditions for the appreciation of literary efforts than Gissing's rooms. They were at a safe distance from the Regent's Canal, which Gissing saw from his own window—"stagnating in utter foulness between coal wharfs and builders' yards"†—and no serious fear of an interruption by drunken Nell need be entertained there.

* *LMF*, p. 53. The original letter is in the Carl H. Pforzheimer Library.
† *Demos*, chap. 3.

T HE CRUDER SENTENCE of death,—condemned upon purely circumstantial evidence, yet condemned justly. Hitherto, whether actuated by obstinate resentment against a world which has never been my friend, or by overmastering dread of the doom which would follow my conviction, I have resolutely kept my secret, uttering a mechanical "Not Guilty" to the last. But the time for earthly resentment is gone by, and, however it may prove on that morning when I issue from the cell to take my last look at the heavens, I now feel that with my last hope of life has vanished my terror at its extinction. I therefore no longer hesitate to yield to the entreaties of the chaplain that I will unburden my soul by confession. I will write in a few words an account of my crime and the circumstances which led to it.

I cannot disguise from myself that one of the motives prompting me to the determination is a lingering particle of self-respect, a desire to make manifest to those whose eyes have been upon me during the unutterable degradation of my trial, and who will pursue me with their interest even to the end of the dread scene still to be enacted, that I have not always been the wretch I now appear, that I have known generous impulses, have experienced keen and honourable ambition; in short, that it has been owing to some fearful and inexplicable destiny rather than to any innate depravity that I have come to spend the last days of an early and vigorous manhood in a condemned cell. My father was a fairly well-to-do tradesman, and, I have always heard, a man of kindly disposition and some intellectual pretensions; unfortunately he died several months before I was born. I say he was well-to-do, but at his death it appeared that nearly all his capital had been invested in the steadily increasing business, and, in consequence, my mother came into possession of but little more than what was realized by the sale of the stock. On becoming a widow she removed from the northern town where she had hitherto lived to a suburb of the metropolis, taking up her abode in the house of her nearest surviving relative, her husband's brother.

I am by nature somewhat superstitious, and from my earliest recollections events have conspired in an extraordinary degree to foster my susceptibility to morbid terrors, till at length, as I look back upon my short life, I cannot help attaching a gloomy significance to even the most ordinary circumstances; every one of my daily acts, words, thoughts recurs to me in the light of an unmistakable prophecy. In this I know I am not alone; I am only one of a number of wretched men, fatally predestined from the hour of their birth. But whereas others may speak of their evil genius as of an invisible spirit which ever hovers around them and guides them to their ruin, *my* fate was singular, in that the evil spirit assumed a human form, and from the first vented its malignity upon me in look and word and deed. This cursed being was no other than my uncle, he with whom my mother came to live after my father's death. I am well aware that most men will be disposed to regard this as an unreasoning prejudice, the reflection upon another of the evil innate in myself. Let them hear my story.

My uncle's name was Eli Charnock, and at the time of my earliest recollection of him he must have been between forty and fifty years of age. In stature he was short and stunted, in form meagre almost to emaciation, and his head was entirely bald. But, to anyone regarding him for the first time, all other peculiarities of person were lost sight of in the contemplation of his face, which was surely the ugliest wherewith man was ever endowed. Viewed in profile it was rather grotesque than repulsive, but when regarded in full it attained to a scarcely conceivable hideousness, mainly owing to the distortion of the eyes which were fixed in an unvarying squint, and which, even in moments of good humour, wore an expression of devilish malice. Doubtless it was in a great measure due to these natural defects that the man had become a confirmed misanthrope, and this notwithstanding the fact that he had from youth upwards prospered marvellously in all his dealings. Up to his fortieth year he had pursued the business of a stock-broker, retiring at length with a considerable fortune, and entering upon a life seemingly devoid of amusement or occupation, but evidently congenial to his temperament. Of his habits I shall presently have to say more; as for his character, I cannot do better than proceed at once to illustrate it by an account of the first occasion on which his influence was exerted upon my life,—the first, and, as I have always thought, the direst instance of his malevolence towards me. For the knowledge of the circumstances I was indebted to my mother, who related them to me upon her deathbed.

The difference in every respect between my father and his

brother Eli was too great ever to permit of any familiar intercourse, even had there not been a special cause of enmity on the latter's side. This was the circumstance of my uncle having been disinherited by his father, who left all his little property to his better disposed son. Once, and once only, did Eli show an apparent desire to heal the breach between himself and his brother, and this happened on the occasion of the birth of the latter's first child, my elder brother. It chanced that at that very time Eli Charnock passed through the town where my parents lived, and, quite contrary to his habits, entered my father's shop to pay a visit. On being shown the new-born infant, he seemed overcome by a sudden impulse of most unwonted tenderness, and stood for some moments regarding it in silence, and with a peculiar benevolence depicted on his generally hateful countenance. All at once he asked whether a name had been chosen for the child, and he was informed that it was to bear its father's name— Abel. Again he was silent, and then, to the surprise of both my parents, begged that it might receive his own name instead, that it might be christened Eli. My father looked questioningly at my mother, and seeing that the proposal was far from agreeable to her, he replied that he feared it was too late to change, that his wife had long since decided to call her child Abel, if it proved a boy, and that it must be hardly just to disappoint her now; then, seeing his brother's countenance darken, he smiled and promised that if he should ever have a second son, Eli should be his name. "This, or none," returned my uncle sharply; and, on my father remonstrating with him for his unreasonableness, he suddenly took up his hat and left the house without a word. Nor did he ever again hold the slightest communication with our family whilst my father lived.

Under these circumstances, it was no agreeable surprise when, on the day of her husband's funeral, my mother saw Eli Charnock enter the room, his features wearing a suppressed grin of satisfaction. He scarcely spoke, but at once took up his residence in the house, and, as my father had unfortunately died intestate, he obtained authority to settle the affairs, with the result which I have already indicated. My poor mother, naturally of a weak and timorous disposition, and at present suffering from the prostration of excessive grief, could offer no objection to any of his proceedings; and at length, despite the disgust and fear with which his presence affected her, and doubtless dreading above all things the being left to struggle for a livelihood in her helpless state, even accepted my uncle's offer of a home in his own house. It is not difficult to account for this apparent benevolence on the part of one whose greatest joy was in evil. Much of Eli Charnock's misanthropy was due to the unconquerable repugnance with which all men regarded him, repugnance which he mistook for settled hatred, and which he accordingly repaid in kind. Though rich, he was not satisfied with his position, longing above all things for authority and an influence from which the relations between himself and the rest of mankind naturally excluded him. In the position of my mother he now saw an opportunity for the prolonged gratification of this desire; she would be a slave at his beck and call, and the prospect of ruling her and superintending the growth of her child he found more pleasing than even that of leaving them to struggle with the hardships of a miserable poverty.

But yet another triumph was in store for him. A very few months after my mother's removal to London she gave birth to her posthumous child. Even this short space of time had sufficed to render the poor woman subject in everything to her so-called benefactor, and even in the choice of a name for her infant she could not venture a thought without previously consulting Eli Charnock. The latter came to her bedside a day or two after my birth, and stood regarding me as I lay asleep with a curious expression of countenance, an expression very different from that with which he had formerly regarded my brother Abel.

"Well, and what name shall the brat answer to?" he asked, with a kind of chuckle.

"You—you would like it to be called"—began my mother timidly; when Eli suddenly interrupted her.

"No, I shouldn't," he said, in his sharp, snarling tone, anticipating her thought. "Let me see," he continued, reflecting. "We've got an Abel; why shouldn't we have a Cain?—Ha, ha!—A good idea!—Yes, yes; Cain it shall be. Cain Charnock. Sounds well, don't it?"

My mother could not utter a word, but closed her eyes and lay back on the pillow, overcome with faintness. Without another word my uncle left the room, chuckling to himself, and muttering, "Cain

Charnock.—Ha, ha!—Cain and Abel, Cain and Abel!" Left to her-self, my poor mother gave way to an agony of tears. The thought of having her child christened Cain, the name of him who, by the murder of his brother, was the first to bring death into the world, upon whose guilty forehead God in anger had stamped an eternal curse,—such a thought was unspeakably dreadful to her. To an extremely devout mind, and one painfully endowed with every variety of feminine weakness, such a proceeding could not but seem a direct tempting of Providence, nay, an absolute defiance of the Almighty's judgment. But, alas! she was powerless to resist. In vain she hoped for a few days that my uncle had but spoken in jest. On the day of the christening he stood as godfather to me, and I received the name of Cain.

I come to the period of my own recollections. My uncle's house was a large one, and much larger than befitted his needs; for he had never been married and was never known to entertain a friend. It was, moreover, furnished from garret to basement in a style of extravagant splendour. Though he himself habitually made use of only one small chamber, which was at once bed- and sitting-room, all the other apartments were nevertheless always kept as if in momen-tary readiness to receive distinguished guests, even the beds being made daily, and, throughout the winter, fires being kept burning in every grate. It was my uncle's daily practice to survey the entire mansion, walking alone through every room, and, I suppose, deriving a species of pleasure from the contemplation of the rich furniture. Pictures there were none, for he took no pleasure in any work of art; but adornments such as vast mirrors, massive and glistening chan-deliers, curtains and carpets of the richest tenture were every-where heaped together; it was in the contemplation of these solid evi-dences of wealth that their master found his delight. The place filled by my mother in this strange abode was that of half housekeeper, half general servant. Besides herself there were two female domestics, and my uncle frequently set himself the task of superintending the work of all the women down to the minutiae of household employments, always treating them as slaves rather than mere menials, and exact-ing from them the most abject servility. As for myself, my earliest recollections are of the most painful description. I well remember that, as often as the master approached the room in which we generally lived, it was my mother's practice to hide me away wherever she could, that I might not fall under my uncle's eyes. For against me he always entertained a special hatred, a hatred which in the commencement could only be explained from his natural malevolence, though, later on, special causes which I came well to understand served to strengthen his aversion. Sometimes when my mother had thus hidden me, he would look round the room, and enquire where I was. In fear and trembling my poor mother called to me to come forth; and then, after receiving a brutal stroke with a cane which the wretch always carried, and which, in his threats, he always referred to as "my namesake," I was set about some menial task quite beyond my strength, my failure to execute which always resulted in more blows.

With my brother things were different. Abel was some year and a half older than myself, and in all things presented a complete contrast to me. In what I am about to say it must not be thought that there enters any feeling of vanity; I tell the plain facts and they are necessary for the comprehension of my strange story. Whereas I was from a child singularly handsome in face, gentle in manners, and of a quick intellect, Abel was ugly, even hateful, in his outward appearance, and in disposition as evil as a child can be. Curiously enough, these unamiable characteristics found a strong recommendation in my uncle's sight; and, in proportion as cruelty, malice and deceitfulness developed themselves in his behaviour year by year, just so did he become more and more a favourite with Eli Charnock, till at length the latter appeared to entertain an absolute passion for his repulsive nephew. The very fact that the fondness was in no way returned even seemed to augment it, and the only occasions on which I saw my uncle manifest keen delight were those when my brother had practised some exceptionally impish trick, or given utterance to some prematurely evil thought. When everyone else in the house cowered before the master's glance, Abel was not only familiar with him, but even went so far as to make him the object of his tricks and the butt of his jokes. Of the peculiar relationship there could be but one explanation. Of all the beings my uncle saw around him Abel showed a marked likeness to himself, both in body and mind. I soon discovered that my personal graces were the object of his vigorous hatred, and I am persuaded that it was the fear of consequences alone which withheld him from mutilating my features and so removing a cause of excessive provocation.

It is by no means my intention to enter into detail in this brief account of my life; after having devoted too much time to the description of my early years, I must pass quickly on to the narration of those few striking incidents which mark my career. My uncle having taken such a liking for Abel, sent him at an early age to a good school and watched with pleasure his progress in study. For my part, though conscious of the activity of my mind and longing for nothing more than an opportunity of learning, I not only received no encouragement to improve myself, but was even threatened with severe punishment if I ever thought of such a thing: my life, I was told, was to be that of a menial, and what had such a one to do with learning? The rebuke was administered on an occasion when, my mother having yielded to my earnest entreaties that she would teach me to read and write, we were surprised by my uncle in the course of a lesson. The result was a severe beating. As I left the room, smarting with pain, I encountered my brother in the passage, and learned from a taunt he threw at me that it was he who had betrayed us. In my nature there was much of strong passion; on this occasion it for the first time broke out in violence. Unable to endure both the injury and the insult with which it was followed up, and maddened all at once by what appeared to be the accumulated sense of manifold injustices, I sprang fiercely upon my tormentor and beat him to the ground. A strong hand seized me and dragged me away, whilst at the same moment I heard my mother's voice calling in agony to me— "Cain! Cain!" I struggled violently to get free, whilst blind with passion, I shrieked again and again, "I'll kill you, Abel! I'll kill you!"

It was my uncle whose hand held me, but, instead of beating me again, as I anticipated, he flung me away from him with an expression of mingled rage and terror on his hideous face which it is beyond my power to describe.

"Take him away!" he cried to my mother. "Take him away, you she-devil; unless you wish me to stamp his young brains out!"

I believe this was the first time that I was led to reflect seriously upon the name I bore, a consequence, in all probability, of hearing my mother call me by it. For the poor woman had perhaps never before thus addressed me, it being her custom to call me simply "dear"; whereas my uncle never lost an opportunity of reminding me that I was the namesake of the first murderer. As soon as I found myself once more alone, I sat down in the gathering darkness of a winter evening, and pondered long upon the subject. Almost absolutely ignorant as I was of all that children generally know, I had yet heard the biblical story of Cain and Abel, not from my mother, who confined what little religious teaching she found an opportunity of giving me to outlines of the New Testament, but from some of the servants, who once told it me, doubtless out of pure good nature, and bade me benefit by the lesson it conveyed. In my ignorance, however, of the rest of the Bible story, I had paid but little attention to the coincidence, and it was only now, as I reflected upon the terrible threat which I had involuntarily uttered, that I first asked myself how I came to be so called. I was just at the end of my tenth year, and though my mode of life had kept me all but completely sundered from the outward world, the reflective tendency of my mind had begun to exert itself in endeavours to understand the reasons of my wretched existence, to account for the extraordinary relations existing between ourselves and Eli Charnock. The same night I sought my mother privately and begged her to tell me why I was called Cain and my brother Abel. She turned pale and looked terrified at my question, then begged me in a whisper, whilst tears ran down her face, never to think of the subject. This, of course, had the effect of making me think all the more. My young heart throbbed with horror as I recalled the violence of passion which had that day possessed me, and reflected the possibility of my being some day led to justify my name. From that moment the idea haunted me. As I grew up I do not think a day passed without my dwelling in thought upon the subject of murder, realizing to myself with dreadful intensity the feelings of a murderer, calculating whether it would be possible for me to commit such a deed, and on the fate which would overtake me in case I did. In the moments of such horrible reflection I have often felt on the verge of madness. Who can say that, at *one* subsequent moment of my life, I was not actually mad?

From that day, too, I noticed a peculiar change in my uncle's behaviour towards me. He began to keep me as much as possible out of his sight; his glances at me whenever we met had in them that peculiar look of terror which I had first noticed when I threatened to kill my brother, and at the same time he took to keeping Abel always with him in his own room. I remember that I had scarcely seen my brother for several months when one day he passed me in the hall whilst I was on my knees doing some menial work, and, as he passed, struck me. Involuntarily, I started to my feet, when he, who seemed to grow more cowardly as he grew older, ran off with a great scream of fright in the direction of his protector's room. This incident was doubtless the cause of my being almost immediately after sent out day after day to work for my living. Out of the few shillings which I earned every week I was made to procure all my food, but was permitted to sleep in an unused stable at the back of the house. This privilege, however, ceased on my reaching my fifteenth year, when I was suddenly bidden to find a home for myself, and threatened with fearful penalties if ever I came near the house, or held any communication with its inmates. Notwithstanding these orders, I ventured into the house at least two or three times a week, for the purpose of secretly seeing my mother, for whom I nourished an increasing love as time went on, pitying profoundly her sad position, though I was utterly unable to do anything to lighten her sufferings. These visits continued, without being discovered, for nearly two years. At length, when sneaking into the house late one night, I was told by the servant who on these occasions always befriended me, that my mother had suddenly been taken very ill, and was in bed. I rushed to her room and found her all but speechless. Had a doctor been called in? I was answered in the negative; whereupon, thinking of nothing but my mother's danger, I flew to my uncle's room and burst into it. My uncle was sitting there with Abel, and, on seeing me, both rose with terrified countenances, the former shrieking out—"A murderer! A murderer!"

"You yourself are a murderer!" I cried in reply. "Send at once for a doctor to see my mother, or I will call in a policeman and charge you with causing her death."

They exchanged a few words in whispers, and then Abel left

the room. In his absence, which lasted some quarter of an hour, I never ceased to overwhelm my uncle with violent reproaches. I observed that he seemed much older and feebler than when I last saw him, and his body trembled. He did not speak a word, but the ever-changing expressions of his countenance could only be compared to those of a fiend in torment. I had grown tall and strong during the last two years, and I doubt whether he would have been a match for me. At length my brother returned with a physician, who at once declared that my mother could not live more than a few hours. I kept by her bedside to the end, and during that brief period she gathered strength enough to relate to me all that which I have given as prior to my own recollections. Then she died. I sought my uncle once more, but he was not to be found; neither was my brother. So I departed from the house, vowing in my desperation that I would one day be revenged upon him who had been the curse of my own and my mother's life.

If it be possible to call happy my portion of a life beginning and ending like mine, I may perhaps say that the six years that followed my mother's death were the happiest I have known. By the exertion of a naturally strong will, I succeeded in gradually attaining at least an average degree of mental cultivation, first of all learning to read, write, and cipher at a cheap night-school, and then occupying all my leisure moments in assiduous reading. The motives urging me to this unusual activity were not, I am bound to confess, wholly pure; for among them was the hope that I might thus be preparing myself to inflict revenge upon my uncle. One would have thought that I should have contemplated punishment for my brother likewise; but of him, of Abel, I did not dare to think. If ever he occurred to my mind, it was in connection with the terrible fears which never ceased to haunt me. I had got rid as soon as possible of my hideous Christian name, calling myself Charles, and, for my surname, I had substituted the name of Hope. In worldly prospects I never ceased to improve, rising with remarkable rapidity from mere manual work to the position of clerk in a City warehouse. In this respect my career has been exemplary, and I may safely point to it to prove how much can be done by resolute hard work. I will grant that I had one circumstance always in my favour,—my personal appearance, which seemed almost immediately to inspire confidence in all with whom I dealt. Many men doubtless envied my handsome face; God knows they had little cause!

Shortly after my twenty-second birthday I took lodgings in a small house in the west of London with a family of the name of Earle. There were father, mother and one daughter; the last a lovely girl of eighteen, her name Winifred. The parents were not pleasant people, their most marked characteristic being avarice; so that I had not been long in the house before I became aware that they were eagerly waiting for the death of a wealthy relative to whose property they had hopes of succeeding. Despite their poverty they were haughty and domineering, and from the first treated me, whose monthly payment they were nevertheless very glad to receive, in a manner which was scarcely tolerable. Indeed I could not have long endured to reside in the house, but for one thing; before I had been there a fortnight I conceived an overpowering passion for Winifred Earle. It is needless for me to depict the course of my love, even if I could bear to summon up at such a moment as this those past hours of almost delirious joy. How I came to be so blest I cannot say; enough that in the end Winifred returned my passion with a fervour scarcely inferior to my own. How did I now curse the tyrant of my early years who had denied me education and thus barred against me those roads to position and happiness upon which my natural abilities would surely have guided me! But Winifred loved me purely for myself, and if I needed any proof that my nature is not wholly bad it would be sufficient to remember that I won the affection of so pure and noble a being. Pure and noble she was, but weak, weak, with a woman's weakness. Oh, Winifred! On you it depended whether I should become a happy man or the doomed wretch I now am! Why did your strength fail in the trial?

Fool that I am! Poor Winifred had no voice in my fate; she did, and could but fulfil the decrees of a cursed destiny. I must hurry to the end of my story, for I have scarcely strength to pen the wretched words. Before long our mutual love became known to the parents, and the natural result followed; I was immediately driven from the house with scorn and insult. But to part thus would have been death alike for myself and Winifred. Despite all impediments we corresponded frequently, and even saw each other once or twice. Some months passed, and I suddenly heard that the expectation of the family had been fulfilled; their wealthy relative was dead, and they had become his heirs. They removed to a fashionable quarter, after which, despite all my efforts, I could not even hear from Winifred. In my despair I thought bitterly of her, feeling sure that the change in her circumstances had proved too much for her fidelity. Nearly half a year passed, and at length, by a desperate effort, I succeeded in obtaining a brief interview. With every sign of anguish she told me that our correspondence had been discovered, that she had been obliged to yield to her parents' severity, most of all, that she had been forced into an engagement with a rich young man, whose character and person were alike hateful to her. The news well-nigh drove me mad. After frenzied appeals, to which she could only reply that she durst not disobey her parents, I broke away in the bitterest anger, invoking upon her the curse of a ruined man.

For a long time I neither saw nor heard of her. My life had all at once changed from that of an ardent striver after worldly success to that of a reckless debauchee. I lost several situations one after another in consequence of my dissipation, but still I went on; in drunkenness and mad revelry was my only oblivion, and oblivion I sought incessantly. One day I met by chance a man-servant whom I knew to be in the Earles' house, and him I eagerly questioned. First of all I asked if Winifred was married, and I heard that she was. Who was her husband? The man replied that it was a very wealthy, but alas a very dissipated young man, by name Mr. Abel Charnock. I staggered back as if he had struck me a blow; but, immediately recovering myself, I urged further questions, the replies to which left me no doubt that Winifred's husband was my own worthless brother, whom I had entirely lost sight of since my mother's death. A cold sweat broke out over all my limbs, and I became deadly faint. How was it that at that moment I heard distinctly my dead mother's voice calling to me, "Cain! Cain!" as she had done on the day when I struck Abel to the ground?

Urged by some demon, I never rested till I had once again resumed my communication with Winifred; the ruin of my own soul was not sufficient, I must even drag another with me to eternal perdition. Let the details be forever hid, and suffice to say that the interrupted passion soon became on both sides more violent than ever, till at length I demanded and received the sacrifice of Winifred's honour. Our opportunities of meeting were ample, for my brother, whom I had not yet seen, was often absent for days and weeks. Whenever he was at home he treated his wife, whom he had married merely for her money, with the brutality which might have been expected from his infamous character. As for my uncle, a righteous retribution had already overtaken him. Winifred (who never knew my real name,) told me that Abel openly boasted of having by degrees gained the mastery over the old man, till at length, by some exercise of extraordinary craft, he had obtained for his own use the whole of his uncle's property. Shortly before the marriage, the old man, already much shattered in mind and body, had been crushed by a paralytic stroke, and was even now lingering out the remnant of his miserable life in squalid lodgings, tended by a hireling in Abel's pay.

I come to the end. Despite, nay, perhaps in consequence of, my guilty triumph, I still continued my habits of debauchery, and was conscious of a rapid deterioration in my health, amounting at length to a slight attack of delirium. When scarcely recovered from this, I rose from my bed and hastened to Winifred. So accustomed had I become to visiting her thus that I neglected all precaution. When I burst impatiently into her chamber, she flew to meet me with horror upon her countenance, and whispered that her husband was at that moment in an adjoining room. Scarcely had she time to conceal me in a closet, when the door opened, and I heard a man's step enter.

"Who was that who just came into your room?" was asked, and I at once knew that the brutal tones could proceed from none but my brother Abel. I trembled, and fell to my knees through faintness.

Winifred replied in a trembling voice that no one had entered.

"It's a lie!" retorted the other, and, as he spoke, he struck her violently on the face. Fierce wrath had suddenly succeeded to my weakness; the blood boiled along my veins. I heard the blow, I heard the poor girl's scream, and the second after I was kneeling upon my brother Abel's breast, squeezing his throat madly, madly with both my hands. Aye, in that moment I was raving mad, and in my ears I heard a sound as though myriads of devils were shrieking "Cain! Cain!" At length I loosed my hold; my brother did not stir. I shook him; he showed no sign of life. Uttering a terrible yell, I rushed from the room and from the house.

The same night Winifred drowned herself, and within a week I was in prison.

The Quarry on the Heath[1]

THE DATE OF this short story is noted by Gissing on the first page of the manuscript as 1881, but the exact month of composition remains uncertain. Apart from his private tuition, he occupied the year in half-hearted attempts to write a novel and in preparing his quarterly articles for *Vyestnik Evropy*. There is no allusion to any piece of short fiction projected or in progress in his letters, but by mid-March, 1882, he had finished a small book entitled *Watching the Storm Clouds,* and it is not unreasonable to think that "The Quarry on the Heath" was written slightly earlier, that is, in the autumn of 1881, after he had lost faith in his previous novel, *Heirs of Poverty*. As the description of the quarry recurs in a subsequent novel mainly situated in Wakefield—*A Life's Morning* (written in 1885, published in 1888)—the setting of his short story may have been suggested to him during his stay in his native town some time after August 20, 1881.

In a letter to Walter T. Spencer, dated September 17, 1926, Algernon Gissing describes "The Quarry on the Heath" as "a MS fragment of a novel which was eventually abandoned."* This is obviously not the case. In all likelihood, Algernon did not read the entire manuscript, for it forms a self-contained, well-rounded whole. He may have been misled by the existence of a rough draft and a partial fair copy, which at first glance look like an attempt at a novel. If a further proof were needed, it lies in the fact that the tale is not divided into chapters.

This document is exceptional in that it is the only instance, to the best of my knowledge, of the preservation of two handwritten versions of a Gissing text. The first draft contains considerable cancellations and additions, testifying to Gissing's serious difficulties with his story and explaining his final decision to abandon the fair copy after transcribing about one-quarter of its twenty-five pages.

The text printed here incorporates the author's last correction. The first draft, if any, is given in a footnote. When there was a second draft prior to the last canceled version, it is recorded in square brackets in the note.

* Gissing Collection, Carl H. Pforzheimer Library, New York City.
[1] "Visited upon the Children" ["Fate"].

REARIER COUNTRY than that around the village of Wastell Heath it would not be easy to discover in England. Flat, woodless, unwatered save by muddy little becks, such features in it as owe their origin to the hand of man only aid to render it uglier and more depressing. The scanty-hedged fields produce cheerless crops, such as turnips and potatoes; the roads run on with monotonous directness, always the same view on either hand; not even a prospect of far-off hills or woods is present for the eye's relief. The village itself consists of perhaps two hundred cottages spread over an area of several square miles; the nucleus being represented by one long hideous row of two-storied dwellings, each with its little patch of would-be garden in front, the various tenements distinguishable by the large number painted in white upon each door. This is Pit Row, a name explained by the proximity of a colliery; the great wheels, the out-houses, and the one tall chimney standing out with painful prominence. Everything around is grimy from the perpetual falling of fine coal-dust. Break a stick out of the stunted hedge and your fingers are sooted; walk about the deserted roads for an hour, and you are uncomfortable with a sense of dirtiness from head to heel. The children playing before the houses of Pit Row are the wretchedest and filthiest little creatures imaginable. The very church, visible a field's length away, is a choice example of modern tastelessness, built of plain stone, with small Gothic windows and a stumpy tower, and standing in the middle of a burial ground full of square head-stones, all black with coal-dust. And hard by it is the parsonage, a low brick house with a tall stack of irregular chimney-pots, not even a garden enclosing its desolation.[2]

[2] (Drearier country . . . desolation). The Rev. Hilton Lashmore was returning towards the close of a winter's afternoon from the death-bed of a remote parishioner. Wastell Heath is a straggling village consisting of perhaps two hundred cottages spread over an area of five square miles, the nucleus being represented by one long, hideous row of two-storied dwellings, each with its little patch of would-be garden in front, the various tenements at first sight distinguishable only by the large number painted in white upon each door. This is called [This was] Pit Row, a name explained by the proximity of a colliery; the great wheels, the out-houses and the one tall chimney standing prominently on a slight elevation, the only one which breaks the dreary flatness for miles around. Everything in the neighbourhood is grimy from the perpetual falling of fine coal-dust; break a stick

Towards this abode the Rev. Edgar Lashmore was making the best of his way at the close of a winter's evening,[3] returning from the death-bed of a remote parishioner. The day had been throughout gloomy, and at present the darkening sky with its one short rift of pale red in the west, the low piping of the wind through the ragged bushes,[4] the absence of any sound from living creature save the dull splash of the walker's footfall on the muddy ground, seemed to harmonize well with the state of Mr. Lashmore's mind. He was a tall, angular man,[5] and walked with his head bent forward; his face was hard and irregular,[6] considerably wrinkled, and with a stern, even repulsive, expression. The nose was long and narrow,[7] the cold, suspicious eyes were set unusually near to each other,[8] and the lower portion of his face, completely shaven, had something intensely animal in its formation. His age was probably not more than five and forty, but his hair was very thin and of iron grey.[9] Perhaps it was the impression of the scene he had just left which gave his face such a fixed look of gloomy brooding. His thin lips kept always tightly clasped, and from time to time their corners twitched downwards with a result not at all favourable to his physiognomy.[10] As he walked,

---

out of the stunted hedge and your fingers were sooted, walk about the deserted roads for an hour and your spirits are crushed beneath a sense of personal hopeless dirtiness from head to heel. Nowhere in England could you find surroundings more unlovely. The very church, visible a field's length behind Pit Row, is the ugliest conceivable building of plain stone, with small Gothic windows and a stumpy tower, standing in the middle of a burial ground full of upright head-stones, all black with grime, whilst hard by it stands the parsonage, a low brick house with a prominent stack of irregular chimney-pots, not even a garden enclosing its naked hideousness.

[3] Towards this latter abode the Rev. Benjamin Lashmore was making the best of his way towards the close of a winter's evening.

[4] the ragged bushes on either side of the road.

[5] He was a tall, rather spare man.

[6] hard, irregular in outline.

[7] The nose was long and thin.

[8] the cold suspicious eyes seemed set unnaturally near each other.

[9] His age might be fifty, and the thin hair at the back of his head was an iron grey.

[10] not all favourable to the reverend gentleman's facial expression. In fact Mr. Lashmore was such a figure as one would have gladly lost sight of after meeting him.

he held his umbrella with both hands transversely behind his back, and occasionally bent it with a sudden exertion of force which timed with the fiercer compression of his lips.[11]

His nearest path at length took him off the main road, and across a tract of ploughed fields, where the way was scarcely marked;[12] he trudged steadily on in complete indifference to the clogging mud which soon plastered his black trousers. When arrived about a quarter of a mile from home, the fields ceased, and he had to traverse a small heath, that which gave its name to the village. In the middle of the heath was a small stone-quarry, long since abandoned, and the hollow at the foot of the rugged wall of rock now converted into a species of dismal swamp, one or two black pools marking themselves out among the foul mud-shallows, their surface at times sluggishly stirred by the wind.[13] On the edge of this quarry stood a rude shed, built of rough-hewn stones, the roof of planks half crumbled away, and the single aperture, on the quarry side, much widened by dilapidation; probably it had been put up for the use of workmen when such were needed there. The clergyman's path brought him close by this shed, and indeed he had just passed it, when he all at once stopped abruptly[14] and turned his head. A voice from within the walls had distinctly reached his ear; as he listened, the voice was again audible. The circumstance seemed to excite his curiosity; he turned,[15] walked with some caution round the corner of the building, and stood in the doorway.

It was still light enough to discern clearly the whole of the interior, and the sight which met Mr. Lashmore's eyes was strange enough, and scarcely one for which he could have been prepared. A

---

[11] compression of his lips. Let us hope Mr. Lashmore was not dwelling upon images of a future world!

[12] His nearest path took him at length off the road [the carriage road], and along the side of a large ploughed field, where the pathway was scarcely marked.

[13] (When arrived . . . by the wind). When at length about a quarter of a mile from home, the fields changed, and he had to pass over a kind of heath in the middle of which was a small stone-quarry long since deserted and itself converted into a species of dismal swamp, with surrounding growths.

[14] he suddenly stopped abruptly.

[15] the voice was again audible. He turned.

young man and a girl stood locked in each other's arms, apparently
in the act of saying farewell, and so wrapt in their emotions that not
until the clergyman had actually entered the hut did they perceive
his presence. Then indeed they started asunder, the girl uttering a
low cry, and for fully a minute all stood motionless.[16] The lovers were
pale as death, the girl holding her hand pressed upon her heart, and
not daring to raise her eyes, the young man, after the first shock,
standing in resolute firmness, his hands clenched at his sides, looking
full into the intruder's face. He was tall and nervously made, with
features far from regular in outline, but open and nobly eloquent,
the dark eyes full of passionate fire. She beside him was very young
and of slight, childish figure. Her countenance showed clearly the
struggle between bodily weakness and spiritual energy, the plaintive,
tremulous lips[17] contrasting with the vivid exaltation which glorified
her eyes and brow. After a moment,[18] she drew a little nearer to her
companion, and silently joined her hand with his.

Mr. Lashmore's eyes fell before the youth's gaze, and he
breathed quickly, the wrinkles of his dark forehead deepening into
fearful lines. He made a quick gesture,[19] as though he would violently
sever their linked hands.

"What does this mean?" he rather muttered than exclaimed, try-

[16] (A young man . . . motionless). A young man and a girl stood locked in
each other's arms, apparently in the act of saying farewell, and so absorbed in each
other's presence that not until the clergyman had actually entered the hut did they
perceive his presence. Then indeed they started asunder, the girl uttering a low
exclamation [a low startled cry], and for fully a minute all stood motionless. The
lovers were an admirably matched pair; the youth tall, nervously built, and with a
dark face full of passionate character, the girl of graceful, lithe mould, not strik-
ingly handsome in feature, but showing a countenance wherein touching and almost
childish sweetness was strongly blended with a lofty firmness. If his eyes spoke
enthusiastic passion [fire] out of depths of wonderful meaning, hers glowed with
unimaginable devotion, now mingled with something like a resolute despair. They
still held each other by the hand, but did not exchange a glance. The youth perhaps scarcely a man in years . . .

[17] She beside him seemed very young and of frail figure, but her countenance
showed a curious mingling of feebleness and clearly the struggle between bodily
weakness and spiritual force, the sweet tremulous lips.

[18] When the first shock passed over.

[19] a quick gesture with one hand.

ing to meet the young man's burning eyes. "What right have you to behave like this? What does it mean?"

He was not fully master of his words, and seemed overcome by some strange emotion which made his tones low and hoarse.

"We love each other, sir,"[20] replied the youth, with clear, manly utterance.[21] "I had no intention of keeping[22] this from you. I should have asked to see you this evening, and have told you our story."

"That is now needless, and I forbid you to approach my house. Do you understand me? I forbid you to come near, to even think of seeing my daughter again. It is impossible, forever impossible![23] You need ask for no reasons; I have none for you but my will. Leave this place, it will be better for you!—Come with me," he added, turning to the girl. "Drop his hand, and come with me!"

The pale lips were calm now, and her eyes as she fixed them upon her lover showed that the strong soul[24] had overcome.

"If I leave him it is only for to-night," she said. "You have no power to part us."

It was darkening in the hut, and the cold, rain-presaging wind from the heath[25] whistled through the crevices drearily; a piece of stone or earth loosened itself from the edge of the quarry, and fell with a hollow splash down into the black pool. For a moment the clergyman held his head down, then, with a sudden effort violently sundered their hands and forced the girl before him out into the open air.[26]

"Come! I command you, come!—And you, follow at your peril!"

There was no resisting his merciless grasp, and the poor child was forced onward at an exhausting speed towards a little gleam of light

---

[20] "It means that we love each other, sir."
[21] intonation.
[22] no intention to keep.
[23] It is impossible.
[24] her strong soul.
[25] the flat fields.
[26] (drearily . . . open air) drearily. The clergyman bent his head for a moment to hide his anguish, then with a sudden effort violently sundered their hands, and forced the girl out into the open air before him.

in the distance[27] which marked the position of the parsonage. Her father spoke no word, and met with no remonstrance. In a few minutes they had reached home.[28]

"Wherever have you been, Bertha!" exclaimed a timid woman's voice when the door opened to them. "And father with you? Why, how foolish of me. It never occurred to me that you had gone to meet father."

"Bertha, go into my room," said the clergyman, briefly, as he closed the door. "Don't stop to take your things off."[29]

Mrs. Lashmore was standing in the doorway of the lighted[30] sitting-room, waiting to usher in her husband and daughter. At the first sound of the former's voice she looked with painful apprehension at him, and now clasped her hands together upon her breast,[31] a picture of wondering anguish. She was a short, frail woman, still somewhat pretty in face, but much marked with care.[32] Her utterance and motions betokened extreme nervousness; at present she was trembling like a leaf, and her clear, simple eyes were full of tears. But she did not venture to speak, and could make no kind of reply to the look[33] of reassurance which Bertha turned to her in entering the study.

Mr. Lashmore turned the key sharply in the door, and began to pace the little room.[34] Bertha stood by the table, on which she rested her hands; once or twice he looked askance at her with lowering eyes.

---

[27] the poor child was forced onwards at an exhausting speed towards the cluster of lights which showed the windows of Pit Row in the distance.

[28] *After this paragraph, the following passage has been omitted from the last version*:

"Is there a fire in my room mother?" ["Is there a fire in my room?"] asked the clergyman briefly, as he closed the door behind him.

"Oh yes, dear; a beautiful one. I told Jane to light it an hour ago, so that it might be well burnt up for you."

[29] "Bertha, go in now. Don't stop to take your things off."

[30] cheerfully lighted.

[31] At the first words the clergyman spoke she had looked with painful apprehension into his face, and now she stood with her hands clasped together upon her breast.

[32] but marked with premature care.

[33] the loving look.

[34] to pace the little room with nervous steps.

There was clearly but little mutual understanding between these two; the parent manifested towards the child an uneasy suspiciousness quite apart from his special thoughts;[35] one would have said he could not bear the pure directness of her look, and felt rebuked by the lofty spirit which was native to her. She, on her side, was cold in his presence, seemed constantly making a vain effort to regard him as a parent, and displayed before his dark look[36] that physical feebleness which she inherited from her mother, and which cost her acute agonies. To-night she was wrought to a high and resolute mood, yet his first words sufficed to make her tremble.

"Can I suppose in you any filial obedience, any sense of religion?"

"I don't know how to answer," she said, grasping the table convulsively. "I cannot trust myself. I must beg you to deal kindly with me,—forbearingly,—with understanding."

"That is no reply to my question. I am at no loss to understand your passion, and I would not willingly be harsh. But there are occasions when[37] a parent cannot reason with his child, when he must demand simple obedience. Are you prepared to promise this?"

"What obedience would you exact?"

"I have told you. From this moment you must renounce this strangely sudden and secret attachment. You must undertake never to exchange another word with that young man."[38]

"You cannot refuse to give me a valid reason. You lay your command on me in a matter in which I cannot control myself, unaided by reason. *Why* must I do this?"

For a moment he looked at her with a face in which wild appeal strove with anger and pride.[39] He seemed on the point of making a passionate entreaty, but his tongue could not utter such words.

"Reason I cannot and will not give you!" he cried, smiting his

[35] mutual understanding between parent and child; the former showed an uneasy suspiciousness quite apart from his present feeling.

[36] his spoken word [his harsh voice].

[37] on which.

[38] another word with—with that young man."
"I cannot. You ask what I cannot promise!"
The word came half choked with a sob, but . . .

[39] angered will [angered pride].

hands together, whilst great beads of sweat stood out on his fore-head. "You must do this because I bid you: that is enough!"

She still held by the table, and trembled.[40] Her large eyes looked wildly out from the death-like face. But, brought to this juncture, her will was as strong as his.

"Then you deal unjustly[41] with me!" she exclaimed, though in a voice which seemed calm after his. "I am no longer a child;[42] at this moment you have no right of arbitrary power to will away my reason or my life.[43] I *cannot* promise to obey you, with no cause given!"[44]

The frightful passion of her father's face[45] made her shrink to-gether in a momentary fear that his upraised hand would strike her.

"Then go,—go to your room! At least in that you shall obey."

He flung the door open, and she fled before him, fled up the nar-row staircase and into the remotest corner of her bedroom, possessed with a fit of terror. Her father strode after her, and locked her in.[46]

Returning slowly to his study he found himself face to face with his wife, who clung about him in agonized weeping.

"For the love of God, Edgar, what has happened?" cried the poor woman, half hysterically. "What has the child done,—oh, tell me what she has done!"

"I can[47] give no explanation; none is necessary. Mind,—you do not speak to her again till I give you permission. Her meals will be sent to her room. Leave me."

Years of trembling obedience had rendered remonstrance im-possible to the simple and soft hearted creature. She crept away, and the study door was locked behind her.

It was about a fortnight before this that the parsonage at Wastell Heath had one afternoon received an unknown visitor, a young man who said he had travelled hither from the south of England for the

[40] She still held by the table, as if to keep herself from fainting.
[41] wrongly.
[42] I am not a child.
[43] to will away my life.
[44] I cannot promise to obey you, with no reason given.
[45] the frightful passion of his face.
[46] *Here the fair copy stops.*
[47] I shall.

express purpose of speaking with Mr. Lashmore. He came in the afternoon, when the clergyman was out, and Mrs. Lashmore, impressed by his gentlemanly demeanour, had requested him to await her husband's return. So he had taken a place in the sitting-room, and the motherly little woman,[48] talking to him the while with country freedom, had made him a cup of tea. In the corner of the window, making use of the last moment of day-light, Bertha sat bending over some sewing. She took no part in the conversation, which turned chiefly on the character of the country round, but from time to time, in reaching her scissors from the little table beside her, cast a quick glance at the stranger, after which her fingers plied the needle with unwonted nervousness and speed. He, too, not unfrequently turned his head towards the window, and once, when his eyes for a second met Bertha's,[49] he lost the sense of a question her mother was asking him, and showed a slight confusion. He appeared to wear mourning, the effect of which being to heighten the paleness of his countenance, and render its spiritual expression yet more striking.

The clergyman reached home in about an hour, and entered the room in his wonted silent manner. When his eye fell on the young man's face he suddenly stood still and remained gazing at him with contracted brows; it was as if some painful memory was struggling for recognition in his brain. When his wife had explained the visit, he bowed slightly, and briefly requested the stranger to come with him into his study. The fire had not yet been lit, and the lamp which Mrs. Lashmore brought showed a bare and cheerless room, in which were[50] two untidy book-cases and a table arranged for writing. The clergyman pointed to a chair, which the young man took; he himself remained standing in silence.

"My name is Cuthbertson," began the visitor. "I have just had the unhappiness to lose my mother; my father died five years ago. On her deathbed[51] my mother spoke to me of a clergyman of your name who lived at a village called Wastell Heath in ——shire, to whom she begged me to give personally, if possible, this little packet. It was

[48] and Mrs. Lashmore.
[49] when their eyes happened to meet.
[50] furnished only with.
[51] to lose my mother; on her death-bed.

sealed and tied in this way when she handed it me. I am myself a teacher at a school in Berkshire, and, as my Christmas holidays began immediately after my mother's death, I have used my freedom to visit you.—I suppose there can be no mistake about the person for whom this is intended?"

Mr. Lashmore had listened with a face which betrayed[52] a terrible struggle to maintain its calmness. Now he held out his hand and took the packet, which bore his full name and address, written in a rather weak female hand. He laid it on his writing-desk, and was silent for some moments.

"Certainly it is for me," he said at length. "I am obliged to you. —Do you think of remaining longer in the neighbourhood?"

The words were spoken forcedly, and as if with no special purpose to avoid the embarrassment of silence.

"Only till Monday,[53] I think," replied the other, rising from his chair with some uneasiness at the clergyman's frigid questioning. "I fear there will be no means of returning to-morrow, as it is Sunday."[54]

"I am sorry I cannot ask you to remain here for the night," said Mr. Lashmore, after standing for a moment[55] in thought. "My house is very small; I have no accommodation."

"Oh, thank you; I have taken a room at the village inn," returned Cuthbertson, distantly.

"You said you were a teacher at a school.—What was your father?"

"He was a medical man."

"How old are you?"

"Twenty-three."

"Have you other relatives?"

"None that I know personally."

Mr. Lashmore looked towards the door, clearly intimating that

[52] showed.

[53] Only till to-morrow.

[54] *After* Sunday *the following passage has been canceled*:
 "I hope you will remain here for the night," said Mr. Lashmore, after walking to the window and standing there for a moment looking out into the blackness. "There is a room at your disposal."

[55] after standing for a moment at the window, looking out into the blackness, for there was no blind.

the interview was at an end. Cuthbertson did not delay, and was conducted at once to the front-door.

"I may possibly call upon you at the inn after evening service to-morrow," said the clergyman, bowing stiffly. And he closed the door.

Mr. Lashmore returned to his study, and took up the packet to examine it. It contained some half a dozen very old letters, still in their envelopes, the dim, yellow writing in a hand which he with difficulty recognized as his own. They were directed to a Mrs. Herbert, at an address in London, and with them lay a note of apparently very recent date directed to himself,[56] in the same manner as the packet. This note he read first, read it with dark movings of his hard face; then crushed it in his hand,[57] and seemed on the point of destroying it; but suddenly he altered his purpose, smoothed it out, folded it, and after a moment's further hesitation, locked it in a drawer. As he did so there came a knock at his door. He made no reply. The knock was repeated, and Mrs. Lashmore's timid voice inquired whether he would not have the fire lit. The room was very cold, but he merely replied with a brief "No!" and, sitting down, took out the old letters one by one. So long did he brood over them, that, when at length he finished the last, the low-ticking clock on his mantel-piece pointed to midnight. Then he rose,[58] laid the letters in the empty grate, and set fire to them with a match, crushing out their ashes with the poker.

On the following day Cuthbertson was at church morning and evening. He sat at a short distance from Mrs. Lashmore's pew, and several times his eyes met Bertha's. As they passed out after the service together with the other worshippers, in all scarcely twenty,[59] the girl and her mother bowed to him, and he returned the bow.

Mr. Lashmore did not fulfil his promise of visiting him that evening, but sent a brief note, in which he excused himself on the plea of engagements, thanked him[60] for his trouble in bringing the packet,

[56] directed to Mr. Lashmore.
[57] *After* his hand *the sentence originally ended as follows*: at length, setting fire to it with a match, let it burn completely away in the empty grate.
[58] Then he rose, and burned these also, slowly, one by one.
[59] together with the handful of other worshippers.
[60] sent a brief note in which he again thanked him.

and expressed a very formal hope that the visit could be repeated if ever the young man found himself again in that part of the country.

Mr. Lashmore was conscientious in the fulfillment of his pastoral duties, though in a hard, loveless way which made him feared rather than respected[61] by all his parishioners, and during the following week he was but little at home. The wet season had brought much sickness into the miserable homes of Wastell Heath; there were many bedsides to be visited, and three or four funerals to attend. One morning he had to pass[62] by a solitary little beer-house about half a mile from the church, and, in passing, caught a glimpse of a face he knew[63] at one of the lower windows. For a moment he stopped, but the face had vanished, and he walked slowly on with troubled countenance. What did it mean? Why was that young man lingering in the neighbourhood, and in concealment, as it appeared? Could he have opened[64] the packet before delivering it, and have learned—?

Bertha had begun to take long walks the last few days, a practice strangely out of accordance with her former habits, and her mother gently expressed her surprise that she should choose this inclement weather, cautioning her anxiously against wet feet and damp clothing. But Bertha only smiled gravely, and shook her head, with some careless remark about feeling the need of exercise. The good mother felt painfully that her child grew more and more distant from her as she grew older, and in these days she would often shed secret tears over the lack of mutual confidence and understanding in the house, for which she was ever in her heart making herself responsible. Between her and her husband there had for years been an insensibly widening gulf; he was never absolutely cruel,[65] but increasingly cold and unsympathetic, wrapped in gloomy egotisms which were to her incomprehensible. She had grown to regard him,[66] like most people with whom he came in contact, with a reverence largely tinctured with fear; his unceasing toil, his restless asceticism more and more

[61] which made him dreaded, if not disliked.

[62] One morning he passed.

[63] a face looking out from the bar-room window.

[64] as it appeared? Did he suspect anything? Had he opened.

[65] there had for years been an inexplicable chasm; she dreaded the cold, hard-featured man.

[66] She had grown to regard him with ...

repelled her wifely affections. With daily pain, too, she observed the relations between him and his child; without really comprehending the deep, impulsive, idealizing nature of the latter, she saw that Bertha likewise feared rather than loved her father, and that too often the fear seemed developing into active dislike. Bertha's position was doubtless the worst of all, since her temperament made her most susceptible to the oppression of her uncongenial surroundings. When nearly two years ago[67] (being then not quite sixteen), she had returned finally from the very indifferent[68] boarding-school where she had received such education as her father could afford her, she had been a not unhappy girl, reticent and finding her chief pleasures in solitary reverie, yet cheerful for the most part in the home circle, and to her mother warmly affectionate. But the dreadful loneliness of their life, the crushing[69] monotony of the scenes which surrounded them, the lack of intellectual resources,—for Mr. Lashmore's library consisted of nothing but works of controversial theology, in literature he took no interest whatever,—soon wrought strangely upon her. She secluded[70] herself in her own corroding thoughts, fed in solitude the visions of a warm, imaginative temperament,[71] and came almost to loathe her existence.

Under such circumstances it needs no great detail of explanation to account for the effect of the young man's visit. In his pale, expressive countenance, his quiet and refined speech, Bertha found from the first moment the embodiment of her ideal; his timid glances towards her as she sat silently apart,[72] and the one meeting of their eyes, spoke to her of his own awakened interest. In very deed the two were drawn towards each other by irresistible passion, every worldly consideration shrunk[73] before their strangely-kindled ardour. They had divined each other's nature; and it was[74] as though some mysterious prompting led them to the meetings in the old hut of the

---

[67] When two years ago.
[68] from the poor.
[69] depressing.
[70] shut.
[71] a warm, artistic temperament.
[72] as she sat apart in silence.
[73] fell.
[74] it seemed.

quarry, where the eloquence of their eyes and the thrill of hand in hand had needed the aid of but few words to knit their union. It was a strange background for the[75] development of such an impassioned drama. The blank, gloomy monotony of their surroundings imparted to their love even from the first something of despair; they clung to each other tremulously, like two spirits of a rarer element,[76] to whom the breath of the coarse world was in itself fatal.[77]

Mr. Lashmore had not as much as suspected the state of affairs which was so startlingly disclosed to him that evening in the hut by the quarry; the lingering[78] of Cuthbertson in the neighbourhood had startled him, but his conscience gave far other explanations than the true one for conjecture to work upon. The discovery[79] came upon him with a double shock, and the night of sleepless agitation which followed made him physically ill. The next morning he went about his work with a ghastly countenance. To his wife he had spoken no word, save shortly to remind her that Bertha must continue in her room; and indications of a pathetic outbreak on the poor woman's part had met with a look which sufficed to impose absolute silence. When he returned at noon there lay on his study table a letter which had arrived during the morning by the hand of a messenger. He opened it, and found a long impassioned appeal from the young man who had mysteriously crossed his path.[80] His love, Cuthbertson wrote, had come upon him with terrible and overwhelming power from almost the first moment of his beholding Bertha. How they had subsequently met and the girl had made known to him an equal passion was scarcely to be described; it was rather like the strong propulsion towards each other of two beings by a mysterious fate, than the ordinary approaches of common experience. To leave the neighbourhood without the assurance of being one day permitted to return and claim

[75] a strange background for such.

[76] like two noble spirits in a world whose.

[77] *This paragraph* (Under such circumstances . . . fatal) *was inserted by Gissing when he had written a few more pages of his story.*

[78] abiding.

[79] The discovery brought. . . .

[80] a long impassioned appeal from the young man with whom he had become so mysteriously connected.

Bertha for his own, would be death to him. He spoke of his descent, which was at least respectable; of his position and prospects, which at all events held out assurances of a modest income before long,[81] and he would be willing to work and wait. He could not but refer to the preposession[s] against him which Mr. Lashmore had seemed to feel even from the first, but he trusted that his best efforts[82] to remove these must surely be successful; he begged for an interview at once, entreated it with the utmost fervour. It was a strange appeal[83] to be addressed to such a man as Mr. Lashmore, to whom the most impassioned flights were all unmeaning, and who, for his own reasons, had a horror of the mere subject[84] of which it spoke. He read the letter impatiently, then burned it, and seemed to purpose no manner of reply.

On the following afternoon,[85] scarcely ten minutes after the clergyman had left the house, there was a knock at the door, to which Mrs. Lashmore herself replied. She was surprised to see the visitor of two weeks ago, and shocked at the change which the interval had wrought in his appearance. He seemed as if just risen from a bed of sickness, and his dark, wonderful eyes shone out with almost ghastly prominence from his pale face. His manner was feverishly nervous.

Mr. Lashmore had only this moment gone out, began the lady, but was interrupted by the youth's quick and broken voice.

"I know it; I have watched for his going. I am taking a great freedom; I entreat your kindness, your sympathy! Let me speak to you only for a moment. You will pity me; you will be like a mother to me; you have a kind, gentle face. Let me speak to you for Bertha's sake!"

The last words were a sudden light in the darkness of the poor woman's silent suffering; she understood at once what had been only a dreadful mystery to her. Not without fearful looks in the direction of the road she admitted the visitor hastily, and led him into her sitting-room. His quick look round the room was followed by an expression of deep disappointment.

[81] which were at least modestly assured.
[82] his efforts.
[83] must surely be successful. It was a strange appeal . . .
[84] loathed and dreaded the very subject.
[85] day.

"She is confined to her room," sobbed the mother, quickly comprehending him. "She may not leave it;[86] I have not spoken to her for two days!"

He took both her hands, and, pressing them in his own, poured out the story of his passion and entreated her favour, her assistance. Weeping, she assured him that she had known nothing of all this, that she would gladly sacrifice everything for her child's happiness, but that she was utterly powerless. Her husband's will was iron. She could not conceive his reasons, and she durst not question or argue with him.

"Speak with Bertha herself!" he urged. "As her mother it is your right to have a voice in her fate. Do you think of what her sufferings are, imprisoned, avoided by all, ignorant of all that is happening! Have you the heart to let her suffer so, you her mother? Can you, dare you, desert her! You are her natural protector, it is your duty to stand by her in affliction.—Perhaps you doubt her love for me, you think I selfishly exaggerate her feelings. Speak to her; break through these dreadful barriers which no one on earth has a right to set between you and her! If you have any pity—"

There was a sudden loud noise upstairs, a hurrying step outside,[87] the door was burst open, and Bertha herself, her hair in disorder, her face wild with past anguish and present hope, rushed into the room. Her quick ear had caught the sound of her lover's voice in the room above, and at length, maddened with excitement, she had forced the frail lock of the door. With a cry of joy she threw herself into the young man's arms, and was passionately pressed to his heart. For a moment they exchanged half-whispered, sobbing words of endearment; then Bertha suddenly turned to her mother.

"I will not leave him again!" she said, in a firm, proud tone. "I knew he would come for me. My father has no power over me; I feared him, but I fear him no longer at Harold's side. I will not stay in this dreadful house; you cannot keep me here—"

A loud double-knock[88] at the front door interrupted her.

"My God! It is your father," cried Mrs. Lashmore, sinking with ghastly face onto a chair.

[86] sobbed the mother. "She may not leave it.
[87] There was a hurrying step outside.
[88] There was a loud double-knock.

The two stood holding each other's hands, Bertha smiling as if in defiance of the worst that might happen. They heard the servant open the door, and they saw the clergyman's tall, dark form enter and stand before them. At the sight of him, his wife covered her face and sank upon her knees.

Mr. Lashmore at first drew back in astonishment,[89] then his eyes flamed with sudden rage. Yet he uttered no violent exclamation, only glared upon his daughter for a moment, then said with forced composure,—"Go back to your room."

"Not again," was the reply,—and Cuthbertson felt her hand quiver and break into moisture, though she spoke so calmly. "You have no reason for treating us in this heartless way, and I will no longer stay under your roof. I can earn my living, and I will do so. Harold, you will let me go away with you, and help me to find a home for the present. I will be no burden to you; I can easily get my bread."

"Edgar!" gasped her mother, rising up and standing before her husband. "You will not drive her away? Have mercy on her and on me![90] Why do you act in this cruel way? Why will you force them to part?[91] They have no thought of marriage at once,—have you, Bertha? You will think differently—"

"Be quiet, woman!" was the short reply. "I tell you a marriage between these is forever impossible;[92] they may not even think of each other. I am responsible for my actions to no one,—but to God. Bertha," he added, approaching the girl, "as you hope to be saved hereafter, I command you to obey me, to let go his hand. The curse of God is on this union!"

Even something of entreaty, spite of himself, mingled[93] with violence. His face was colourless and the sweat stood out on his forehead.[94]

"Those are only words," returned the girl, scornfully. "You must satisfy my reason before I obey you."

[89] Mr. Lashmore was at first astonished.
[90] Have mercy on me.
[91] Why will you part them?
[92] is impossible [can never be].
[93] Even something of entreaty mingled.
[94] *These two sentences were added later.*

There was a silence, in which the man's countenance expressed a dreadful struggle;[95] then it settled into resolve.

"If I satisfy *him*," he said, deliberately,[96] pointing to Cuthbertson, "if *he* is content to renounce you,—is it enough?"

"If he is satisfied to leave me," was the solemn reply, "I shall not force myself upon him."

She smiled gravely at Harold[97] as she spoke, and he returned the smile.

"Come with me then," said Mr. Lashmore, motioning to Cuthbertson. The latter exchanged a quick whisper with Bertha, and followed into the study.

The two stood facing each other in the darkening room,[98] and to the young man's agonizing impatience it seemed as if the silence would never be broken. He looked towards the window, and noticed that with the approach of night had come a wintry storm; the dull sky was flecked with falling snow. The breath of both was visible[99] in the freezing atmosphere.

"If I prove to you that this connexion is impossible," began the clergyman at length, his voice lowered as if in caution, but uncertain with fierce feeling, "do you give me your word to leave this place at once,[100] to hold no manner of communication henceforth with[101] anyone in the house, and to write a line for the girl, here in my presence, forbidding her to think of you?"

"If you satisfy me, I promise it all; but—"[102]

"Stop, that is enough. Then I will tell you that your love for her is incestuous. You are her brother. I am your father, not the man you have always thought of as such."

Cuthbertson made no motion, but stared[103] into the speaker's

[95] in which the man's face expressed a dreadful determination.

[96] slowly.

[97] She smiled at Harold.

[98] in the dimly lighted room.

[99] rose visibly.

[100] *After* at once *the sentence ended thus*: and never let your hated face be seen again by me or mine; and, what is more, that you will disclose to no one the secret of what I tell you, but you will write a line for the girl here in.

[101] [with my daughter]

[102] "If you satisfy me, I promise it" ["If you satisfy me, I promise it all"].

[103] The listener made no motion but looked.

face with an expression half of horror, half of incredulity. At once Mr. Lashmore stepped to a drawer, unlocked it, and took out the crumpled note which he had so nearly destroyed.

"You could recognize your mother's handwriting?" he asked.

"Certainly."

"Then read this. It was in the packet you brought to me."

There were only a few lines, at the head a date only a few months before the writer's death. "I am near to my end, but I must speak once more before I go; I have kept silence for nearly twenty-three years.[104] The letters in this packet will be brought to you by your own son; no one has ever read them but myself, and now you can destroy them. I left you free; did I not? I have not remained[105] faithful to you, for I was a weak woman to struggle against the world, and the boy needed a father. That father is dead, and Harold will soon be alone. How shall you act towards him, I leave to your own heart.—Emma."

The paper dropped to the ground, and Harold stood in reverie. All at once a number of curious and hitherto unexplained circumstances of his life crowded upon him,—a chance word puzzled over from time to time, a glance, an air of mystery which had at times seemed to hang about his home. These came back to him now with such vivid force that, with his mother's words before him, there was no room left for doubt.

"You betrayed my mother, then!" he exclaimed, suddenly, with passion. "You betrayed and deserted her!"

"Say what you like," was the reply, given with something of brutal carelessness, the result of an endeavour to keep down the anguish of shame. "But now that you are satisfied, fulfil your promise. Here is paper. Write what I bid you."

The revelation had conquered Harold's reason, but could not subdue his passionate love. With white lips and hand which trembled so much that the words it traced were scarcely legible, he wrote this: "We must never see or think of each other again. Good-bye, forever. Harold."

[104] I am near to my end, but I wish to send you a last message, after a silence of nearly twenty-three years.

[105] by your own son; I have not remained.

And, a moment after, mother and child, waiting in anguish in the dark sitting-room, heard steps pass quickly along the passage, then the front-door open, then its closing. And the clergyman returned to them alone, a lamp in his hand.

"Harold will think over my words," he said, with calm gravity, "and will let you hear from him in the morning."

There was no reply from either, and he went back to his study. For him the long hours that followed brought thoughts and feelings such as lay waste a life and make it forever after a barren wilderness. With fearful vividness came back to him every circumstance of his sin, every feature of his baseness. He was a young man again, living in the home of his widowed mother, and with them an orphan cousin, scarcely more than a child, whom they had taken out of charity. He felt over again, burning through his flesh, that fierceness of animal desire,—love his nature had never known,—which had left him no rest till the girl had become his, body and soul.[106] He recalled every diabolical art which he had practised to make her love him; he realized—and it was agony to him—the infinite superiority of her nature to his own, the possibilities of blessedness which even after the crime might have been his, had he but possessed the honour and the courage of a man. Even in those days he had been fanatically superstitious,—religious, he would have said,—and then, as now, he had regarded this hideous sin as the result of direct temptation of the Evil One; if he had wrought his will, it is surely conceivable with what mental tortures the crime had been accompanied.[107] And in what followed there was the same diabolic contradiction, the same perception of his duty, with fatal inability to perform it. The girl had vanished from her home, no one but himself knew why or whither. He had found her an abode where she lived under an assumed name, and for a very short time[108] after the birth of her child he continued to write to her. Then came events which rendered the continuance of the connection irksome to him beyond measure. He had tried the result of keeping silence, had let her see that he no longer cared for her; and the girl was too proud to utter a word of complaint, to make a single

[106] till he wrought the girl's ruin.
[107] had been immediately accompanied.
[108] He had found her an abode, and for a very short time.

appeal to his honour or compassion. She had, as she now said, left him free, seeing that he desired it. But she had never entirely lost sight of him, and had known to the last his position and abode. And now, whether intentionally or not, she had inflicted upon him a fearful retribution. It might [be] she had thought he would feel some natural love towards the child whom he had deserted almost as soon as it was born, and would be glad of an opportunity to give Harold some kind of protection and help. As it was, she had created[109] in him the bitterest feelings of hate. The man's perverted heart loathed her memory for the pain it gave him, loathed his son for the[110] agonies of conscience which the youth had re-awakened. His God was a God of terrors, and he felt himself among the reprobate. Surely the poor dead woman was sufficiently avenged.

The next day was Sunday. Bertha had not slept at all,[111] and her face was like that of a dying creature; her mother was all but prostrate with illness, not having dared to ask her husband for a word of explanation.[112] When the pretence of breakfast was over, Mr. Lashmore went into his study and returned with a small folded note in his hand, which he held out to Bertha.

"This was left with me for you last night," he said. "I thought[113] it better you should have the night for reflection before receiving it."

The girl read Harold's farewell, and seemingly it produced no effect upon her. She remained still seated by the window, her eyes fixed before her, but with a vacant rather than an anguished look. Her mother came and took the paper from her hand, and read it; then went away sobbing. But Bertha did not move.

"You will stay with her this morning," said Mr. Lashmore to the poor woman, when it was time for him to leave for the service. And he walked away to the church with a freer step than of late.

The mother, when they were left alone, at first began a few words

---

[109] some kind of help. In truth she had created.
[110] for the conscience-smitten . . .
[111] had not slept during the night.
[112] her mother was almost helpless, not having dared to speak to her husband for a word of explanation.
[113] he said, "but thought.

of faltering consolation, but Bertha silenced her with uplifted hand[114] and a low "Hush!" Mrs. Lashmore[115] took a seat beside her and closed her eyes in dreary pain.

After a while Bertha moved and turned towards her mother, whose eyes were still closed. The loosely hanging arms and regular breathing showed that weariness had at length overcome her, and she was asleep. At once the girl rose and, with quick, noiseless steps, passed from the room. Quick as thought she had put on her hat and straightway left the house. Snow had ceased to fall during the night, and the surface was now hard frozen, but the leaden, lowering sky surely presaged another storm. Running with all her speed, Bertha was rapidly out of sight of the parsonage, and drawing near the heath where the old quarry was. Often she slipped and tumbled, but scarcely seemed to pause; she reached the hut, panting, and with wild eyes sought through its shadow, calling the while, under her breath, "Harold! Harold!" But the hut was empty, and the fresh snow which had fallen through its wrecked roof showed no sign of a foot-print. She wandered out again, and stood on the edge of the quarry. What was it that caught her eye down[116] below there, that strange object frozen up[117] in the midst of the pool? Surely it was a face, just rising above the snow-covered ice, and itself flecked with white,—a human face![118] Unconscious of what she did, the girl had in a moment made her way round the end of the quarry, and was springing over the frozen pools, which cracked at the head but yet bore her. She was on her knees by the face, had passed her hand over it. Then the dead stillness of the winter morning was pierced by a terrible shriek.—

Morning service was going on in the ugly little church,[119] where some[120] twenty persons sat shivering in the clammy cold, whilst Mr. Lashmore read on unceasingly in his deep, unvarying, dismal tones.

[114] with a slightly uplifted hand.
[115] Mrs. Lashmore sat in.
[116] What was that down.
[117] frozen up amid the pool.
[118] a human face.
[119] in the ugly little church which, in the absence of any source of warmth.
[120] where scarcely

He had reached the Communion, in which the responses were accompanied by a thin, tuneless organ, wretchedly played. And he had come to the words: "For I, the Lord thy God, am a jealous God, and visit the sins of the fathers upon the children, unto—"

His voice was interrupted by a loud, wild laugh, such a laugh as chills the blood with sudden horror. Looking down into the church, he saw his daughter Bertha standing at the entrance, her eyes[121] wandering[122] in the meaningless glare of madness, and her features distorted with a ghastly mirth. Peal followed on peal of laughter, ringing[123] with horrible echo through the bare aisle. That Sunday the Communion was never finished.

Poor Harold had not been so thoughtlessly cruel as to seek a voluntary death in the quarry pools. Leaving the parsonage in a state of mind not far from madness, he had rushed forth,[124] driven by his agony, over the neighbouring fields, heedless of track or direction; there was momentary ease for him in battling with the thick snow-drifts, the icy wind was welcome to[125] his cheeks and forehead. It had grown quite dark, but he was unconscious of this, and pushed fiercely on, straight before him. For more than an hour he wandered in this way, often falling, at times forcing a way through unseen obstacles, still impelled[126] as if by furies. And so at length chance had brought him to the edge of the quarry. The wild storm beat in his face; he neither saw nor thought of what was in front of him; and only a hollow splash of water,[127] a brief cry, told that he had perished in the darkness.

[121] her face and manner bespe [*sic*] . . .
[122] wandering about in.
[123] ringing horribly in the . . .
[124] rushed forth in the . . .
[125] welcome on.
[126] draw[n]
[127] splash of water, scarcely audible for . . .

The Lady of the Dedication

OF THE EIGHT PIECES in this volume, this is one of the most difficult to date. A precious clue is offered by the signature itself which, as it does not contain the initial R, cannot be dated 1881 or the earlier part of 1882, as suggested by the style and general atmosphere. Gissing informed his brother of his decision to discard the initial of his second Christian name in a letter dated December 27, 1882,* but this date is not rigidly fixed; for instance, "The Hope of Pessimism," written in late September and early October, 1882, is signed "George Gissing," while the middle R appears in letters to Algernon as late as March 7, 1883. The most likely date of composition seems to be the autumn of 1882. By September 3, he had completed the first version of his now lost novel *Mrs. Grundy's Enemies.* Then, after moving to 17 Oakley Crescent, Chelsea, and writing his essay on pessimism, he turned to his last Russian article for *Vyestnik Evropy,* which appeared in the November issue (272: 385–400). As he did not begin *The Burden of Life,* later retitled *The Unclassed,* until the end of 1882, "The Lady of the Dedication" was probably written in November or December of that year.

It might be objected that Gissing could not have written two pieces as different in tone as the somber philosophical essay and this youthfully optimistic short story in immediate succession. However, there is a similar contrast in 1879, with stories like "My Clerical Rival" and "My First Rehearsal" confronting "The Last Half-Crown" and "Cain and Abel."

The biographical material available does not indicate whether Gissing tried to have this manuscript published. Its nineteen pages are obviously a fair copy in a hand that betrays no hesitation.

---

* Trace W. McGregor Library, University of Virginia, Charlottesville, Va

A T THE HOUR of eleven before noon Mr. Swanwick's study was ordinarily secure from intrusion. Mr. Swan-wick—without having recourse to direct misrepresen-tation, unworthy of a man of culture, a whilom poet, and actual editor of the *Narthex,* a popular magazine of various literature—gently fostered in his family circle the belief that the hours between breakfast and lunch were devoted by him to that severe labour which had prematurely interspersed his dark locks with iron-grey, and had even bestowed a tinge of the same upon his comely whiskers. Nature works to one end in magnificent ways, and it is true that more commonplace explanations might have been offered of these greetings from old age on the threshold of our friend's forty-fifth year. Be that as it may, I have only to report that, on the present morning, the hour of eleven, ringing with presto timefulness from the clock on the mantelpiece, found Mr. Swanwick buried very deep in a very easy chair, and engaged in no more taxing occupation than the perusal of a newspaper. His pipe had just gone out, and, after a succession of fruitless puffs, he was bracing himself to the effort of reaching after the matches, when Mrs. Swanwick entered the room. She held a book in her hand, and her face was bright with a look of pleasure, almost of enthusiasm.

Mr. Swanwick strung his slackened sinews with the graceful readiness of a man not easily to be taken at a disadvantage, and had his pipe alight at least two minutes sooner than he could have hoped.

"Been going through the provisions of the Land Bill," he re-marked with a shade of weary thoughtfulness on his brow, accom-panied by a slight motion of the lips, which suggested something else. "It gives an opportuneness to my work on Modern Agrarian Legis-lation."

"This is the first I have heard of any such work," said his wife, looking at him with a shrewd twinkle in her eyes.

Mr. Swanwick had got his pipe alight, and, as he carefully deposited the match-end on a little tray, he smiled.

"To what am I indebted—"

"O, Edward, what a delightful book this is!" Mrs. Swanwick ex-claimed, holding up the volume she had brought with her. "For once, the 'great big stupid' is really right. I have laughed and cried over it,

—positively cried, and you know I am not given to the melting mood."

"I see no traces of recent emotion."

"It is the noblest and sweetest story since the 'Vicar of Wake-field,'—I say it and believe it! Confess, now, that it mastered you. 'Something pretty,' forsooth, you said, when you gave it me to read. 'Something the women are sure to like.' But you know very well it is more than that. And it's a first work, isn't it? Who is 'Robert Adler'? Do you know anything of him?"

"There was talk about him at the Club last night. Brownwigg says it went to seven houses before it got into their hands. At first they wanted the author to spin it out into the conventional three volumes, but he refused. They gave him fifteen pounds for it, White tells me."

"And is that all he will get,—such a success?"

"Probably. But it has made his name. He has just sent in a tale for the *Narthex*. A month ago I should have returned it without reading; now I shall print it without reading; that's all the difference."

"That is a shameless confession, upon my word! I've a good mind to send it as an interesting anecdote to some weekly *chronique scandaleuse*. And yet you pooh-pooh authors who complain of editorial carelessness."

Mr. Swanwick curled his lips.

"See what reward one gets for ingenuousness. The fact is, the fellow writes a microscopic hand. I've had his MS. before, and really couldn't undertake to read it."

"But it's your duty to read contributions, Sir! If you lack time and patience,"—Mrs. Swanwick glanced meaningly at the newspaper —"give the things to me, and let me be your taster. Who knows what misery you cause by these heedless rejections! I'll be bound the stories you sent back would have increased the circulation of the magazine."

"Just as likely they were worthless. There's promise in this book, no doubt; but I shouldn't wonder if it is his first and last; so often happens.—Do you know, I thought of asking him to lunch, when I write to accept his story."

"Do so, by all means. I feel sure he is young and in need of help."

"Pity I am neither the one nor the other!"

Mrs. Swanwick uttered a contemptuous little sound, and stood turning over the leaves of the volume.

"The style is perfect; there are sentences here and there of exquisite beauty.—Who is 'E. E. L.,' I wonder?"

"E. E. L.?"

"Didn't you notice the Dedication? Look. 'E. E. L.—To you, and to you alone, this and all.' "

"Mighty disrespectful to the public."

"Maybe; but it is something for her to be proud of; she will be a happy girl."

And Mrs. Swanwick stood dreaming for a moment, as women do in thinking of such things.

"She?" exclaimed her husband. "Why she, necessarily?"

"Edward, I will disown you! And you once wrote poems!"

"Mea culpa, mea culpa!"

"You never dedicated a book to me."

There was tenderness in her voice and eyes, spite of the half-mocking smile.

"No, I never did. I will repair the omission. My work on Modern Agrarian Legislation—"

"Announced to appear on the Greek Calends,"—

There was a noise outside, as of children running down stairs with laughter and merriment. Mrs. Swanwick went to the door.

"Don't take them very far this morning, Ellen," she said; "it will certainly rain.—Godfrey, you had better not take your ship; wait for a finer day."

"O but, mamma," cried out a hearty little voice, "I'm going to race with Johnny Wilson's cutter. I'm sure it won't rain."

"Are you? Come here, a moment. Eddy will take the ship, and you'll catch them up directly."

She brought into the room a boy of seven, a joyous little fellow with her own dark eyes and already something about his lips of that easy humorousness which marked his father's countenance.

"Now, stand here," she said, fixing him in front of the easy chair, "and recite the piece I heard last night; as well as you can, now."

There was a moment of shamefaced hesitation, but the youngster seemed to derive encouragement from his father's smile. He began, with a prettily modulated voice, and with much justice of expression, that song of Herrick's:—

> "Her eyes the glow-worm lend thee,
> The shooting star attend thee;
> And the elves also,
> Whose little eyes glow
> Like the sparks of fire, befriend thee."

All three verses were recited without fault, and Godfrey looked up for commendation.

"And who is it by?" asked his mother.

"By Robert Herrick."

"Good. Now run after the others, sweetheart."

The child ran away, and Mrs. Swanwick closed the door behind him.

"When did you teach him that?" asked her husband, who looked pleased with the performance.

"I didn't teach him at all, and that's why I wanted you to hear him. Ellen taught him the piece, and told him who it was written by."

"Ellen? Where the deuce did *she* get it from?"

"That I understand as little as many other curious things about the girl. Really, Godfrey repeats it well, and it's all her instruction."

"I didn't know she was a girl of education. Didn't you say she came from a work-room?"

"Yes, she has been a slave of the needle all her life. There was something in her that interested me from the first. She spoke so frankly. She knew nothing of the duties of a nurse-maid, but felt so sure, she said, that she could soon learn everything,—as indeed it has proved. Then she had showed such good sense in wishing to get out of that wretched work-room life and take a situation; that kind of wish is very uncommon, such girls look down on service."

"*Nigro simillinia cygno.* Then it seems that she whiled away the super-abundant leisure of her former life over the pages of the Elizabethan poets. Somewhat unusual that, eh?"

"I can't understand it. She knows such uncommon things, and is at the same time so ignorant. I have been talking with her this morning a little, but couldn't discover much. I know she writes and spells poorly."

"Case of reserved potentialities, as the scientific men might say. —She's rather good-looking, isn't she?"

"Don't affect a modest diffidence in your judgment. Yes; she is neither pretty nor handsome, but has that kind of bright intelligence and quiet goodness in her face which means more than either one or the other. She won the affections of the children in a day, and I have faith in the little people's instincts."

"Especially when they coincide with your own, Emily.—But look at the clock, as Ingoldsby says.—Am I to ask Adler, then?"

"Do so, by all means."

So, by the last post that day, there was delivered at a lodging-house in the neighbourhood of Tottenham Court Road a letter, which contained a cheque and an invitation to lunch with the editor of the *Narthex* at his residence in Kensington. The room in which sat the recipient of this letter was not very cheerful; it was a small bedroom at the top of the house, barely furnished, but at the same time having something of the appearance of a study; a tall book-case, well filled, concealed a portion of the ugly wall-paper, and on the rickety round table was a writing-slant, covered with papers. Robert Adler was not at this moment engaged in literary composition; nor were his thoughts, though he seemed absent enough, busy with plots and dialogues. In very deed, he was considering how he might avoid the necessity of going to bed with a most unpleasantly hearty appetite. With one hand he kept turning over and over in his pocket the sum of four shillings and sixpence, the possession of which did not help him to the attainment of his end, seeing that the coins were due to his landlady on the following morning. He looked round the room. Unless he parted with some of his books, there was absolutely nothing convertible into a supper. His overcoat, happily not needed in these summer days, had disappeared a week before, and was at present represented by a yellow "duplicate" in his waistcoat pocket. Other clothing he had none, save what he wore. Was there any volume less dear to him than the rest? The rows made up on the whole but a ragged regiment; most of the books had been picked up for a song at this or that book-stall, and to retail them would be productive of little but the bitterness of the loss. The faces of all were dear to him; not one of these "affable familiar ghosts" whose presence he would not miss. And yet it was not only a question of to-night's supper, but of food throughout the ensuing week. For some months he had been employed at a translation-office, his payment for the rendering into English of multifarious French and German documents being fifteen shillings a week. The office suddenly finding his services superfluous, he was reduced to the present pass. Yet on the table lay a pile of newspapers and reviews, each of which contained a highly laudatory notice of his book; and at this moment he was doubtless the subject of conversation in not a few genial circles, where appreciation of literature was heightened by the soothing effects of recent dining.

Never mind how a young man of education and talents came to be living thus from hand to mouth. It was not exactly his own fault, unless we may impute to a man as a crime the possession of a restless heart and impetuous qualities little consistent with prudence. For some years he had been feeling his way in pen-work, yet now that he seemed to have hit the right track at last, it was very doubtful whether he might not starve before gaining that temple of letters wherein the money-changers have made themselves chief-priests. He lacked assurance, and could not easily bring himself to beg the aid of those who would perhaps have given him a hand by the way. He was, moreover, somewhat indolent, and readily discouraged. The return of a manuscript would check his efforts for weeks. Nor was his writing of that kind which finds acceptance at the hands of editors; the beauties of his work were too delicate for the eyes of those who read as they run; they would only be appreciated when the accredited surveyors of literature had at length set up a finger-post in his honour, crying to all and sundry "Halt!"

Robert had heard the postman's knock at the street door, but it had so often awakened in his heart false echoes of hope that to-night in his perplexity he scarcely heeded it. Yet surely there was someone coming upstairs. Doubtless the letter was for the old gentleman on the second floor. No; the second floor was passed. A tap at his own door; an envelope rent open; then the miraculous scattering of clouds, and the rising of the sun in the night-time.

When he returned to his room, an hour after, he unlocked a drawer and took out a letter which he had half written the day before. He sat down to continue it, and wrote thus:

"Good fortune makes past evil pleasant both to think and talk of. An hour ago I was in the worst straits I have ever known, hungry and hopeless; at present I have a cheque for ten guineas in my pocket, and before me a very agreeably worded invitation to lunch with the editor who has accepted my story. I need not hide from you now what you would otherwise have never known. I have lost my translation work, and am adrift once more; but not, you see, without hope of better things.

"But this is not all. I am astonished to find that the editor who writes to me is no other than Mr. Swanwick,—*your* Mr. Swanwick. When I sent my story to the *Narthex* I had of course no suspicion of this. And here he asks me to come and see him at his house. In the first moment of surprise I thought it would be impossible to accept his invitation. How could I sit down at ease as a guest in the house where you are regarded as a servant? But, after all, I know it would be not only unwise, but unjust, to neglect this opportunity. It will doubtless mean all sorts of possibilities to me, and the more of such that present themselves, the nearer will be your day of freedom and of my crowning happiness. Fortunately, I shall not see you. That indeed would be beyond my power, to pass you by without a word or a look,—you, dear one, in whose presence my heart is fire, whose image I cannot call before my thoughts without throes of passionate joy.

"How little they think that it is *you* who are meant in the Dedication of my book, that without you the book would never have been written, that to you—modest, simple, low-voiced little girl—is owing all the tenderness of thought, the sweetness of utterance, which they no doubt praise like the rest! I am willing to believe all you tell me of the kindness of Mrs. Swanwick; she thinks, no doubt, that she is very good and condescending to you. She little imagines that you are the love-crowned lady of a heart which bends before you in devotion such as she never inspired, that you are throned upon heights beyond the reach of her thought, that your name will some day twin with mine on the lips of those whose praise is fame. I shall smile as I sit at their table, thinking of all this; outwardly my attention will be with them, my heart will be with you.—But it is wrong to seem to speak contemptuously of these people. How can they know all the hidden beauty and wealth of your nature? Who does know you but I myself, I, to whom you have granted to read your soul, whom you have blest beyond all utterance with the rapture of your love?"

Well, well; no need to quote the whole letter, which was not a short one. After midnight, Robert went out to post it, and wandered for a time about the still streets, his eyes and thoughts among the clustered beacons of heaven.

Mr. Swanwick had the presence and tone of a man whose natural geniality has ripened in the sunshine of worldly success. He had known hardships, though not of long duration, in days gone by, and in the office of assisting a struggling youth of promise he found a pleasure which had something over and above that of the complacent patron. Robert Adler made a good impression upon him. He liked a man who met his look unfalteringly, and, at the first moment of meeting, the young author's gaze was as steady as his own. In the course of half an hour's conversation before lunch, the favourable impression was strengthened. Adler had in his voice and features that bright confidence which is the reflex of a heart aglow with noble instincts. His reception had speedily put him at his ease. When Mrs. Swanwick presently entered the study, she smiled to find how nearly she had hit the mark in her preconception of their visitor's appearance. He was, in fact, the author of his book, and it is pleasant to have one's ideals realized once in a way.

After lunch, Robert was led out into the garden behind the house, where the sun lay dreaming on lawn and flower-pot. As it happened, the children were at play here, the little boy whom we know, and his younger brother and sister; their nurse was with them. The gravel-path led by the group. Mr. Swanwick, being in the midst of talk, just nodded and smiled to the little ones; his companion, however, raised his hat, presumably to the nurse-maid, who turned away with a very slight flush, almost instantly dispelled. Mrs. Swanwick was just then coming out of the house, and observed this occurrence.

She mentioned the incident to her husband that evening.

"Piece of *gaucherie,* I suppose," was Mr. Swanwick's suggestion.

"That is the name we give to natural politeness. I think none the worse of him for it."

Mrs. Swanwick was thoughtful.

"Did he speak to you at all of his private circumstances?" she went on to ask.

"He was reticent, but I should judge they were none too brilliant. My offer to take a serial for the *Narthex* made his eyes flash."

A few days later, Mrs. Swanwick chanced to go up to the nursery at an unusual hour of the evening, shortly after the children had been put to bed. The door was a little open, and she entered without noise, her approach unnoticed by the person who sat alone in the room. The nurse-maid was sitting over some sewing, her attention, however, not wholly devoted to the needle, for, on the table before her, a book was propped up, and she every now and then gave a moment to the open page.

"What are you reading, Ellen?" asked Mrs. Swanwick, in her usual kind voice, when she had drawn near still unobserved.

The girl started and rose from her seat, at the same time laying her hand upon the book with a quick, frightened movement, as though she had been detected in a forbidden occupation. Her eyes fell before her mistress's rather keen look, and she reddened painfully.

"Let me see," said the lady, holding out her hand, smiling. "Surely there is nothing to be ashamed of."

Ellen handed her the volume, and stood, with hands before her, her look cast down. She was pale now, and trembled a little.

"Why," exclaimed Mrs. Swanwick, "I have read this book myself, and liked it very much. Everybody is talking about it, and of the author. I believe you saw him the other day; do you remember—"

Ellen stood pale as a ghost. She had raised her eyes, and their expression checked the speaker.

"Ellen," Mrs. Swanwick said, meeting the girl's strange look with a quiet and kind gaze, "what are your initials?"

She tried to speak, but the moving of her lips was voiceless.

"Your name is Ellen Lake. Does your second name begin with an E?"

"Yes, ma'am."

"So your initials are E. E. L.?—I wonder whether you know anything of a person with the same initials, who stands at the beginning
of this book and no doubt is very much ashamed to find herself in
such a conspicuous position?"

It was spoken in a tone of humorous gravity which Ellen perhaps
did not quite understand. At all events, the sewing she held dropped
to the ground, and tears started from her eyes.

"Why do you cry, Ellen? Don't mind my silly way of speaking.
Am I right? Is this book dedicated to you?"

The girl looked up, and, with something of unconscious pride in
her dim eyes, murmured a very low "Yes."

"And is that a thing to cry about? Why, you ought to be one of
the happiest girls in England. You are distressed that I have discovered your secret. Can't you trust me with it, Ellen?"

For a few moments, and in spite of all efforts to command herself,
the girl sobbed, her face hidden in her hands. Mrs. Swanwick com-
forted her with a mother's soothing kindness, and before long brought
a pleased smile to the gentle countenance.

"But this is a romance," she said at length. "It is as interesting
and delightful as the book itself. Sit down quietly, now, and talk to
me a little; tell me something about yourself, will you? Or am I
asking too much? Indeed, it is not mere curiosity; I am really interested in you; how could I help being? Try to speak to me as a friend,
and be sure that I should respect your confidence."

It was not difficult for Mrs. Swanwick, warm-hearted and full
of sympathetic intelligence, to attract the girl's trust. Without losing
the modest reserve which indicated the worth and delicacy of her
nature, Ellen told her story simply, glancing for an instant now and
then at the listener's face, and finding encouragement in its expression. An every-day occurrence in its commencement, her acquaintance
with Robert Adler had developed in an unusual way, and led to anything but commonplace results. They had lived in the same lodging-
house, each quite alone; upon frequent recognition had followed
mutual interest; then came the first spoken words; then a drawing
nearer on both sides, beyond the power of either to resist; then the
moment which put hand in hand on the threshold of a new world.

"I cannot tell you all his kindness to me," she said. "He gave me books, and taught me how to understand them; he gave me a new mind. Though I was nothing but a friendless work-girl, he treated me from the first with the respect he would have shown to a lady. In a life where it was so hard to keep one's self-respect, he made me strong to bear every kind of misery. I had often and often been despairing, when work was hard and payment so poor; but he was as poor as I, and had suffered even more, yet he had not lost courage. I distrusted him at first; I couldn't help it; but he was so different from anyone I had ever known, and I came slowly to understand him. He said I helped him in his work, and to think that I could do so made me very happy. Still, the better I understood him, the more I came to see how good and clever he was, the more fearful I grew; it seemed impossible that I should ever be worthy of him. But I said to myself that I would try, and I tried my best. But I felt I ought to make a change in my every day life; the companions I had to be with made everything harder for me; I needed to be with better people. Then I thought that I would leave the work-room, and find a place in some family, never mind what it was; it would be better. Robert was glad when I told him; he, too, felt it would be better. And in that way, I came here. I was happier from the first day. You were so kind to me, and the children made my days so cheerful. The time goes so quickly, and I know that Robert is making his way. He will soon be a great man. I am glad of it, so glad; but it often makes me afraid. I can't hope to be ever worthy of him."

Mrs. Swanwick's promise to respect Ellen's confidence naturally did not prevent her from telling her husband the whole story the same night. Mr. Swanwick listened with the calm of a humourist, whose experience of life teaches him to be surprised at nothing.

"Well, does it make any difference?" he asked.

"Yes, I think it does. She must be helped in some way, and I have a plan."

"As a matter of course. Does it involve transfer of stock? My income is limited, you know."

"Be serious, Edward, and listen. You know that your mother would be glad of someone to read to her, and that kind of thing; she was hinting as much to me the other day. What if I propose Ellen? It would give the girl a sort of education in the things she needs; she would have leisure for reading, and the position would be altogether more suitable. Don't you think it's a good idea?"

"How delightful to be philanthropic at others' expense! Yes; I think it will do very well."

"And you will see what you can do for Mr. Adler?"

"O, let the rascal look out for himself. He's no worse off than I was at his age."

Mrs. Swanwick sighed.

"What a pity I wasn't a work-girl! How delightful to have worked and starved and hoped!"

"Humph!" was her husband's reply.

Mutimer's Choice

ITS GREATER MATURITY alone would prove that "Mutimer's Choice" was written after "The Quarry on the Heath" and "The Lady of the Dedication." The use of Chelsea and Battersea for the setting also indicates that these places were still fresh in Gissing's memory when he wrote his story. In all likelihood, it is the materialization of an idea which he had expressed to his brother on June 27, 1884: "Shall hope to come down [to Wakefield] on *Monday week* by an early train, if you are quite sure that it will be convenient. Can occupy the interval by writing a short story I have in mind."* Various details support this suggestion. Gissing was then contemplating writing short stories for Bentley until the fifty-pound advance he received for the never-to-be-published *Mrs. Grundy's Enemies* was repaid. There is no other story that can be dated late June or early July, 1884, and its hero bears the same name as the protagonist of *Demos,* the subject of which was chosen at the same period, though it was not written until the end of the next year. He seems to have given the protagonist of his short story the name first intended for the hero of his novel, after he decided to suspend work on the latter.†

It is very doubtful whether the nineteen-page manuscript was submitted to an editor. Gissing was expecting that Bentley's magazine, *Temple Bar,* was about to publish another story "Letty Coe," which he had written in the first half of June and had sent to Bentley as soon as it was completed. As Bentley tried to gain time by keeping silent and turned a deaf ear to his proposal to make up for the fifty pounds by spinning out tales for *Temple Bar,* Gissing very likely kept "Mutimer's Choice" until he became indifferent to, or dissatisfied with, the story.

---

* Yale University Library

† A similar situation occurred later with the short story entitled "Rash Miss Tomalin," whose heroine's name was used for one of the leading characters of *Our Friend the Charlatan* (1901). When the story was accepted for publication, he had to change the surname of the heroine to "Rockett." The title then became "A Daughter of the Lodge" (*Illustrated London News,* August 17, 1901, pp. 235–37).

HE RINGERS of St. Mary's of Battersea were putting in their practice with a will to-night, and the bells seemed bent on making up for their shortcoming in the matter of quality by volume of voice. The peal rang out clamorously over the broad reach of the river, and the gusty south-west wind, which ever and anon lashed with rain the black water speeding at flood by the wall of the church-yard, flung the notes away to Chelsea, where distance endowed them with melody. Here, in the shadow of the steeple, the hour-long clash and jangle was, at the best of times, anything but conducive to harmonious thought, and when two minds were already set at var-iance the bells became so many spirits of mischief, every throat of them provocative of discord.

"Drat the bells!" exclaimed Mrs. Mutimer. "They fair split one's head."

She spoke just to break the silence, for, in spite of St. Mary's peal, an oppressive quietness filled the room; for the last quarter of an hour neither she nor her husband had uttered a word, and to both of them the sound from without seemed only to intensify the obstinate muteness they preserved. James Mutimer was sitting at table, some bread and butter and a cup of tea before him, but since he drew up his chair he had neither eaten nor drunk; one of his hands was playing unconsciously and nervously around the rim of the saucer, with the other he shaded his face, his elbow resting upon the table. His wife was sitting near the fire, her hands idle upon her lap; one of her feet kept tapping lightly on the fender. As she spoke, she turned her eyes slightly towards her husband; seeing that he paid no attention, she set her forehead in a still deeper frown and again looked into the fire. The face was that of a rather pretty young woman, or would have been so if she had allowed its lines to rest in their natural curves of beauty; as she turned away after the vain attempt to draw her husband's attention there was a spiteful twisting of the lips, a sharp compression of the nostrils, and a lowering of the eyebrows, all of which united to produce an expression very little at home upon a pretty face; if you had been watching her thoughtfully, you would have divined in this moment not a few disagreeable pos-sibilities for the development of the countenance when years should have made it less mobile.

Another five minutes passed in that clanging silence, then Mrs. Mutimer could bear it no longer. She rose and went to where her hat was hanging from a peg.

"I'm going out," she said, carefully arranging her hair with steady fingers before proceeding to put on her hat.

"Where to?" asked her husband, putting down the hand from his face and looking up at her.

"I'm going over to mother's; dessay you can do without me."

"No, I can't," he replied; "I want to talk to you."

At that moment the bells ceased. As if relieved, Mutimer rose with a sigh, and walked to the fireplace. He was a tall, strong man of five and thirty, dressed in the substantial workaday attire of an artisan; the floor of the little room creaked under his step, and his head was not so very far below the ceiling. Hearty enough in appearance, his bearded face yet wore a cast of trouble which seemed to date further back than the annoyance of the past hour; the eyes which turned slowly, as if under a certain embarrassment, and fixed themselves steadily upon his wife, were the clear open eyes which speak intelligence and honesty; feeling was in them, too, for all that they had a look of grave displeasure. He was doing his best to master the sensation of strangeness caused by the sound of his own voice, and the fingers which had before played about the saucer now plucked at his beard.

"What's the good o' talking?" said his wife, contemptuously, but replacing her hat upon its peg, when she had first blown a speck of something off her feather.

"A good deal, it seems to me, Bella," replied Mutimer, his voice shaking a little upon her name. "We've got to put this matter straight, you see. I've no wish to speak unkindly to you, but speak plainly I must. If we're to go along as man and wife should there must be confidence between us, and I want to know how I'm to feel confidence in you after this."

"To hear you talk," broke out Bella, in a tone which promised little for the success of her husband's calm manner of facing the situation, "I might a'been stealing. You'd better have a policeman up, an' give me in charge."

"You've been guilty of something quite as bad," returned Mutimer, with a sudden sternness which for an instant overawed her. "You've abused my confidence, and, when I find it out, instead of being sorry you fly into a bad temper. You make your fault all the worse."

"So 'ud any woman get angry when a man makes all this kick-up about a few shillings. You're mean, Jim, that's what you are!"

He kept silence for a moment. His face paled, then reddened; the words were as hard to bear as if a man had struck him.

"You must say what you like," he began again, as soon as he could trust his voice. "For all that you're in the wrong, Bella, and you must know it. What I want is to have you confess it; till you do that, you're no true wife. See here. I come home one day and find you in a new dress, a dress that I didn't like; it seemed to me too fine for one in your position. When I ask where it comes from, you tell me your mother's given it you. And I believed you, because I wouldn't doubt your word. Well, the time goes on, and now I come home and find this tally-man waiting for me. You and he have fallen out, it seems, and he rounds on you. The dress was got of him, not from your mother at all; you've been paying him with money you put down to all kind of false accounts; and now that you can't pay him any more, he comes and tries to get it out of me. It seems to me, Bella, that there's both stealing in all this and something worse too."

She had taken up a piece of ribbon and kept smoothing it over her fingers. The pretty face was less pretty than ever; it was hardening itself into self-will and rancour. But she did not seem disposed to speak.

"You say I'm mean," Mutimer went on. "If so, I don't put the same meaning to the word as you do. I've grudged you nothing we could afford—"

"You have!" she broke in quickly, snatching at the opportunity. "You wouldn't let me buy that bracelet at the pawn-shop, for all it was so dirt-cheap."

"You're right. And I refused because it doesn't become a workingman's wife to wear such things. I did my best to make you understand me, and I thought I succeeded."

"It was meanness, that's what it was," said Bella, with the inconsequence which maketh a wise man mad. "An' somebody else said it was at the time, what's more."

This was added with a certain intention which had its effect in hardening the lines of Mutimer's mouth and bringing his clear eyes to a close, stern focus upon her face.

"And who was that?" he asked, quietly.

There was no reply.

"Do you hear me?" Mutimer said, sternly. "Who was that?"

"Well, if you want to know, it was Bill Snowdon."

She tried to meet his look as she said this, but failed. In the necessity of doing something, she began to remove the tea-things. The clatter seemed to jar upon Mutimer's nerves, and for the first time he spoke irritably.

"Then I think Bill Snowdon had better have minded his own business, and I shall tell him what I think of him."

"You can tell him what you like.—If I'd married him, he wouldn't a' blowed me up like this, all about a few shillings."

The last sentence was an after-thought. As he heard it, Mutimer turned away, rested his elbow on the mantel-piece, and again hid his face with his hand.

There came a knock at the door, and, in reply to Bella's summons, a good-looking young fellow showed his face. He was very wet from the rain, and, before entering, stood and shook his soft hat in the passage, laughing in a cheerful way as he did so. Then he came in and held out his hand to Bella, who reddened and looked down as she gave her own. The expression of her features had changed with miraculous suddenness; the lines had resumed their curves of beauty, and taken moreover the graceful addition of a pleased smile. This seemed to be involuntary, for, as the visitor turned to meet her husband, there came back the look of half-fearful, half-indignant apprehension which had risen to her face when she heard the knock.

Mutimer had faced round at the interruption. His eyes fixed on the young man, and then watched both him and Bella keenly whilst the two were shaking hands. When his own turn came, he hesitated for a just appreciable moment, but ended by giving the greeting, though in silence.

"Who'd a' thought it 'ud rain to-night!" exclaimed the visitor, who was none other than the Bill Snowdon of whom there had been question a minute or two ago. "I had to come over to see about an order, and as I was close by I just thought I might give you a look in."

"You'll have a cup o' tea?" Bella asked, beginning to move about quite briskly. "We've only just this minute got up."

"No, no, Mrs. Mutimer; I won't trouble you, many thanks."

"Trouble! It's no trouble at all. It's here on the hob.—Jim didn't care for his to-night."

What a different woman! Her husband's eyes followed her as she moved about the room, and his face grew darker, but less stern.

"Wouldn't take his victuals an' drink!" cried Snowdon, laughing. "What's amiss Jim? You don't look up to high-water-mark."

"I've got a headache," Mutimer replied, and, as Bella proceeded to pour out a cup of tea, into which she had put three large pieces of sugar, he went to the window, pulled the blind a little aside, and look[ed] out into the darkness.

Young Snowdon tried to talk in the wonted cheerful way, but he soon understood that his jokes and laughter fell flat. Mutimer spoke a word or two now and then, but for the most part sat silent by the fire, glancing occasionally at his wife in a furtive way which was unnatural to him. At length he grew restless.

"Well," he said, rising all at once, "I'll go a little way with you, if you're ready. I don't hear the rain now."

Snowdon showed a little surprise at this summary dismissal, but took his hat readily. Again he shook hands with Bella, and again Bella reddened slightly and looked down.

The two men walked out of the house together. Snowdon was turning in the usual direction, but his companion stopped him.

"I want a word or two with you, Bill," he said. "Let's just go round the corner here; there's a quiet spot."

A few steps brought them to the river-side. Though the rain had ceased and the wind fallen somewhat, it was still a black night. The scattered lights on the opposite bank, and the stray gleaming here and there from a moored barge, alone pierced the veil of the darkness. There was no traffic near at hand, and the wash of the river below was almost the only sound.

"What's up, Jim?" Snowdon asked, apprehensively, when he had waited a few moments for an explanation and Mutimer still remained silent.

"I'll tell you," the other replied, speaking very calmly. "Do you think it's right for a man to say to a woman about her husband that he's a mean fellow, and so try to make her despise him?"

"What do you mean, Jim? Who's been a-saying so?"

"You know, it seems, that I refused to let Bella buy a bracelet a bit ago?"

Bella had indeed mentioned this to Snowdon, and he now confessed his knowledge; he did so under his voice.

"And then you told her it was mean of me?"

"Did she tell you that?" asked the other, after a pause.

"She did."

Snowdon knew well enough that he had never allowed such words to escape him, whatever he might have thought. He did not know at first what to say.

"Do you think it right, Bill?" Mutimer asked again, perhaps a little more severely.

"No, it wasn't right, Jim, and I beg your pardon for it. I hadn't ought to a' said anything o' the kind. It was thoughtless of me."

"Well," said Mutimer slowly, "it seems to me it was a bit worse than that. Never mind, however; that's all I wanted to ask you. And now I've just one thing more to say: you must come no more to see me and my wife, Bill Snowdon.—You understand that?"

Snowdon said nothing.

"Bella had the choice better than a year ago," Mutimer pursued, "and she chose me. I don't quite know why she did, now I think back over it, but that's neither here nor there. We're man and wife, and we've got to do our duty to each other. Part of my duty to Bella is to protect her, and I must do my best to carry it out."

"Why," stammered the other, "you don't surely think—"

"Never mind what I think. If you're an honest man, you'll turn this over a bit and see what I mean.—Well, I think that's all."

Snowdon held out his hand; he had seemed about to speak, but thought better of it. Mutimer shook hands in silence, and the men parted.

From that night the shadow deepened upon Mutimer's face. He had never been a man of many words, but his companions in the yard where he worked as a stone carver had already noticed a change in him since his marriage, the growth of a reserve which meant more than mere thoughtfulness; and now it was clear enough to those who saw him every day that something was going wrong with him. At home, on the other hand, he was more lively than had been his wont. No word was exchanged between him and Bella on the subject of young Snowdon's suddenly ceasing to visit them, frequent as those visits had hitherto been; nor was the discussion which had led to this result renewed by either. Mutimer had set himself the task of modifying his own character, at his age no easy thing. He said to himself that his habitual gravity, and his habit of taking little things seriously, had had the effect of estranging Bella, whose nature was the very antithesis of his own. He seemed always to have missed his mark when trying to impress her with the strength and tenderness of his love; he would try to adapt himself more to her modes of thought and feeling. But the effort it cost him to face a task which in his heart he felt to be hopeless was a new source of sadness in the hours when with chisel in hand, he measured in his thoughts the results of his endeavours on the day before, and looked forward to their renewal when he returned home. Forced into a sudden understanding of his wife's character by circumstances which made it indispensable to his peace that he should mould her to his own idea, his earnest and steadfast, but too unpliable, nature tortured itself in the perception that he had been hitherto blind to the reality, that all his hopes were based on a delusion. The piece of deceit which Bella had practised upon him assumed to his mind an importance it would have had for few men of his class, and the anger aroused in him by her way of meeting his discovery was anything but the irritated egotism of the uneducated man; her dishonesty came upon him like an unexpected flaw in a fine piece of marble which was destined to noble uses, her perverse ill-temper aggravated him by its accentuation of the defect he would so gladly have passed over and have tried his best to forget. A deep distrust of the woman he loved had perforce taken possession of him, and it rankled in his nature like a disease. Distrusting her, he distrusted himself as never before, saw the distance between her and himself as he had never yet seen it. His very efforts to abridge the distance made it greater; his ceaseless observation of her taught him to recognize in every thought she gave utterance to how hopelessly her heart was alienated from him. He knew that Bella fretted; he knew that any relapse from his own enormous patience would in a moment renew the scene, so horrible to him, of that night which had seen their first open quarrel. With such persistent forbearance on his part, and in the absence of any strong initiative in Bella's character, there were laid the foundations of a lifetime of commonplace un-happiness. That Mutimer was spared this was due to accident, which put before him a choice of a strange kind, and offered him an easy way out of his troubles.

He rose one morning at the usual early hour, and, without dis-turbing Bella, as his custom had always been, lit the fire and made his own cup of tea. Then as soon as he was ready to set forth, he stepped into the bedroom to say good-bye to Bella if she should be awake, or, if not, to kiss her in her sleep. His entrance into the room seemed to have aroused her; she started up and, with a frightened look, asked—

"What have you been doing to Bill Snowdon?"

Mutimer was silent, gazing at her in surprise. It was the first time she had mentioned the name since Snowdon's last visit, more than a month ago.

"I've been dreaming," she said, turning away her face, and still trembling.

"What did you dream about?" Mutimer inquired, forcing his voice to express nothing but good-humoured kindness.

Bella hesitated a little, but at last told him that in her dream she had seen him roll a great piece of stone upon Snowdon and crush him beneath it.

Mutimer laughed a little, but made no comment. He kissed her and went out into the pale morning light, himself pale and wretched.

Shortly before mid-day, just as Bella was making dinner ready, a knock came at her door and there entered a man whom she recog-nized as foreman in the stone-yard. His face wore an expression which made her look at him inquiringly, unable to use her voice.

"I'm sorry to bring you a piece of bad news, Mrs. Mutimer," the man said, turning his cap in his hands and looking about the room uneasily.

"About Jim?" she asked.

"Yes. You needn't frighten yourself too much, but he's rather badly hurt, had an accident in the yard."

"Is he killed?" Bella inquired, with a self-possession which did not seem to be exactly the result of effort.

"No, no; he ain't killed; not so bad as that. The chain gave way on a crane just when they was lifting a big block, and it fell on him. He's hurt about the legs. They've took him to St. Thomas's Hospital."

Bella thought at once of her dream, and the strangeness of the coincidence occupied her so much that she could only stare at the messenger in wonder. But all at once fright took hold of her. She put on her hat and ran sobbing to the house of her mother, which was only a little distance off.

The accident had happened an hour ago, and James Mutimer was now lying in the hospital ward, his legs frightfully crushed. Both would have to be amputated; so at all events reported Bella's mother, who went at once to St. Thomas's to make inquiries. But at the same time she brought back information that Mutimer's employer, who had accompanied the mutilated man to the hospital, had, on hearing the result of the first examination, at once made an offer of all the reparation in his power; Mutimer having been reduced to lifelong helplessness by a fault in the machinery of the yard, his wages should be continued to him as long as he lived. If he succumbed under the operation, his widow would have the benefit of the promise. Mutimer, Bella was assured, had been made aware of this at once, lest he should suffer unnecessary anxiety on his own or on her account. She was to see him on the following morning; till then it would be better to leave him in quiet.

Through the night Mutimer lay in silence and heard the great bell across the river strike hour after hour. A few intervals he had of semi-unconsciousness, when the agony seemed to set his brain on fire; but these could not have lasted long; he did not miss one of the pealing quarters. No groan came from his lips; only now and then he caught his breath convulsively and closed his eyes. At times the silence of the long dim ward was broken by a moaning, or by a low call for one of the nurses, who moved about with noiseless tread.

About midnight a new case was admitted, a lad who for a while uttered shrill cries; but his pain was assuaged, and the silence came back. Mutimer lay and thought, thought over an alternative which had been put before him, and in which he must decide by the morning. Would he consent to lose both his legs? If not, there was no doubt as to the issue; he would die. He looked steadily at the choice, as it was his wont to face every difficulty, and by pure force of will he overcame those fits of weakness which threatened to deprive him of his thinking-power.

Big Ben had struck four o'clock when Mutimer suddenly raised his hand and called quietly for the "sister" of the ward.

"I wish to see two people before making up my mind," he said in his weak voice.

"Who are they?"

"My wife first of all; then a friend of mine called Snowdon. Could you send for him, if I give his address?"

The request was acceded to. As the operation was to be performed, if at all, in the course of the day, Snowdon was telegraphed for at an early hour. Mrs. Mutimer was expected about nine o'clock.

Something of the restfulness of resolve came over the sufferer when he had spoken with the sister; a thin veil of sleep fell upon his senses, sleep which yet did not banish all consciousness of his position, though it deadened the racking pain. He opened his eyes at times and observed the progress of daylight. And at one of these awakings he saw his wife standing beside the bed.

He held out his hand, making it as steady as he could. Bella took it for a moment; then dropped it again. She had a scared look, and her eyes were wandering about the ward. Mutimer smiled sadly at her, but she did not bend down her face to his.

"What a face you've got!" she exclaimed. "I shouldn't have known you."

He kept his eyes fixed upon her. There was a terrible pleading in his gaze, but the effect of it was only to frighten her.

"Can you speak, Jim?" she asked, in an awed whisper.

"Yes, dear."

"Have they cut your legs off?"

"Not yet."

She looked about again and shuddered. Again he held his hand to her; she gave her own, but very soon withdrew it. And still he watched her.

"Don't look at me like that!" she whispered, fearfully. "I don't seem to know you."

She sobbed, and a few tears fell. Mutimer's eyes gleamed; he seemed to try to raise himself.

"Bella!"

"Yes, Jim."

"You remember your dream?"

"But it wasn't *him*!" she replied quickly.

Perhaps he had expected some other kind of reply. For the first time his gaze strayed from her. Her voice drew it back.

"Do you think they'll really pay you just the same?" Bella asked.

"Maybe I shan't live through it," he answered, quietly.

"O, but they said they'd pay *me*, all the same," Bella rejoined, as if to reassure him.

Mutimer closed his eyes.

"I can't do nothing for you, can I, Jim?" she asked, presently, when he seemed to have forgotten her presence.

"You can kiss me, Bella, and say good-bye."

She bent down, and, as she did so, saw a tear come from under his closed eyelids. His lips were very cold. Bella hastened out of the ward, trembling.

Half an hour later, another visitor was at the bedside. Snowdon took the faint hand and grasped it warmly.

"Jim, old man," he said, with a lump in his throat, "this has cut me up. I wish to God nothing hadn't come between us! I feel as if I'd somehow caused it."

Mutimer shook his head and smiled.

"Bear up!" said the young man, fairly sobbing. "You'll have good friends by you. It might a' been something worse."

Mutimer motioned him to bend nearer.

"If I don't come through it," he said, "will you—will you be good to Bella?"

Snowdon started and met the wide eyes with embarrassment and doubt.

"Will you make her a good husband, Bill Snowdon?" the sufferer asked, his voice hoarse with smothered emotion.

"Don't talk like that, Jim! You *know* you'll come through it. For God's sake—"

Mutimer interrupted him by holding out his hand again.

"Good-bye," he said, hurriedly. "I sent for you to say that. A dying man's words stick in the mind, and they have power either to bless or to curse.—Good bye!"

When the surgeon entered the ward, shortly after this, the sister went up to him, and, nodding in Mutimer's direction, said,—

"He refuses the amputation."

"Indeed? Perhaps he'll alter his mind yet."

"I think not. There's something strangely resolute about him."

And the sister was right.

Their Pretty Way

UNLIKE ALL THE PRECEDING PIECES, this short story belongs to Gissing's middle period of production. It was written at Eversley, Worple Road, Epsom, a place to which he had moved in September, 1894, after he and his irascible wife had become tired first of Exeter, then of Brixton. For a couple of years he had been writing short stories between periods of concentration on longer fiction. Domestic unrest, which was detrimental to the concentration of energy required by three-deckers, told less heavily on his *nouvelles*.

His contributions were now sought by editors and even publishers. On September 17, 1894, his friend C. K. Shorter, who edited the *Illustrated London News,* the *English Illlustrated Magazine,* and the *Sketch,* had asked him for some more short stories, and on the twenty-eighth, he had received from his literary agent—William Morris Colles—a similar request for two short tales. He promised them in a fortnight. "Simple Simon," composed in two days, September 30–October 1, was the first. Colles was so delighted with it that he immediately asked Gissing "for as much more of that sort as I can send him" (Diary, October 3, 1894). The next day he sat down to his desk and wrote "Their Pretty Way," the idea of which had occurred to him when Colles' note had reached him. The manuscript was despatched the same evening.

Apart from one insignificant allusion to it in a letter to his agent dated December 14, 1895,* it seems never to have emerged from obscurity. There is apparently no other instance of a short story of Gissing's mature years which failed of publication, though a good many were rejected several times. The three-page manuscript, which bears no printer's marks, is certainly a fair copy.

* Carl H. Pforzheimer Library.

S THEY WERE to be married about the same time, Henry Wager and Joseph Rush, friends from boyhood, agreed to take a home and share it together. After much consultation with their future wives, young ladies keenly sensible of social distinctions, they chose a house in Brixton,—imposing, spacious and convenient for double occupancy. It was perhaps unfortunate, to begin with, that Wager's resources (he had just begun business as a chop-merchant in the Borough) enabled him to spend more on furniture and decoration than his friend could reasonably afford, Rush being only cashier to a firm of wholesale cheesemongers in Tooley Street; but the buoyancy of prenuptial days permitted this detail to pass without remark. On their return from the honeymoon, the ladies embraced with effusion, and spent their first day at home in exclaiming delightedly at each other's domestic appointments, in admiring each other's wardrobe, and in forecasting a long lifetime of rapturous intimacy.

Mrs. Wager had dark tresses, a tall, slender form, and somewhat acute features: she was nine-and-twenty. Mrs. Rush, younger by five years, exhibited a fluffy growth of pale-brown hair, had a face of rather infantile prettiness and frisked about with the graces of a plump lamb. Their names being Elizabeth and Theresa, they decided to call each other Muriel and May.

"They seem to hit it off very well," remarked Wager to his friend, when for a day or two they had been witness of affectionate demonstrations. And Rush, whose temper was less sanguine, answered fervently "First rate!"

As might have been anticipated, the earliest note of dissonance that sounded amid these ideal harmonies came from below-stairs. The ladies had engaged two servants, who were expected to devote themselves impartially to both their mistresses. Given a quartette of females each of whom was but a little lower than the angels, this arrangement might have worked fairly well; in a Brixton household it naturally led to trouble within the first week. Coming home one evening in expectation of a quiet dinner, the husbands found a scene of disorder; each was taken apart by his tender spouse, and, spite of hunger, compelled to hear a catalogue of complaints against cook and housemaid. Practical men, they pooh-poohed the difficulty, talked about system and firmness and the like, and turned towards the dining-room with resolute joviality.

"Things'll work themselves right," said Wager, carelessly, as he smoked with his friend afterwards. "The girls have to get used to housekeeping. Take my advice, Jo, and don't pay much attention to this kind of thing. It isn't our department."

Rush acquiesced, subduing his nervousness. He had begun to understand, for his own part, that housekeeping on the present scale was decidedly more expensive than his calculations supposed. That night, he and his Theresa put aside their lovers' babblement for dialogue of a less agreeable nature. Mrs. Rush had but the vaguest ideas of domestic economy; when her husband insisted on speaking gravely of sordid matters, she pouted, rambled into all manner of irrelevant subjects, and at length, accusing him of never having loved her, burst into tears. Joseph, whose soft heart and irresolute will put him at a great disadvantage in junctures such as this, passed a restless night and came down next morning with no appetite for breakfast.

The servant difficulty, more serious as days went on, was soon complicated with heart-burnings between the newly-married women of which their husbands for awhile heard and suspected nothing. Friends and relatives called, and had their calls returned; a river of gossip was set flowing, and ere long showed a decidedly turbid course. To Mrs. Rush's ears came remarks on the inferiority of her furniture and her dress when compared with her darling Muriel's possessions. Mrs. Wager heard it whispered that her sweet May was complaining of slights and injustices experienced in the common home. One evening, Joseph found his wife in her bedroom, with red eyes and flabby cheeks. She would not dine; she was not well; she— in short she wished she might soon breathe her last.

"Come, come; what's all this about?" exclaimed Joseph good-naturedly. And he referred to the state of her health. Already there was question of the state of both ladies' health,—a fact which their husbands would not henceforth have much chance of forgetting.

"That woman has been horrid to me!" sobbed Theresa, after five minutes' entreaty that she would explain herself.

"That woman? Who?"

Joseph was astounded to learn that Mrs. Wager had been thus

designated. Half an hour's talk resulted in other disclosures which no less perturbed him. Impossible, his wife declared, to go on living thus. She was despised and insulted—openly, flagrantly! The servants (a new pair) regarded her even less than those who had been dismissed. And, with autumn advancing, she had not yet purchased a single article of new attire, whereas Mrs. Wager had spent the last three days in shopping, and at least half a dozen parcels had been delivered to her. It was enough to make one think of suicide! Why had Jo married her, if he meant only to plunge her into degradation!

"Look at my dresses! Look at my old waterproof! And I feel ashamed to take my sister into the bedroom, with that mean carpet!—"

Rush felt the perspiration rising to his forehead. This helpmate he had chosen promised to help him only too effectually in one particular—the spending of his income. But before long the dialogue ended, he had promised that Theresa should have a ten-pound note to lay out in garments of the new fashion, that she might hold her own with Mrs. Wager.

A week later, Mrs. Wager's state of health necessitated fresh visits to big shops across the water. Again parcels arrived, and again Joseph found his wife possessed with thoughts of self-destruction. The two men had carefully avoided speaking to each other of the discords no longer disguised from them, and the result was that they talked much less frequently and less cordially than of old. Both had long since repented their domestic experiment, but they would not confess. Wager contrived to spend very little time at home; he had many friends, and was to a large extent resuming his bachelor life, of course with the consequence that his wife grew bitter against him, and yet more against Mrs. Rush. Joseph, less courageous, came home at regular hours, and bore the brunt of miseries. His wife ruled him through his fears; Mrs. Wager, on the other hand, sought more subtly to manage her husband through his pride and his passions.

So it came to pass that, less than four months after marriage, Joseph Rush was driven to the inevitable step. Before speaking to his wife, he made avowal to Wager that the expenses of this mode of living were too high for him; he must find a separate abode.

"I shouldn't wonder if you're right, old fellow," said his friend. Neither spoke of their wives' discussions.

Had matters ended thus, it had been well. But on learning that she must go into a small house, whilst her rival would henceforth occupy the whole of this "desirable residence," Mrs. Rush fell into a voiceless fury. She resolved not only to quarrel violently with her erewhile darling Muriel, but that her husband and his old friend should be set at variance, the fiercer the better. And this she brought about with little difficulty. When for two or three days the house had been thrown into furious disorder, Henry Wager and Joseph Rush sought a colloquy late at night. Hitherto, in talk with their wives, each had tried to make peace by defending the wife of the other against more or less virulent charges, a masculine method which, needless to say, made things worse by adding to the caldron of strife the fresh ingredient of jealousy. But to-night Wager began by saying abruptly:

"Look here, old chap, you must really put a stop to your wife's talk. She has been saying all sorts of ill-natured things about Lizzie. Of course I know that it isn't easy—"

Rush, driven to desperation, broke in hotly.

"Why, confound it, Wager! I'm told that your wife has spoken abominably—to the servants too—about Theresa. You certainly oughtn't to allow that. Your wife is very much older, and—"

Now it happened that Mrs. Wager, having crept down from her bedroom to hear if possible what the men were talking about, heard this last remark through the keyhole. And it also happened that, as she stood listening, and quivering with rage, Mrs. Rush, who suspected that this was to be a night of crisis, also crept downstairs, and caught her enemy eavesdropping. In consequence, the men presently became aware of angry voices in the hall. They moved to the door, and forthwith the two couples were involved in loud reproof and recrimination. Where both women had determined that their husbands should come into conflict, such issue was inevitable. The old friends said harsh things to each other, made charges and comparisons not easily forgiven. Had their social standing been one grade lower, they would have come to blows; for this, they had too much self-respect.

But it was impossible that they should live together for another day under the same roof. Next morning, Rush took his wife into temporary lodgings, and in a week or two their goods were removed to a modest house half a mile away. The men of necessity corresponded, but they would not meet (out of shame quite as much as anger), and did not see each other again for a long time.

Though removed from contact with her old rival, Mrs. Rush still endeavoured to vie with her at all events in pursuit of the fashions. The little house and the solitary servant ate into her soul; but her dress when she received visitors, and that in which she showed herself abroad, became little inferior to Mrs. Wager's equipment. When Joseph declared that ruin stared him in the face, his wife fell into hysterics, and shrieked about the state of her health. In the fulness of time this plea became no longer valid, but with the birth of a child Joseph found the demands upon his purse still increasing. Mrs. Wager also had a baby, and common friends reported the magnificence of its *layette*. Again and again Rush yielded, until, one morning of late summer, his old friend Wager, unfolding the newspaper at breakfast, uttered a horrified exclamation.

"What is it?" asked his wife, who by this time had learnt the limits she might not pass in resistance to her husband's will, and on the whole was better for it.

"Why, good heavens, Jo Rush has been arrested for embezzlement!"

Had she dared, Mrs. Wager would have screamed delight. Ha! there was an end of that odious Theresa and her pretensions to cut a figure! But Wager's eye counselled a decent dissimulation.

"Oh, never!—I must go and see that poor silly creature—"

"You must do nothing of the kind," replied her husband, sternly.

Nor was this amiable suggestion ever put into practice.

For many months, Joseph Rush disappeared from among his friends. It was not known to Mrs. Wager that, among the people who took care of Mrs. Rush and her child, Henry was the main, though a secret, benefactor. Neither did she learn, long after, by what instrumentality Joseph received a new start in life. It had been her devout hope that no such chance would ever be granted him, that he would remain an outcast, and drag his wife down to the gutter. Darling "Muriel" would have gloated over the certainty of such a prospect for her sweet "May." Yet the fact was, that on a certain day two men encountered by appointment in a retired place, and, as they beheld each other, one of these men could not restrain his tears, whilst the other grasped him strongly by the hand.

"It's all right, Jo. I was a cursed fool to behave to you as I did. Women! Women!"

And the other, hearing himself addressed in honest words of friendly encouragement, looked up again, and once more hoped.

Index

THE JOHNS HOPKINS PRESS

Designed by Arlene J. Sheer

*Composed in Caslon Old Style text and display
by Typoservice Corporation*

*Printed on 55-lb. Perkins and Squier, Old Forge,
by The Murray Printing Company*

*Bound in Interlaken ARCO Vellum
by Moore and Company, Inc.*